Discourse, Communication and Tourism

TOURISM AND CULTURAL CHANGE
Series Editors: Professor Mike Robinson, *Centre for Tourism and Cultural Change, Sheffield Hallam University, UK* and
Dr Alison Phipps, *University of Glasgow, Scotland, UK*

Understanding tourism's relationships with culture(s) and vice versa, is of ever-increasing significance in a globalising world. This series will critically examine the dynamic inter-relationships between tourism and culture(s). Theoretical explorations, research-informed analyses, and detailed historical reviews from a variety of disciplinary perspectives are invited to consider such relationships.

Other Books in the Series
Irish Tourism: Image, Culture and Identity
    Michael Cronin and Barbara O'Connor (eds)
Tourism, Globalization and Cultural Change: An Island Community Perspective
    Donald V.L. Macleod
The Global Nomad: Backpacker Travel in Theory and Practice
    Greg Richards and Julie Wilson (eds)
Tourism and Intercultural Exchange: Why Tourism Matters
    Gavin Jack and Alison Phipps

Other Books of Interest
Classic Reviews in Tourism
    Chris Cooper (ed.)
Dynamic Tourism: Journeying with Change
    Priscilla Boniface
Managing Educational Tourism
    Brent W. Ritchie
Marine Ecotourism: Issues and Experiences
    Brian Garrod and Julie C. Wilson (eds)
Natural Area Tourism: Ecology, Impacts and Management
    D. Newsome, S.A. Moore and R. Dowling
Progressing Tourism Research
    Bill Faulkner, edited by Liz Fredline, Leo Jago and Chris Cooper
Recreational Tourism: Demand and Impacts
    Chris Ryan
Shopping Tourism: Retailing and Leisure
    Dallen Timothy
Sport Tourism Development
    Thomas Hinch and James Higham
Sport Tourism: Interrelationships, Impact and Issues
    Brent Ritchie and Daryl Adair (eds)
Tourism Collaboration and Partnerships
    Bill Bramwell and Bernard Lane (eds)
Tourism and Development: Concepts and Issues
    Richard Sharpley and David Telfer (eds)
Tourism Employment: Analysis and Planning
    Michael Riley, Adele Ladkin, and Edith Szivas

For more details of these or any other of our publications, please contact:
Channel View Publications, Frankfurt Lodge, Clevedon Hall,
Victoria Road, Clevedon, BS21 7HH, England
http://www.channelviewpublications.com

TOURISM AND CULTURAL CHANGE 5
Series Editors: Mike Robinson and Alison Phipps

Discourse, Communication and Tourism

Edited by
Adam Jaworski and Annette Pritchard

CHANNEL VIEW PUBLICATIONS
Clevedon • Buffalo • Toronto

Library of Congress Cataloging in Publication Data
Discourse, Communication and Tourism/Edited by Adam Jaworski and Annette
Pritchard.
Tourism and Cultural Change: 5
Includes bibliographical references and index.
1. Tourism. 2. Tourism–Social aspects. 3. Discourse analysis. 4. Intercultural
communication. I. Jaworski, Adam. II. Pritchard, Annette. III. Series.
G155.A1D572 2005
910'.01'4–dc22   2005004536

British Library Cataloguing in Publication Data
A catalogue entry for this book is available from the British Library.

ISBN 1-84541-020-3 /EAN 978-184541-020-9 (hbk)
ISBN 1-84541-021-1 /EAN 978-184541-021-6 (electronic)

Channel View Publications
An imprint of Multilingual Matters Ltd

UK: Frankfurt Lodge, Clevedon Hall, Victoria Road, Clevedon BS21 7HH.
USA: 2250 Military Road, Tonawanda, NY 14150, USA.
Canada: 5201 Dufferin Street, North York, Ontario, Canada M3H 5T8.

Typeset by GCS Ltd.
Printed and bound in Great Britain by the Cromwell Press.

Contents

Part 4: Performance and Authenticity

Acknowledgements

We are grateful to David Botterill, the Welsh School of Hospitality, Tourism and Leisure Management, University of Wales Institute of Cardiff for bringing us and our Departments into contact. We would also like to thank Nigel Morgan who provided some useful comments on the structure of the book and much needed encouragement.

AJ gratefully acknowledges support for this work by funding from the Leverhulme Trust to the Centre for Language and Communication Research, Cardiff University, for a larger project on *Language and Global Communication* (grant F/00407/D) (www.global.cf.ac.uk). He also thanks his colleagues at the Centre for the opportunity of taking a research leave in 2003/04, which facilitated work on this volume.

Last but not least, we thank all the authors for their contributions, and all at Channel View for their support and cooperation.

AJ and AP
Cardiff, June 2004

Contributors

Irena Ateljevic, Department of Travel & Tourism, Auckland University of Technology <irena.ateljevic@aut.ac.nz>

Hywel Bishop, Centre for Language and Communication Research, Cardiff University <bishoph1@cardiff.ac.uk>

Nikolas Coupland, Centre for Language and Communication Research, Cardiff University <coupland@cardiff.ac.uk>

Kelly Davidson, School of Media and Performing Arts, University of Ulster at Coleraine <kellyjdavidso16@hotmail.com>

Stephen Doorne, School of Social and Economic Development, University of South Pacific, Suva <doorne_s@usp.ac.fj>

David Dunn, West Kilbride, North Ayrshire <dunn.dr@virgin.net>

Peter Garrett, Centre for Language and Communication Research, Cardiff University <garrettp@cardiff.ac.uk>

Adam Jaworski, Centre for Language and Communication Research, Cardiff University <jaworski@cardiff.ac.uk>

Chris Kennedy, Centre for English Language Studies, University of Birmingham <c.j.kennedy@bham.ac.uk>

Sarah Lawson, Centre for Language and Communication Research, Cardiff University <lawsons@cardiff.ac.uk>

Nigel Morgan, The Welsh Centre for Tourism Research, University of Wales Institute, Cardiff <nmorgan@uwic.ac.uk>

Camille C. O'Reilly, School of Sociology & Social Policy, University of Surrey Roehampton <camilleoreilly@hotmail.com>

Uta Papen, Department of Linguistics and Modern English Language, Lancaster University, <u.papen@lancaster.ac.uk>

Annette Pritchard, The Welsh Centre for Tourism Research, University of Wales Institute, Cardiff <apritchard@uwic.ac.uk>

John Urry, Department of Sociology, Lancaster University <j.urry@lancaster.ac.uk>

Introduction

Discourse, Communication and Tourism Dialogues

ANNETTE PRITCHARD and ADAM JAWORSKI

Scope, Aims and Approaches

This book brings together two distinctive cultural formations: discourse and tourism. Both fields have accumulated critical and theoretical bases in their own right, but the ways in which the two interact have received much less attention. Certainly, there has been little dialogue between scholars who primarily study discourse (language in particular) and communication, and those whose primary focus is tourism. In creating and presenting such dialogues, this book aims to make a contribution to the emerging debates surrounding discourse, communication and tourism. The study of these research fields extends across disciplinary boundaries and each has attracted the attention of a range of different specialists. This diversity is also reflected in the mix of disciplinary labels derived from our contributors' departmental affiliations, which include: English Language; Language and Communication; Media and Performing Arts; Sociology; Social Policy; Social and Economic Development; Travel and Tourism. Despite the seeming mix of priorities and methodologies highlighted by this disciplinary diversity, all the authors share a common interest of placing discourse and communication at the centre of studying tourism, be it by theorising the relation of traveller/tourist to space, representations of the tourist experience, mobility-related identities, or ways of enacting the tourist experience, which are also the broad themes of the book.

As a result, the reader will soon discover that there is no single topic for study, nor just one theoretical and methodological approach adopted in the chapters to follow. Indeed, the reader of this collection might be bewildered at its seemingly eclectic choice of issues and by some of the juxtapositions of its chapters: historic and contemporary; global and local; representation and appropriation; reflexivity and subjectivity; images and words, and so on. Rather than ignore such diversity, our intention in this introduction is to highlight how the multiplicity of tourism experiences and performances can be variously explored through discourse and communication. Discourse, including language, defines experience and performance, and by empowering action or inaction, naturalises social relations. But discourse and communication are also products of social relations and we need to explore and understand how their meanings have been constructed and used across the totality of human experience – and that includes tourism experiences.

This book addresses three central questions. First, it asks how discourse, understood here as a semiotic system, be it textual-linguistic, visual-pictorial, or, in a broader sense, any other system of signification (see next section), shapes tourism and the tourist experience. Secondly, it asks how tourism shapes and has shaped our discourses about peoples and places over time. More specifically, the book examines how discourse and communication shape the identities of hosts, tourists, destinations and tourist attractions, modes of transport, and so on. At the same time, it is also concerned to explore how tourism and travel create their own systems of signification, providing keys for the construction of self and others. Finally, it addresses the notion that tourism is a literal embodiment of travelling theory; being both an agent and channel of globalisation, and the site and subject of various competing discourses effecting change and transition, whilst also echoing the imperialist discourses of the colonial age.

The analytic interrelationship between tourism, discourse and communication offers a useful transdisciplinary mix of assumptions and techniques for a sustained and critical exploration of the possibilities, tensions, conflicts and representations which characterise a phenomenon which is frequently described as one of the most important global industries and cultural activities. For its part, communication refers to the practices, processes and mediums by which meanings are produced and understood in a cultural context and could include almost anything – from a wave of the hand to the system of interconnected computers that constitute the internet. Such an all-encompassing definition means that communication is a fundamental concern of disciplines across the humanities and social sciences. Yet, although discourse and communication are of central importance in tourism studies, they remain relatively unexplored and undertheorised among tourism researchers, and the specific links that have been made between language and tourism have for the most part ignored the vast tradition of discourse and communication studies (see next section) and remained resolutely non-empirical (cf. Dann, 1996; Cronin, 2000). Likewise, the disciplines which have discourse and communication at the heart of their interest, i.e. sociolinguistics and discourse analysis, have only recently recognised the domain of tourism as an important context for the study of interpersonal and intergroup relations, especially along the lines of international/intercultural contact afforded by globalisation.

Therefore, this book constitutes a timely opportunity to explore and theorise the complex and multifaceted relationships between the three crucial concepts which constitute its title. Through discourse we communicate our positions, allegiances and patterns of dominance and disempowerment. Through exploring communication between hosts and tourists we can access and theorise notions of identity, difference, otherness and community. Together, discourse and communication are thus vital prisms through which we can examine tourism, and this book is the first publication which brings together scholars from sociolinguistics and critical tourism studies.

The collection offers an international and wide-ranging coverage, exploring tourism communication experiences around the world and examining the representation of tourist destinations in Europe, Africa, Asia and the Pacific. The contributors draw their data from different sources including: participant observation; interviews with hosts, tourism operators, tour guides and tourists; experimental design; tourist photographs, diaries and travelogues; postcards, brochures and flyers. Likewise, the contributors utilise a variety of theoretical paradigms and frameworks of analysis including: post-modern and reflexive ethnography, sociology, social semiotics, genre and discourse analysis. Thus, it does seem that many in this collection are responding to Jamal and Hollinshead's (2001: 78) call for 'a dialogue in travel and tourism research … on the multiple approaches, theories, practices, methods, techniques that can assist those of us in tourism studies to do justice to the research topic and research questions we formulate and pursue.'

As a collection, the chapters in the volume also deal with the full range of tourism types, e.g. package tourism, backpacking/independent travel, cultural/heritage tourism, agri-tourism, ethno- and eco-tourism, day tourism/hiking, and/or different genres of tourism representation. They variously explore the vehicles and creative dimensions of tourism communication (e.g. television holiday programmes, promotional materials of tourism organisations, tourist guides, postcards, internet sites, etc.), discourses of tourism representation, tourism products and the discourses that underpin tourism activity. In sum, this volume addresses a number of key areas in the exploration of the relationships between communication and tourism including the following key themes and issues: intercultural communication and tourist agency; representations of tourist destinations, hosts and tourists; genres of tourism representation and the making, remaking and performance of identities, peoples and places.

Discourse

By producing this book, we also sought to respond to the growing importance of the 'discursive turn' in social theory. There is not enough space to provide an adequate overview of the notions of 'discourse' and 'discourse analysis' in this introduction, although we would like to introduce at least a few concepts and issues which are of particular relevance to the chapters below.

Discourse is a complex, contested concept which is evolving and assuming an increasingly significant role in social science research. Definitions of discourse and discourse analysis, such as the following one, tend to be complex and multifaceted: 'a very narrow enterprise that concentrates on a ... conversation between two people. Others see [it] as synonymous with the entire social system' (Howarth, 2000: 2). This breadth and polyvalency of discourse and discourse analysis has been often discussed and commented on. For example, Schiffrin *et al.* (2001: 1) observe that most definitions of discourse 'fall into three main categories ... : (1) anything beyond the sentence, (2) language use, and (3) a broader range of social practice that includes nonlinguistic and nonspecific instances of language' (see also Jaworski & Coupland, 1999, 2002; Coupland & Jaworski, 2001).

What these broad definitional categories make clear is that discourse can be studied from a range of methodological perspectives; starting from a relatively narrow linguistic/textual view (e.g. Stubbs, 1983; Fasold, 1990), to the 'critical' approach of discourse as 'social practice' (Fairclough, 1992). The latter perspective draws heavily on the work of Pierre Bourdieu (e.g. 1991) and Michel Foucault (e.g. 1970, 1972) whose interest in discourse is not so much in empirical examination of actual, interactional data, but in discourse as an abstract vehicle for social and political processes.

As Coupland and Jaworski (2001) have pointed out, discourse does indeed require both the local approaches to the study of language in use, face-to-face interaction, and close textual analyses of all sorts of linguistic and non-linguistic representations as sites of socio-cultural significance, as well as attending to the global dimensions of discourse patterns, which inscribe large-scale norms, values and ideologies. 'The most incisive approaches to discourse are those that combine the detailed analysis of language, in particular instances of its use, with the analysis of social structure and cultural practice' (Coupland & Jaworski, 1992: 134).

The above formulation suggests that discourse is not synonymous with or reducible to language, which, of course, is not a new idea. Foucault (see above) viewed discourse as inclusive of non-verbal elements ('gesture') and, more generally, as the way people organise social life, institutions, and so on. For Halliday (1978), language is only one of the semiotic systems used by humans to 'mean'. Following on from these ideas, and from the work of other semioticians (e.g. Barthes, 1973, 1977), discourse analysis started more systematically to embrace the study of modalities other than language, for example, visual images (Kress & van

Leeuwen, 1996, 2001), music and other non-linguistic sounds (van Leeuwen, 1999), non-verbal communication and body image (e.g. Goodwin, 1981, 2000; Coupland & Gwyn, 2003). It is apparent that in numerous chapters in this book, discourse is also treated as a multimodal resource. For example, in Chapter 1 (John Urry), 'landscape' can be viewed as a discourse for the organisation of 'land' under tourist gaze. Various other chapters in the book involve analyses of multimodal texts, in which spoken and/or written language co-occurs with visual images such as postcards (Pritchard & Morgan), graphic design in promotional brochures (Papen), televisual image (Dunn), as well as posters, spatial arrangements and artefacts (Coupland, Garrett & Bishop, this volume).

The 'discursive turn' in social sciences mentioned above is closely linked to the now common assumption in discourse analysis and other fields that discourse not only reflects but also shapes social reality, our identities and our relations with others including patterns of power, dominance and control. Put differently, our social lives are constructed in and through language/discourse, whether in the moment-to-moment social interchanges of everyday talk or in the beliefs, understandings and principles that structure our lives. Such constructionist positions (cf. Shotter & Gergen, 1989; Shotter, 1993) have been largely associated in discourse analysis with notions of identity formation, ideology construction and representation.

An early version of the constructionist approach to interpersonal communication was formulated by Goffman (1959, 1967, 1974) in his work on 'self-presentation' and 'interaction order', which he elaborated on using his famous theatrical metaphor. In Goffman's framework, social actors engage in conversation as a series of ritualised processes for a specific 'dramatic effect'. Thus, targeting specific audiences, interactants produce successions of interdependent performances in which they construct and project desirable versions of their identities. Goffman's and, more recently, Butler's (1990) work on *performativity* (which draws heavily on Austin's 1961 seminal work on performative speech acts) have led to a large body of discourse analytic research on the discursive construction of identities, for example, in relation to gender (e.g. Cameron, 1997; Coates, 1996, 2002); ethnicity (Tannen, 1981), and age (e.g. Coupland *et al.*, 1991; Coupland & Nussbaum, 1993). Similar approaches have also emerged in tourism studies (e.g. Edensor, 1998, 2001; Bærenholdt *et al.*, 2004; see also Doorne & Ateljevic; Coupland, Garrett & Bishop, this volume).

Another important notion in discourse analysis, especially its more critically inclined varieties, has been that of *ideology* (cf. Billig, 1990, 1991; van Dijk, 1998), i.e. 'any constellation of fundamental or commonsensical, and often normative ideas and attitudes related to some aspect(s) of social "reality"' (Blommaert & Verschueren, 1998: 25). In other words, ideology is a set of social (general and abstract) representations shared by members of a group and used by them to accomplish everyday social practices: acting and communicating (e.g. Fowler, 1985; Billig *et al.*, 1988; van Dijk, 1998). These representations are organised into systems which are deployed by social classes and other groups 'in order to make sense of, figure out and render intelligible the way society works' (Hall, 1996: 26). And, importantly, as has been argued by van Dijk (1998), for example, it is indeed through discourse and other semiotic practices that ideologies are formulated, reproduced, reinforced as well as subverted. Again, much work in discourse analysis has dealt with the issues of ideology especially in politics and the mass media (e.g. Fowler *et al.*, 1979; Fairclough, 1995), and in relation to discriminatory discourses such as racism (e.g. van Dijk, 1991) and sexism (e.g. Pauwels, 1998). In parallel, critical tourism studies, sociology and anthropology have been engaged in the study of tourism ideologies, largely in the context of post-colonial patterns of power and dominance, often based on analyses of texts and images (e.g. Morgan & Pritchard, 1998). The notion of ideology is implicitly or explicitly central to most chapters in this collection (see, especially, Davidson; Dunn; Papen; Pritchard & Morgan; Jaworski & Lawson).

Discursive accomplishment of ideology is an important strategic task in political and non-political domains because its acceptance by the audience, including mass media audiences, ensures the establishment of group rapport. As Fowler (1985: 66) puts it, through the emergence of a 'community of ideology, a shared system of beliefs about reality' creates group identity. This point highlights another important feature of discourse, i.e. its social character or group orientation. In discourse studies and sociolinguistics, the term 'communities of practice' has recently gained much currency as it identifies groups of people who 'come together around mutual engagement in some common endavor' (Eckert & McConnell-Ginet, 1992: 473). Such 'common endavor' may involve motherhood, or shopping, or body culture (Holmes & Meyerhoff, 1999; Coupland & Coupland, 2000), or specific ways of 'doing' tourism. We have touched on this aspect of social activity above, discussing the performative aspect of constructing social identities (including tourism), although the emphasis here is on participants' developing shared ways of linguistic and other discursive patterns of behaviour, and the interaction between the micro- (interpersonal) and macro- (institutional) structures of engagement. It is in this sense that various groups and sub-groups of tourists and hosts can also be viewed as members of global and local communities of practice (Lawson & Jaworski, forthcoming). In the present volume, there is much emphasis on how people come together as groups or how they set boundaries around themselves by deploying specific discursive resources to enact particular versions of being tourists (e.g. Davidson; Dunn; O'Reilly; Doorne & Ateljevic; Kennedy) or hosts (e.g. Coupland, Garrett & Bishop; Jaworski & Lawson).

One term which is inextricably linked with the notion of discourse is *genre*. Traditionally, it has been used to designate different types of literary writing, e.g. novels, sonnets or ballads (Bakhtin, 1981, 1986). More recently, the term has been applied to different forms of media, professional and other 'everyday' types of discourse such as general conversation, story-telling, gossiping, and so on (Fiske, 1987; Swales, 1990; van Leeuwen, 1993) as different ways of acting and organising networks of social practices (Fairclough, 2003). In their analysis of inflight magazines as a genre of a globalised travel industry, Thurlow & Jaworski (2003: 582) follow Swales' (1990) definition of genre as a distinctive text type 'characterized in term of: (a) its central purpose, (b) its prototypical content and form, and (c) its being conventionally recognised and labelled as such by the discourse community of which it is a part'. Kennedy (this volume) offers a corpus linguistic analysis of one such, relatively stable genre of tourism writing: the holiday postcard, through which he demonstrates one way in which mainstream tourists realise discursively their roles as 'tourists'. However, as many authors have commented on, texts are usually *heteroglossic* or multi-voiced (Bakhtin, 1981, 1986) in the sense that they 'mix' or 'hybridize' different genres (Fairclough, 1995, 2003; Thurlow & Jaworski, 2003), which allows them to orient to their multiple stances and goals. The chapter by Dunn, for example, illustrates how a seemingly uniform genre of the television travelogue may change its effects depending on whether it veers towards the documentary film, educational programme or entertainment.

Several chapters in our book use elicited data such as narratives and accounts (Davidson; O'Reilly; Jaworski & Lawson), which are commonly recognised genres of representing people, states and events, or more generally – experience (Labov & Waletsky, 1967; Edwards, 1997). It is by accessing such overt formulations of the experience of self and other in the context of tourism that allows us to tease out some of the underlying principles of this social activity, and to engage in a critical debate of its sources, consequences, inevitability and possible ways of contestation. As a special case of such self-reports, Jaworski and Lawson (this volume) concentrate on the participants' accounts of their own uses of language and communication, or their metadiscourses, which are sites of what Schieffelin *et al.* (1998) refer to as 'language ideology', that 'intersection of language and human beings in a social world' (Woolard, 1998: 3).

Discourse and the Study of Tourism

In the preceding section, we have introduced several examples of work in which tourism has engaged with various aspects of discourse study, although, as has already been stated, to date there has not been much dialogue between discourse analysts and other theorists working in the area of tourism, even though the question of 'meaning' in tourism has been of interest to semioticians and anthropologists for a considerable length of time (cf. Culler, 1981; Kirshenblatt-Gimblett & Bruner, 1992), and has long been of central concern. In fact, much tourism study has been so divorced from any social theorising that critics have pointed to a growing dissatisfaction with the theoretical bases of tourism scholarship in general (e.g. Aitcheson, 2000) and with the 'lack of receptivity to intellectual currents in the "parent" disciplines' in particular (McNamee, 2000: 125). At the same time, many of these 'parent' disciplines have been remarkably reluctant to engage with tourism as a field of study. As a result, since our knowledge and understanding of the social world is largely shaped and mapped by social science (Delanty, 1997), there is a real sense in which the social sciences and humanities themselves have played an active role in marginalising the study of tourism. To take just one example from the discipline of history, Walton has pointed out that historians have consistently ignored tourism. Thus, the British seaside has yet to produce a historiography to challenge that of the British cotton industry and yet the former has had a much greater and long-lived impact on Britain's culture, economy and society (Walton, 2000).

Having said that, it is impossible not to acknowledge, albeit in the sketchiest of ways, a large body of work on tourism, travel, mobility, etc. which has engaged with the notions of discourse, communication, interaction, representation, ideology and so on, although usually without reference to discourse analysis as a method of close analysis of texts, be it spoken, written, visual or otherwise as outlined in the previous section. Most notably, the sociological work of Urry (2002 [1990]), MacCannell (1999 [1976]), Lash and Urry (1994), Hannerz (1996), and others have placed tourism on the map of critical social scientific investigations. Another huge area of influence has been anthropology and ethnography, e.g. Clifford (1988, 1997), Kirshenblatt-Gimblett (1998). In recent years, cultural geographers, art historians and cultural and American studies scholars have turned their attention to tourism (e.g. Edensor, 1998; Desmond, 1999; Osborne, 2000; Crouch & Lübbren, 2003). Numerous important anthologies spanning several disciplines have brought together different methodological perspectives and analytic foci, among them Boissevain (1996); Selwyn (1996); Rojek & Urry (1997); Smith (1989); Dann (2002).

Morgan and Bischoff (2003: 295) have recently suggested that 'by connecting more fully with the wider debates in the social sciences and embracing pluralist, multi-dimensional epistemologies already in evidence elsewhere, tourism studies has the opportunity to create a richer, more inclusive and more innovative research base.' Whilst it is true that much remains to be done, cross-disciplinary work is gathering pace. Such work has also been reflected in the 'proliferation of new journals that are orientated towards theoretical and critical works in methodological issues in tourism studies' (Jamal & Hollinshead, 2001: 66). This is a trend which is set to accelerate since, as much of the world itself shifts from a production to a service economy, social science's preoccupation with production and politics is increasingly being challenged so that the cultural arenas of cuisine, leisure and tourism are gradually becoming respected fields of enquiry. Moreover, the ability of the social scientist to break the ties of previously powerful epistemological straitjackets is being increasingly encouraged by the fracturing of formerly stable divisions between academic disciplines (Seale, 1998). In such a climate of epistemological exchange and synthesis, we would suggest that the variegated, complex and interdisciplinary nature of the fields of discourse, communication and tourism make them particularly well placed to contribute to these contemporary epistemological and ontological debates within the social sciences.

Introducing the Chapters

The book is divided into four non-discrete parts: 'The Semiotics of Tourist Spaces, Landscapes and Destinations'; 'The Discursive Construction and Representation of the Tourist Experience'; 'Identities on the Move'; 'Performance and Authenticity'. We are, however, conscious that many of the chapters make interesting contributions to a number of the conceptual frames identified and we would therefore invite the reader to engage with the collection with this in mind.

Part 1 consists of three chapters which explore discourses of tourism spaces. Cultural geographers, amongst others, have established that space and place are complex concepts, cultural constructions that are subject to change and negotiation (Shields, 1991; Rogoff, 2000). Places are thus constructed inter-subjectively and express powerful psychological, ideological and emotional meanings and confrontations. John Urry's contribution develops his long-standing interest in tourists' experiences of place and he considers here how places are visually consumed by visitors (cf. Urry, 1995). Noting the key shift from land to landscape, Urry discusses how historically places of land became places of visual desire for rich, primarily male, Europeans. The development of photography proved central to this transition and gave rise to the 'endlessly devouring tourist gaze' (p. 21). Urry's chapter thus highlights the ways in which, through globalisation, mediascape realities and electronic consumerism, tourist places are being recast as places of consumption and mobility, as places which lack any uniqueness and are defined by abstract characteristics which mark their similarity or difference to other places.

Kelly Davidson continues the theme of the consumption of place by focusing on how particular travel discourses construct backpacker understandings of India. Davidson demonstrates how, in their search for the 'real India', backpackers are actively and reflexively engaged in producing new identities and imagined communities; identities and communities which 'have the potential to transgress the boundaries of fixed national and Western identities' (p. 28). In this journey, space is central and Davidson explores the discourses which stimulate the 'alternative' travellers' desires to problematise older preconceptions of the Western 'self' and Indian 'Other.' This chapter provides a fascinating insight into 'alternative' travel discourses and practices (travel as pilgrimage, pleasure, countercultural mythologies and utopianism), exploring how travellers actively negotiate their relationships with 'India'; how representations of Indian Otherness frame their enactment of transgressive identities and influence their desires for intercultural understanding and the transformation of self.

Annette Pritchard and Nigel Morgan shift the focus on space to explore how differences between identities were marked out and defined through linguistic and visual representation on early 20th-century postcards. In particular, they interrogate the comic postcard as an everyday cultural text that has both reflected and shaped particular discourses of place and identity. They argue that postcards provide rich cultural reservoirs of popular perceptions and emotional geographies of people and places and, as 'commonsense' understandings of ethnographic knowledge, constitute a 'moment' in the circularity of knowledge and power and contribute to the tourism-representation dialectic. Pritchard and Morgan do this by focusing on early 20th-century comic postcards of Wales, demonstrating how these visual narratives form a long tradition of certain imaginings of place, culture and nationhood. As they conclude, however, the meanings generated by texts can be contested, ambiguous and polysemic, and they caution readers and researchers against one dimensional interpretation.

The two chapters in Part 2 focus on the discursive construction and representation of the tourist experience, examining the ideologies and discourses which inform tourist promotional texts such as brochures and TV holiday programmes. Uta Papen examines the construction of place myths in Namibian tourism brochures. Namibia provides a particularly interesting case study as an emergent tourism destination giving rise to 'competing discourses' between black, largely urban community tourism and white, post-colonial, predominantly safari-oriented tourism. Interestingly, despite the stated orientation of the texts in question, Papen demonstrates how both types of texts remain dependent and closely associated with the dominant tourism discourses of the latter variety. She explores how the texts themselves are strongly influenced by the asymmetrical relationships of power that characterise the Namibian tourism sector. Significantly, she concludes that whilst the community-based tourism initiatives appear to promote a post-colonial cultural diversity, in essence they present simplified and homogenised pictures of local life and history.

In contrast, David Dunn focuses on a well-established tourism destination – Venice. His examination of three television travelogues on Venice spanning three decades in the latter part of the 20th century reveals changing conventions and signifying practices that underpin UK television holiday programmes over time. His discussion demonstrates how the presenters act as mediators of the destination and the tourism experience, and how resorting to different semiotic resources and inter-textual links they construct their own and the implied tourist's (i.e. the viewer's) persona as either 'traveller', 'tourist' or 'post-tourist'.

Part 3 of the collection explores issues of identity and self within the framework of globalisation. Tourism is itself both a manifestation and an aspect of globalisation and experiences of globalisation vary in terms of whether one is a recipient of global tourism flows or part of the flow itself. The two chapters in this part examine the experiences of both the host recipients (Jaworski & Lawson), and those who are part of the international tourism flow (O'Reilly). Focusing on the local, Adam Jaworski and Sarah Lawson examine the discourses surrounding Polish agritourism in order to unravel the tensions between global tourism and local consumption. They begin by exploring how Polish agritourism promotional materials draw on global discourses of ecotourism, reflecting 'responsible' concerns for the local, the environment and ultimately the planet. In both the promotional material and their subsequent investigation of hosts' accounts of their interaction with visitors, however, they identify the tension between 'traditional/rural' and 'modern/safe', the promise for example of 'raw earthy authenticity, and the security of a flushing toilet and a hot shower' (p. 129). Thus, in the hosts' accounts of host-tourist interactions, Jaworski & Lawson explore the concepts of identity, difference, otherness and community.

Camille O'Reilly then shifts the discussion to explore the impact of backpacker travel on travellers' ongoing development of self-identity. Through the accelerated processes of globalisation, backpacker travel and the attraction of an encounter with the exotic 'Other' have become increasingly accessible and desirable to many people. In a wide-ranging discussion, O'Reilly focuses on the mechanisms travellers' use to identify themselves and their narrations of their experiences. The labels back-packers use to describe themselves are value laden and emotionally charged and sometimes generate significant debate. O'Reilly thus demonstrates that there is much in a name in her discussions of individuals and her examinations of internet sites which enable travellers to access wider discourses. She shows how the pejorative nomenclature of 'tourist' is largely eschewed in favour of the more positively valued 'traveller', embodying ideals of independence, freedom and mobility and drawing on discourses of adventure and exploration (and more unwittingly of colonialism and imperialism). O'Reilly concludes that travelling is both a state of mind and a lifestyle which travellers can draw on to reinvent their identity at a collective and individual level. The travelling process (inception, journey and return) thus emerges as a vital element to developing and experimenting with one's sense of self, which is in turn central to identity narrations.

The three chapters which comprise the final part of the collection build on such discussions of identity by foregrounding concepts of performance and authenticity. Stephen Doorne and Irena Ateljevic pay tribute to Goffman's (1959) emphasis on the dramaturgical nature of social life in their examination of backpacker performances in the Fiji Islands. Here 'performance' provides a powerful critical conceptual framework in which tourism practices and processes such as identity construction, cultures of consumption and communication can be observed. As these authors demonstrate, stages are set, characters are cast, and roles are learned, performed and produced. Travellers identify and carefully capture (in photographs and stories) the stages upon which they choreograph being a backpacker, whilst character identities are negotiated in a number of sensual and embodied practices (including deportment, dance, dress, sexual behaviours and alcohol and drug consumption), and performances are crafted using a variety of props and costumes. Interestingly, it seems that backpacker scripts rarely confront the asymmetric power relations that facilitate their individual travel experiences and, as O'Reilly and Doorne and Ateljevic note, the variety of roles and characters which travellers assume provide, in part, a rehearsal for their return home.

The book's penultimate chapter shifts the focus on performance to an exploration of authenticity. Authenticity is a complicated, highly contested concept which has provoked significant debate and approbation in tourism studies. It is always defined by its binary opposite – inauthenticity – 'fake' as opposed to 'real'. In tourism (as some of the chapters suggest here), 'Third World' and rural cultures are often held by consumers to be 'more authentic' than their more shallow, media and consumption-driven Western/urban counterparts. Nikolas Coupland, Peter Garrett and Hywel Bishop explore discursive frames and authenticities in Welsh mining villages. In doing so, they confront tourism research's increasingly sterile engagement with the concept of authenticity, arguing that tourism's tendency to 'frame the debate through totalising and critically precious questions like: Is heritage tourism inauthentic?' (p. 199) is ultimately self-defeating. Instead they argue that authenticity issues do define much that is distinctive in some heritage tourism's design, implementation and experience. Their detailed textual analysis of spoken, written and other visual data demonstrates that the Welsh mining attractions under investigation are informed by 'different, internally coherent systems of authentic experience' (p. 200). Thus, the authors discuss the varied cultural performances of the heritage sites, likening them to theatrical rather than museum spaces (where 'display' rather than 'performance' is the core activity; cf. Kirshenblatt-Gimblett, 1997) and reveal that there are many routes into what should more appropriately be termed *authenticities* as opposed to *authenticity*.

The concluding contribution of the collection builds on the preceding analyses of textual forms of tourism communication through its examination of a much-neglected area of research – the practice of postcard sending. As Chris Kennedy observes, postcards continue to operate as significant communication devices between those away on holiday and those who remain at home. Yet, despite this, there has been relatively little research on the linguistic aspects of holiday postcards. Kennedy's focus on the sending of postcards as a literacy event is thus a welcome and timely contribution. Highlighting the socio-cultural importance attached to postcards and their transmission, Kennedy explores how postcards serve a relational social purpose designed to foster positive relationships. The language used reflects particular discourse communities, or communities of practice (cf. above) – in Kennedy's case university students who exhibit a high degree of shared knowledge, interests, tastes and lifestyles, similarities which are subsequently reflected in the substantial levels of interactivity between the postcard writer and reader. Kennedy's evaluation of the linguistic content of the postcards demonstrates how these apparently innocuous ephemera reveal significant information about the attitudes of senders and recipients towards each other, the activities they engage in and the events they experience.

References

Aitcheson, C. (2000) Poststructural feminist theories of representing Others: A response to the 'crisis' in leisure studies' discourse. *Leisure Studies* 19, 127–44.

Austin, J.L. (1961) *How to Do Things with Words*. Oxford: Clarendon Press.

Bakhtin, M.M. (1981) *The Dialogic Imagination: Four Essays*. Edited by M. Holquist. Translated by Vern W. McGee. Austin, TX: University of Texas Press.

Bakhtin, M.M. (1986) *Speech Genres and Other Late Essays*. Translated by Vern W. McGee. Austin, TX: University of Texas Press.

Barthes, R. (1973) *Mythologies*. London: Paladin.

Barthes, R. (1977) *Image, Music, Text*. London: Fontana.

Bærenholdt, J.O., Haldrup, M., Larsen, J. and Urry, J. (2004) *Performing Tourist Places*. Aldershot: Ashgate.

Billig, M. (1990) Stacking the cards of ideology: The history of the Sun Royal Album. *Discourse & Society* 1, 17–37.

Billig, M. (1991) *Ideologies and Beliefs*. London: Sage.

Billig, M., Condor, S., Edwards, D., Gane, M., Middleton, D. and Radley, A.R. (1988) *Ideological Dilemmas*. London: Sage.

Blommaert, J. and Verschueren, J. (1998) *Debating Diversity: Analysing the Discourse of Tolerance*. London: Routledge.

Boissevain, J. (ed.) (1996) *Coping with Tourists: European Reactions to Mass Tourism*. Oxford: Berghahn Books.

Bourdieu, P. (1991) *Language & Symbolic Power*. Edited and Introduced by John B. Thompson. Translated by Gino Raymond and Matthew Adamson. Cambridge: Polity Press.

Butler, J. (1990) *Gender Trouble: Feminism and the Subversion of Identity*. New York: Routledge.

Cameron, D. (1997) Performing gender identity: Young men's talk and the construction of heterosexual identity. In S. Johnson and U.H. Meinhof (eds) *Language and Masculinity* (pp. 47–64). Oxford: Blackwell.

Clifford, J. (1988) *Predicament of Culture: Twentieth-Century Ethnography, Literature, and Art*. Cambridge, MA: Harvard University Press.

Clifford, J. (1997) *Routes: Travel and Translation in the Late Twentieth-Century*. Cambridge, MA: Harvard University Press.

Coates, J. (1996) *Women Talk: Conversations between Women Friends*. Oxford: Blackwell.

Coates, J. (2002) *Men Talk: Stories in the Making of Masculinity*. Oxford: Blackwell.

Coupland, J. and Coupland, N. (2000) Selling control: Ideological dilemmas of sun, tanning, risk and leisure. In S. Allan, B. Adam and C. Carter (eds) *Communication, Risk and the Environment*. London: UCL Press.

Coupland, J., Coupland, N. and Grainger, K. (1991) Intergenerational discourse: Contextual versions of ageing and elderliness. *Ageing and Society* 11, 189–208.

Coupland, J. and Gwyn, R. (eds) (2003) *Discourse, the Body and Identity*. Basingstoke: Palgrave Macmillan.

Coupland, N. and Jaworski, A. (2001) Discourse. In P. Cobley (ed.) *The Routledge Companion to Semiotics and Linguistics* (pp. 134–48). London: Routledge.

Coupland, N. and Nussbaum, J.F. (eds) (1993) *Discourse and Lifespan Identity*. Newbury Park, CA: Sage.

Cronin, M. (2000) *Across the Lines: Travel, Language, Translation*. Cork: Cork University Press.

Crouch, D. and Lübbren, N. (eds) (2003) *Visual Culture and Tourism*. Oxford: Berg.

Culler, J. (1981) Semiotics of tourism. *American Journal of Semiotics* 1, 127–40.

Dann, G.M.S. (1996) *The Language of Tourism: A Sociolinguistic Perspective*. Oxford: CAB International.

Dann, G.M.S. (ed.) (2002) *The Tourist as a Metaphor of the Social World*. Wallingford: CAB International.

Delanty, G. (1997) *Social Science: Beyond Constructionism and Realism*. Milton Keynes: Open University Press.

Desmond, J.C. (1999) *Staging Tourism. Bodies on Display from Waikiki to Sea World*. Chicago: University of Chicago Press.

Eckert, P. and McConnell-Ginet, S. (1992) Think practically and look locally: Language and gender as community-based practice. *Annual Review of Anthropology* 21, 461–90.

Edensor, T. (1998) *Tourists at the Taj: Performance and Meaning at a Symbolic Site*. London: Routledge.

Edensor, T. (2001) Performing tourism, staging tourism: (Re)producing tourist space and practice. *Tourist Studies* 1, 59–81.

Edwards, D. (1997) *Discourse and Cognition*. London: Sage.

Fairclough, N. (1992) *Discourse and Social Change*. Cambridge: Polity Press.

Fairclough, N. (1995) *Media Discourse*. London: Edward Arnold.

Fairclough, N. (2003) *Analysing Discourse: Textual Analysis for Social Research.* London: Routledge.

Fasold, R. (1990) *The Sociolinguistics of Language.* Oxford: Blackwell.

Fiske, J. (1987) *Television Culture.* London: Routledge.

Foucault, M. (1970) *The Order of Things: An Archeology of Human Sciences.* London: Tavistock.

Foucault, M. (1972) *The Archeology of Knowledge.* London: Tavistock.

Fowler, R. (1985) Power. In T. van Dijk (ed.) *Handbook of Discourse Analysis, Volume 4* (pp. 61–82). London: Academic Press.

Fowler, R., Hodge, B., Kress, G. and Trew, T. (1979) *Language and Control.* London: Routledge & Kegan Paul.

Goffman, E. (1959) *The Presentation of Self in Everyday Life.* New York: Anchor Books.

Goffman, E. (1967) *Interaction Ritual: Essays on Face-to-Face Behavior.* New York: Doubleday.

Goffman, E. (1974) *Frame Analysis: An Essay on the Organization of Experience.* New York: Harper & Row.

Goffman, E. (1983) The interaction order. *American Sociological Review* 48, 1–17.

Goodwin, C. (1981) *Conversational Organization: The Interaction between Speaker and Hearer.* New York: Academic Press.

Goodwin, C. (2000) Gesture, aphasia and interaction. In D. McNeill (ed.) *Language and Gesture* (pp. 84–98). Cambridge: Cambridge University Press.

Hall, S. (1996) The problem of ideology: Marxism without guarantees. In D. Morley and K.H. Chen (eds) *Stuart Hall: Critical Dialogues in Cultural Studies* (pp. 25–46). London: Routledge.

Halliday, M.A.K. (1978) *Language as Social Semiotic: The Social Interpretation of Language and Meaning.* London: Edward Arnold.

Hannerz, U. (1996) *Transnational Connections: Culture, People, Places.* London: Routledge.

Holmes, J. and Meyerhoff, M. (1999) *Communities of Practice in Language and Gender Research.* Special Issue of *Language in Society* 28 (2).

Howarth, D. (2000) *Discourse.* Milton Keynes: Open University Press.

Jamal, T. and Hollinshead, K. (2001) Tourism and the forbidden zone: The underserved power of qualitative inquiry. *Tourism Management* 22, 63–82.

Jaworski, A. and Coupland, N. (1999) Introduction: Perspectives on discourse. In A. Jaworski and N. Coupland (eds) *The Discourse Reader* (pp. 1–44). London: Routledge.

Jaworski, A. and Coupland, N. (2002) Discourse analysis and conversation analysis. In K. Malmkjært (ed.) *The Linguistics Encyclopedia* (2nd edn) (pp. 114–19). London: Routledge.

Kirshenblatt-Gimblett, B. (1997) Afterlives. *Performance Research* 2, 1–9.

Kirshenblatt-Gimblett, B. (1998) *Destination Culture: Tourism, Museums, and Heritage.* Berkeley, CA: University of California Press.

Kirshenblatt-Gimblett, B. and Bruner, M. (1992) Tourism. In R. Bauman (ed.) *Folklore, Cultural Performances and Popular Entertainments: A Communications-centred Handbook* (pp. 300–7). New York: Oxford University Press.

Kress, G. and van Leeuwen, T. (1996) *Reading Images – The Grammar of Visual Design.* London: Routledge.

Kress, G. and van Leeuwen, T. (2001) *Multimodal Discourse: The Modes and Media of Contemporary Communication.* London: Arnold.

Labov, W. and Waletsky, J. (1967) Narrative analysis: Oral versions of personal experience. In J. Helms (ed.) *Essays in Verbal and Visual Arts* (pp. 12–44). Seattle: University of Washington Press.

Lash, S. and Urry, J. (1994) *Economies of Signs and Spaces.* London: Sage.

Lawson, S. and Jaworski, A. (forthcoming) Narrative acts of group identity: Backpacker-travellers as a global community of practice.

MacCannell, D. (1999) *The Tourist: A New Theory of the New Leisure Class* (2nd edn.) Berkeley, CA: University of California Press. [First published in 1976.]

McNamee, M. (2000) Just leisure? The ethics of recognition. *Leisure Studies* 19, 125–6.

Morgan, N.J. and Bischoff, E. (2003) Editorial. *Tourism and Hospitality Research* 4, 293–6.

Morgan, N. and Pritchard, A. (1998) *Tourism, Promotion and Power: Creating Images, Creating Identities*. Chichester: John Wiley.

Osborne, P.D. (2000) *Travelling Light: Photography, Travel and Visual Culture*. Manchester: Manchester University Press.

Pauwels, A. (1998) *Women Changing Language*. London: Longman.

Pritchard, A. and Morgan, N. (2000) Privileging the male gaze: Gendered tourism landscapes. *Annals of Tourism Research* 27, 884–905.

Rogoff, I. (2000) *Terra Infirma: Geography's Visual Culture*. London: Routledge.

Rojek, C. and Urry, J. (eds) (1997) *Touring Cultures: Transformations of Travel and Theory*. London: Routledge.

Schieffelin, B.B., Woolard, K.A. and Kroskrity, P.V. (eds) (1998) *Language Ideologies: Practice and Theory*. New York: Oxford University Press.

Schiffrin, D., Tannen, D. and Hamilton, H.E. (2001) Introduction. In D. Schiffrin, D. Tannen and H.E. Hamilton (eds) *The Handbook of Discourse Analysis* (pp. 1–10). Oxford: Blackwell.

Seale, C. (ed.) (1998) *Researching Society and Culture*. London: Sage.

Selwyn, T. (ed.) (1996) *The Tourist Image: Myths and Myth-making in Tourism*. Chichester: John Wiley.

Shields, R. (1991) *Places on the Margin: Alternative Geographies of Modernity*. London: Routledge.

Shotter, J. (1993) *Conversational Realities*. London: Sage.

Shotter, J. and Gergen, K.J. (eds) (1989) *Texts of Identity*. London: Sage.

Smith, V. (ed.) (1989) *Hosts and Guests: The Anthropology of Tourism* (2nd edn). Philadelphia: Pennsylvania University Press.

Stubbs, M. (1983) *Discourse Analysis*. Oxford: Blackwell.

Swales, J.M. (1990) *Genre Analysis: English in Academic and Research Settings*. Cambridge: Cambridge University Press.

Tannen, D. (1981) New York Jewish conversational style. *International Journal of Sociology of Language* 30, 133–49.

Thurlow, C. and Jaworski, A. (2003) Communicating a global reach: Inflight magazines as a globalising genre in tourism. *Journal of Sociolinguistics* 7, 581–608.

Urry, J. (1995) *Consuming Places*. London: Routledge.

Urry, J. (2002) *The Tourist Gaze* (2nd edn). London: Sage. [First published in 1990]

van Dijk, T.A. (1991) *Racism and the Press*. London: Routledge.

van Dijk, T.A. (1998) *Ideology*. London: Sage.

van Leeuwen, T. (1993) Genre and field in critical discourse studies. *Discourse & Society* 6, 81–106.

van Leeuwen, T.A. (1999) *Speech, Music and Sound*. Basingstoke: Macmillan.

Walton, J. (2000) *The British Seaside: Holidays and Resorts in the Twentieth Century*. Manchester: Manchester University Press.

Woolard, K. (1998) Language ideology as a field of inquiry. In B.B. Schieffelin, K. Woolard and P.V. Kroskrity (eds) *Language Ideologies: Practice and Theory* (pp. 3–47). New York: Oxford University Press.

Chapter 1

The 'Consuming' of Place

JOHN URRY

Wordsworth's The Brother 'signifies the beginning of modernity ...
a time when one stops belonging to a culture and can only tour it'
(Buzard, 1993: 27)

'A view? Oh a view! How delightful a view is!'
(Miss Bartlett, in A Room with a View; Forster, 1955 [1908]: 8).

Sharon Macdonald recounts a common story she heard told on the Isle of Skye in
Scotland. 'There was an old woman ... living in township X. One day a couple of
tourists come by and start asking her questions.
"Have you ever been outside this village?" ...
"Well, yes. I was at my sisters in [neighbouring township]" ...
"But you've never been off the island?"
"Well, I have, though not often I suppose."
"So, you've been to the mainland?" She nods. "So you found Inverness a big city
then?"
"Well, not so big as Paris, New York or Sydney, of course ..."'
(Macdonald, 1997: 155)

'Wow, that's so postcard' (visitor seeing Victoria Falls.
(Quoted in Osborne, 2000: 79).

Visual Consumption

For a decade or so I have been interested in how it is that visitors (and
indeed local people) experience place. One way of formulating this is
through the idea of *Consuming Places* (Urry, 1995), that visitors especially
through a visual gaze or appropriation increasingly consume places. But
what does this mean exactly, and what are the implications that places are
visually consumed?

First, we should distinguish, loosely following Wordsworth, between
land and landscape as distinct forms of belongingness to place (Milton,
1993). The former, *land*, involves conceptualising land as a physical, tangible resource that can be ploughed, sown, grazed and built upon. It is a
place of work conceived functionally. As a tangible resource, land is
bought and sold, inherited and especially left to children, either directly

or through the rights established resulting from the use of land over lengthy periods of time. To dwell on a farm is to participate in a pattern of life where productive and unproductive activities resonate with each other and with very particular tracts of land, whose history and geography will often be known in intimate detail. There is a lack of distance between people and things.

The practice of land is quite different from that of *landscape*, with the latter entailing an intangible resource whose definitive feature is appearance or look (Milton, 1993). The notion of landscape emphasises leisure, relaxation and visual consumption by visitors. From the 18th century onwards a specialised *visual* sense developed – this was based upon the camera obscura, the claude glass, the use of guidebooks, the widespread knowledge of routes, the art of sketching, the balcony, photography and so on (Ousby, 1990). As a consequence of this specialised visual sense areas of wild, barren nature, once sources of sublime terror and fear, were transformed into what Raymond Williams terms 'scenery, landscape, image, fresh air', places waiting at a distance for visual consumption by those visiting from towns and cities of 'dark satanic mills' (1972: 160; Macnaghten & Urry, 1998). By 1844 Wordsworth was noting that the idea of landscape was only recently developed. So that by the mid-19th century houses were increasingly built with regard to their 'prospects' as though they were a kind of 'camera' (Abercrombie & Longhurst, 1998: 79). The language of views thus prescribed a particular visual structure to the very experience of place as land gave way to landscape (Green, 1990: 88). As Miss Bartlett declares in *A Room with a View*: 'A view? Oh a view! How delightful a view is!' (Forster, 1955 [1908]: 8).

Thus in the case of the English Lake District, there was a complex multi-layered making. A place of 'land', according to Daniel Defoe of inhospitable terror, came to be transformed into 'làndscape', a place of beauty and desire (Urry, 1995). Similarly, even before the end of the 18th century the Alps had been regarded as mountains of immense inhospitality, ugliness and terror. But they too became 'civilised'. Ring describes how the Alps 'are not simply the Alps. They are a unique visual, cultural, geological and natural phenomenon, indissolubly wed to European history' (2000: 9). And also by the end of the 18th century the land of 'tropical nature' of the Caribbean had been romanticised by European travellers who began to see the scenery as though it were a 'painting', as landscape (Sheller, 2003). And there are diverse other examples of how places of land became places of visual desire, as the inhospitable was turned into landscape, especially for rich (male) European visitors.

Photography is central to this shift from land to landscape. Indeed tourism and photography could be said to commence in the 'west' in their modern form around 1840. Louis Daguerre and Fox Talbot announced their somewhat different 'inventions' of the camera, in 1839 and 1840. In

1841, Thomas Cook organised what is now regarded as the first packaged 'tour', the first railway hotel was opened in York just before the 1840s railway mania, the first national railway timetable, Bradshaws, appeared, Cunard started the first ever ocean steamship service, and Wells Fargo, the forerunner of American Express, began stagecoach services across the American west (Lash & Urry, 1994: 261). The year 1840 then is that moment when the 'tourist gaze' emerges, involving the combining together of the means of collective travel, the desire for travel, the techniques of photographic reproduction and the notion of landscape. As a visitor to Victoria Falls subsequently declared: 'Wow, that's so postcard' (quoted in Osborne, 2000: 79) as landscape rather than land is all the rage.

But while 1840 marks the beginning of the modern era in terms of landscape, of an endlessly devouring tourist gaze, there are some distinct variations in the consuming of place. There are varied tourist gazes (see Urry, 2002 [1990]). With the most powerful, *romantic* gaze, solitude, privacy and a personal, semi-spiritual relationship with the object of the gaze are emphasised. Visitors expect to look at the object privately or at least only with 'significant others'. Large numbers of strangers visiting, as at the Taj Mahal, intrude upon and spoil that lonely contemplation desired by western visitors (famously seen in the Princess Diana shot at the Taj; Edensor, 1998: 121–3). The romantic gaze involves further quests for ever new objects of the solitary gaze, a process like the sorcerer's apprentice, consuming and then devouring the very places sought out for the romantic gaze.

By contrast the *collective* tourist gaze involves conviviality. Other people also viewing the site are necessary to give liveliness or a sense of carnival or movement. Large numbers of people that are present can indicate that this is the place to be. These moving, viewing others are obligatory for the collective consumption of place, as with central London, Ibiza, Las Vegas, the Sydney Olympics, Hong Kong and so on. Baudelaire's notion of flânerie captures this well: 'dwelling in the throng, in the ebb and flow, the bustle, the fleeting' (Tester, 1994: 2).

Analogously, there is the *spectatorial* gaze that involves the collective glancing at and collecting of different signs that have been very briefly seen in passing, at a glance such as from a tourist bus window (Urry, 1995: 191).

Then there is the notion of the *reverential* gaze used to describe how, for example, Muslims spiritually consume the sacred site of the Taj Mahal. Moslem visitors stop to scan and to concentrate their attention upon the mosque, the tombs and the Koranic script (Edensor, 1998: 127–8).

Likewise, an *anthropological* gaze describes how individual visitors scan a variety of sights/sites and is able to locate them interpretatively within a historical array of meanings and symbols. Some tour guides may themselves provide accounts that interpret sights/sites historically and interculturally.

Somewhat related is the *environmental* gaze. This involves a scholarly or NGO-authorised discourse of scanning various tourist practices for their footprint upon the 'environment'. On the basis of such reflexivity it is possible to choose that with the smallest footprint and then recommend that through various media to like-minded environmentalists (as with the UK-campaigning organisation, *Tourism Concern*; Urry, 1995: 191).

And finally, there is the *mediatised* gaze. This is a collective gaze where particular sites famous for their 'mediated' nature are viewed. Those gazing on the scene relive elements or aspects of the media event. Examples where such mediated gazes are found would include locations in Santa Monica and Venice Beach where many Hollywood films are set.

Consuming Objects and Services

I have so far talked about the consumption of place, and brought out the role of the visual and landscape within that consumption. However, two further points need to be noted. First, I show in this section how place is not an abstract Cartesian space, defined by various geometric coordinates. Rather place is a centre of many material activities, especially the production and consumption of specific and often distinct goods and services.

Second, in the next section I show how places are in a way themselves mobile, in a set of relationships with other places and this makes them move, nearer and farther in a system of differences. Places are only contingently fixed and stable destinations.

First, then, a huge array of places across the globe are being generally restructured as places of consumption, or what Fainstein and Judd term 'places to play' (1999). Place after place we might say are locations within which very many goods and services are compared, evaluated, purchased and used. Places to play are places involved in producing distinctions of taste resulting from consuming, and anticipating the consumption, of an incredible array of goods and services.

Especially significant here are consumer services which can be deemed central to particular places, such as art galleries in Paris, theatres in London, casinos in Las Vegas, Broadway shows in New York, skiing in the Alps, country house hotels in the English Lake District, exotic sex tourism in Thailand, water sports in the Caribbean and so on. Through the often active consuming of certain services the place itself comes to be consumed. The service in question is metonymic of the place, with the part, the service, standing for the whole.

The consuming of place involves the consumption of services and sometimes of goods that are deemed specific to that place, e.g. cheeses in France, malt whisky in Scotland, chardonnay in Australia and so on. But of course with goods, the growth of global markets has partly reduced this specificity of goods that are often now available across the world, especially in airport shops that have become a kind of 'global super-market'. Even so the marketing of place will still often invoke images of particular products, of popular music records in Liverpool, wine in the Loire, industrial museums in northern England, cream teas in Cornwall and so on. But even with the global marketplace there is still thought to be something authentic about consuming particular goods or services in specific places.

Also images of place are fundamental to the symbolic branding of many goods and services. So the background of major cities (e.g. Rome, London, New York, Paris) is used to imply a cosmopolitan product, the background of the countryside a natural product, the background of mountains a pure product, the background of former industrial area a heritage product and so on.

Two further points need to be noted. First, there is often a contradiction between the consumption of place *and* the consumption of specific goods and services. Thus the items of consumption may not be available, or the services have become too commercial, or the service delivery has become too expensive or too low quality, or the shops have turned into souvenir shops. There are many ways in which the consuming of place is contra-dicted by the actual consumption possibilities within that place, especially since commercially oriented companies pursuing short-term goals will often be providing such consumption possibilities. Such companies may be poor at ensuring the appropriate quality of the service delivery, or of attracting a suitable set of other consumers that are consistent with that place's marketing. So consuming place through consuming certain kinds of goods and services is shot through with contradiction and ambiguity (see Urry, 2002: Chapter 4).

Second, services for visitors are increasingly generated not by com-merce but by collective enthusiasts. Especially in the UK, many groups of enthusiasts have documented, laid out for display, and sought to bring in visitors to see, touch, hear and remember 'their memories'. Raphael Samuel writes of how:

> the 'heritage' which conservationists fight to preserve and retrieval projects to unearth, and which the holiday public or museum visitors are invited to 'experience' – is in many ways a novel one. Though indu-bitably British ... It has little to do with the continuities of monarchy, parliament or British national institutions ... It is the little platoons, rather than the great society, which command attention in this new version of the national past. (Samuel, 1994: 158)

One interesting 'little platoon' established the Aros Heritage Centre on the Isle of Skye in Scotland (see Macdonald, 1997; Dicks, 2000). Its two founders thought that establishing such a commercially oriented Centre would help to strengthen Gaelic language and culture. But Aros possesses few 'authentic' exhibits to be put into a museum. Aros mostly consists of 'reproductions' since Gaelic culture was a poor culture with few physical remains.

Also the 'story' that it tells links together the decline of Gaelic culture with the history of resistance of the people both to the English and to Scottish clan chiefs. The Gaelic heritage story does not presuppose a pristine, untouched and authentic culture. Gaelic heritage is rather a story of contact and relations with numerous outsiders – and such a story highlights resilience, resistance and the appropriation of elements from beyond Gaelic culture. Thus Gaelic heritage is a hybrid and did not exist in some authentic state before visitors began to arrive. Gaelic places are thus places of movement and both visitors and locals have made Aros for visual consumption.

Mobile Places

Hetherington develops this notion of place as a 'place of movement'. Imagine, he says, that places are metaphorically like ships (Hetherington, 1997: 185–9). They are not something that stays in one place but move around within networks of agents, both humans and non-humans. As noted in the case of Gaelic heritage, places are about relationships, about the placings of materials and the system of difference that they perform. Places should be thought of as being located in relation to sets of objects rather than being fixed through subjects and their uniquely human meanings and interactions.

And places even based upon a high degree of geographical propinquity normally depend upon mobilities. There are countless ways of a sense of dwelling being reinforced through *movement* within a place's boundaries, such as walking along well-worn paths. But any such community is also interconnected to many other places through movement. Raymond Williams in the novel *Border Country* is 'fascinated by the networks men and women set up, the trails and territorial structures they make as they move across a region, and the ways these interact or interfere with each other' (Pinkney, 1991: 49; Williams, 1988).

Some of this movement of place itself can be seen in the history of the English Lake District (see Urry, 1995: Chapter 13). This area in the northwest of England only really became part of England when many visitors, particularly artists and writers, began to travel to it especially from the metropolitan centre at the end of the 18th century and especially in the 19th century. These visitors moved the landscape of the Lake District closer to the centre of England through the concepts of the picturesque and the sublime that came to structure the very experience of place. Land got changed into landscape because of the artists and writers who moved the Lake counties *into* English culture.

Many of the key writers were deemed to be local, from that place, and became known as the 'Lake poets'. They became celebrities in an area that had previously not had national celebrities. These writers were major tourist attractions especially for metropolitan visitors; by the 1840s Wordsworth was receiving 500 visitors a year at Rydal Mount. And after their death the Lake poets were transformed into literary shrines and memorialised as core figures now at the very heart of English literature. These visitors had brought the peripheral and background area of inhospitable terror, of land, closer to the centre, almost part of a metropolitan nature. This is very similar to the processes involved in metropolitanising nature around Paris also in the mid-19th century (Green, 1990: 88).

Place and Landscape

In *Howard's End* E.M. Forster noted that certain kinds of place have come to be nomadic or cosmopolitan in character. He argued that '[u]nder cosmopolitanism ... we shall receive no help from the earth. Trees and meadows and mountains will only be a spectacle ...' or landscape (E.M. Forster, 1931: 243; see Szerszynski & Urry, 2002, for related research). Certain local places seem quintessentially cosmopolitan; other places not. And certain sorts of places come to be seen as detached from nature and the physical environment. Nature is transformed into landscape, containing images of trees, meadows and mountains that are to be known about, compared, evaluated, possessed, but not according to Forster places that can be 'dwelt-within' as land.

It seems that, as visuality has become central to the consumption of place, so it has turned into an abstracted, somewhat disembodied quality or capacity. There is thus a tendency for *all* places in the end to become cosmopolitan and nomadic. The related shift to a *visual* economy of nature – the assumption that nature and place are above all to be looked at rather than used and appropriated – assists this 'de-substantialisation' of place. A given locality becomes not a unique place, with its own associations and meanings for those dwelling or even visiting there, but a particular combination of abstract characteristics that mark it out as similar or different, as more or less scenic than all sorts of other places.

The language of landscape is thus a language of mobility, of abstract characteristics. It is not just that such mobility is necessary if one is to develop the capacity to be reflexive about landscape. It is also that landscape talk is itself an expression of the life-world of mobile groups, including both tourists and environmentalists. If places are increasingly visually consumed, this is a consumption of movement, of bodies, images, information, moving over, under and across the globe and subjecting it to abstract characterisations. Those mobilities, a 'fluid modernity', have produced a widespread capacity for aesthetic judgement that has in turn fed into and animated the environmental movement.

And yet this is judgement from afar, not necessarily 'grounded', a judgement possessive and abstract. In *The Beaten Track*, Buzard notes how Wordsworth's *The Brother* 'signifies the beginning of modernity ... a time when one stops belonging to a culture and can only tour it' (Buzard, 1993: 27). And yet it leads to the consuming up of place after place through an unrelenting visual economy of signs. Places can indeed be consumed, wasted, used up as they are merely a set of abstract characteristics. Consuming places can literally consume places as the tourism industry rushes headlong in a search for a new room with a view before it gets immediately 'postcarded'. And in consuming places we too are consumed. The consuming of place as landscape is thus our destiny and our dilemma. It cannot be avoided.

References

Abercrombie, N. and Longhurst, B. (1998) *Audiences*. London: Sage.

Buzard, J. (1993) *The Beaten Track*. Oxford: Clarendon Press.

Dicks, B. (2000) *Heritage, Place and Community*. Cardiff: University of Wales Press.

Edensor, T. (1998) *Tourists at the Taj*. London: Routledge.

Fainstein, S. and Judd, D. (eds) (1999) *The Tourist City*. Cornell: Yale University Press.

Forster, E.M. (1931) *Howard's End*. Harmondsworth: Penguin.

Forster, E.M. (1955 [1908]) *A Room with a View*. Harmondsworth: Penguin.

Green, N. (1990) *The Spectacle of Nature*. Manchester: Manchester University Press.

Hetherington, K. (1997) In place of geometry: The materiality of place. In K. Hetherington and R. Munro (eds) *Ideas of Difference*. Oxford: Blackwell/ Sociological Review.

Lash, S. and Urry, J. (1994) *Economies of Signs and Space*. London: Sage.

Macdonald, S. (1997) A people's story: Heritage, identity and authenticity. In C. Rojek and J. Urry (eds) *Touring Cultures* (pp. 155–75). London: Routledge.

Macnaghten, P. and Urry, J. (1998) *Contested Natures*. London: Sage.

Milton, K. (1993) Land or landscape: Rural planning policy and the symbolic construction of the countryside. In M. Murray and J. Greer (eds) *Rural Development in Ireland* (pp. 120–50). Aldershot: Avebury.

Osborne, P. (2000) *Travelling Light. Photography, Travel and Visual Culture*. Manchester: Manchester University Press.

Ousby, I. (1990) *The Englishman's England*. Cambridge: Cambridge University Press.

Pinkney, T. (1991) *Raymond Williams*. Bridgend: Seren Books.

Ring, J. (2000) *How the English Made the Alps*. London: John Murray.

Samuel, R. (1994) *Theatres of Memory*. Verso, London.

Sheller, M. (2003) *Consuming the Caribbean*. London: Routledge.

Szerszynski, B. and Urry, J. (2002) Cultures of cosmopolitanism. *Sociological Review* 50, 461–81.

Tester, K. (ed.) (1994) *The Flâneur*. London: Routledge.

Urry, J. (1995) *Consuming Places*. London: Routledge.

Urry, J. (2002) *The Tourist Gaze* (2nd edn). London: Sage. [First published in 1990]

Williams, R. (1972) Ideas of nature. In J. Benthall (ed.) *Ecology. The Shaping Enquiry* (pp. 146–64). London: Longman.
Williams, R. (1988) *Border Country*. London: Hogarth Press.

Chapter 2

Alternative India: Transgressive Spaces

KELLY DAVIDSON

> *As Said's remarks about the Orient indicate, the site and space of*
> *otherness is also the site of dreams, fantasies, obsessions, myths –*
> *a site where transgression (for the Western subject) is possible*
> (Venn, 1992: 50)

Introduction

The notion of 'Real India' is somewhat of a travel cliché; nevertheless the belief that it can be revealed through the process of travel still preoccupies many Western visitors. This chapter makes suggestions about the ways contemporary 'alternative' travellers understand India through travel discourse and practice and how they make sense of their experiences in spatial terms that rely on a particular form of 'planetary consciousness'(Pratt, 1992: 29–30). Alternative travel, which includes long-haul, budget travel, independent backpacking and overlanding, has emerged as a specific conceptual and organisational niche in the global tourism market. Its unique selling point is the idea that travelling is an important route to overturning the ways of relating to other cultures that have been circumscribed by the West's systematic accumulation of knowledge about the world. In this respect it is constituted as an oppositional cultural practice. Those who participate orientate themselves towards 'new' forms of intercultural understanding by seeking out experiential cross-cultural encounters that have the potential to transgress the boundaries of fixed national and Western identities.

Despite alternative travellers' shared conviction in the 'honesty' of their chosen mode of travel, those who spend time in India can be characterised by their differences, as much as by their similaritites. This chapter is based on the findings of an ethnographic research project that reveals marked differences in the personal and social investments various participants make in the process of travel, and in the ways that they spatialise this process within and through India's budget travel sites. It dwells upon the issue of *utopics*, whereby travellers project utopian social visions onto their representations of India's geography as specific symbolic sites and incorporate them into their own narratives of belonging and becoming. Going 'on the road' is seen as essential to the production of new identities and imagined communities, as travellers negotiate difference along India's budget trails; equally important is the finding that it is often the *spaces* (contexts, environments) in which these encounters take place that fashion the types of transgressive identities that they embrace (see Urry, this volume).

India: A Discursive Regime

India has a long history in the Western imagination. Since 1498, when Vasco da Gama sailed into the coast of Kerala, Indian settings and people have provided a vast reserve of stories, images and myths for the Western traveller. The various representations that have appeared in historical, institutional and aesthetic texts during this time do not, of course, provide transparent access to any external 'reality' of India. Rather, the tropes, narratives and discourses inscribed in these textual signifying practices work to provide a coherent 'regime of truth' (Foucault, 1980) for their audiences, until even a casual observer might assume some neatly ordered entity that may be called 'India'.

The romantic images that the 'West' has projected onto India over time have conferred on it, as with other parts of the 'Orient', a very specific identity. This is dominated by the idea that India has an elusive, enigmatic quality that threatens to slip out of the grasp of analytical reason. This has not, of course, stopped other artists and travellers from trying to qualify their impressions of India in 'objective' terms. This desire to reveal India's fundamental essence has preoccupied Western cultural mediators, from Hegel to Mill, Forster, Kipling, and latterly Malle and Jhabvala. Since each version is only partial, it should be surprising that most visitors who return from India claim to 'know' it well. The predominant image that has emerged is that of a land of fascinating contradictions: of disease and exoticism, lavish opulence and grinding poverty, unspoilt tribals and social repression. This perceptual framing makes critical analysis difficult in the sense that almost anything can be read onto India, but over time two particular ways of understanding India have come to dominate. In one, India is passive and spiritual; in the other it is constructed through the trope of chaos and irrational violence. On the surface these discourses appear to be diametrically opposed. Nevertheless, whether they celebrate or lament the characteristics they perceive within Indian culture and civilisation, they set up clear differences between this 'organic' India and a 'cultured' West.

Today these established representations have been revitalised across a range of Indian and overseas tourist advertising which promotes the idea of travelling in India as a life-changing experience (see Morgan & Pritchard, 2001: 279–80). Even Lonely Planet Publications' guidebook, *India: A Travel Survival Kit* (Crowther *et al.*, 1993: 1104), the 'backpackers' Bible' for 'free-thinking' travellers, reinforces the convention of India's essentially vital quality, that can be known through sensory metaphors. The editorial claims that India 'somehow gets into your blood ... it's a total experience, an assault on the senses' (1993: 16). Such myths form much of the cultural baggage that contemporary visitors bring to India, as a means of interpreting their cross-cultural travel experiences. What is at stake is how their ways of being-towards-the-locals are complicit with, or contest the clearly ethnocentric worldview that has produced India as the oriental 'Other'. As Edward Said (1978, 1994) has pointed out, any concepts, trends and mythologies that organise 'First World' people's interactions with India are inevitably bound up with a residue of imperialism and the hegemonic power to be in, and define, 'other' cultures. Indeed most contemporary images of India emerged through the history of European colonisation of India, where the identities of coloniser and colonised were forged and where the colonial struggle was expressed in Europe's romantic fiction as the clash between a rational, progressive culture and an exotic, but turbulent nature.

Recent studies within the sociology of tourism argue that an equally problematic romanticism underpins contemporary travel practices. Several theorists have reinterpreted popular myths about the nature of 'real travel' by stressing how travellers' motivations, meanings and actions are grounded in the broader structures of power, economic and material interests from which they speak (Munt, 1994; Desforges, 1998; Urry, 2002 [1990]). Of interest is the growing specialist market impulse for 'getting back to nature', expressed in a renewed desire for 'authenticity' and in an exponential rise in interest for visiting 'Third World' countries (Munt, 1994: 103–23). This romantic insistence on aesthetic pleasure and the sacralisation of other countries often conceals implicit ideological concerns with domination. In this sense the discourse and practices of contemporary Western travellers may mirror earlier exploratory missions that represented non-European countries through naturalistic metaphors and thus constituted the world as a 'marvellous possession'. Nevertheless, as Said (1994: xxix) reminds us, all cultures are 'hybrid, heterogeneous, extraordinarily differentiated and unmonolythic'. The cross-cultural travel that many of today's travellers engage with gestures towards a different political project. The 'imaginative pleasure-seeking' that informs their experiences in India is fuelled by other ideological premises and claims to problematise older preconceptions about the Western 'Self' and Indian 'Other'.

The Framing of Alternative Travel

In recent years, tourism sociologists, social geographers and cultural theorists have become interested in the cultures and activities of adventure travellers and independent travellers on the global 'shoestring' trails. What unites this significant body of work is a desire to understand how these popular modes of travel frame understandings of the postcolonial world and incorporate their travelling experiences into their own conception of self-identity. Two particular academic trends have come to dominate. Firstly, following Urry (1995: 211–29), several sociologists (Munt, 1994; Hampton, 1998; Desforges, 1998, 2000) have adapted aspects of Bourdieu's (1989) social critique of hegemonic taste cultures to examine how the discourse of alternative travel used by backpackers and adventure travel operators serves to confer symbolic distinction on their preferred travel practices, enabling them to avail of the privilege that goes hand in hand with entry into an empowered social class.

Luke Desforges (1998: 191) argues that 'long-haul travel is at the centre of a largely white middle-class identity and its representations of the world beyond home', that independent travellers frame the world as a place to be collected and later used to extend their privileged identities at home. Ian Munt (1994: 101–23) also sees alternative travel as a predominantly middle-class form of tourist consumption that depends on the construction of Third and Fourth World authenticity to attest to the perceived superiority of their own character, lifestyle and orientating practices (see also O'Reilly, this volume). The long-haul journey is intellectualised as a process of self-education into the backstage lives of other peoples in destinations that are imagined as sites for adventurous exploration and achievement. Further, this adventure rhetoric allows participants to cash in on their travel experience by using it as an entry-level qualification into the travel industry, social welfare and development sectors.

A different perspective on the relationship between long-haul travel and identity is found in Anne Beezer's analysis of adventure travel rhetoric. By emphasising the process through which individual and social identities are constituted *through* travel and experience of other countries, Beezer (1993: 119–30) draws interesting links between the discourse of alternative travel and postmodern theories of identity. For Beezer the 'planetary consciousness' of alternative travel purports to change the goalposts of Western travellers' experiential and interpretative process in countries on the European 'pleasure periphery'.

According to Beezer the fascination that underpins much long-haul travel is the deeply held conviction that travelling offers a way to finding a route towards the construction of new identities, rather than a way to confirm older, 'rooted' ones. From this central premise, Beezer identifies three key features of postmodern travel discourse that construct travel as an alternative way of orientating oneself in the world. Firstly, the discourse depends on the 'real' traveller as 'nomadic subject', for whom travelling is a form of resistance against the authoritative legislation that organises people spatially, especially within the boundaries of the nation-state. As developments in telecommunications and international transport systems 'shrink' distances between local and global spaces, old ties of belonging and identity are being dissolved. For some, this process signifies a loss of power and certitude that must be reclaimed; for others the social and cultural changes brought about by the condition of post-modernity offer opportunities to seek out new forms of 'imagined community'. One such example would be the emergence of a European identity which is developing as a consequence of short-term mobility and its relationship to the transformation of familiar social identities. (Urry, 1995: 169). A second aspect of alternative travel discourse is the pursuit of 'difference'. Kobena Mercer (1990: 58–60) argues that difference is the privileged metaphor of modern societies. This is based on the understanding that the modern 'Self' is becoming increasingly creole as new social movements, diverse ethnicities, migrant groups and languages radically alter the social and political landscape of the sovereign nation-state. If the world is also broadly imagined as a series of differences, it follows that many people view travel as an educational short-cut into encountering difference on a global scale. Thirdly, alternative travel discourse still relies on the concept of authenticity, given its curiosity with encountering other people's 'backstage' lives. Yet this concern with the 'real' is employed within an interactive narrative; alternative travellers are interested in integration, not observation and in experience, rather than objectification. In this respect alternative travellers seek to reinvent adventure in a way that avoids the limiting perceptions characterised by earlier exploration narratives and by contemporary tourism.

The discourse, and the theory which has produced the notion of alternative travel, imagines the actual experiences and intercultural encounters that this involves in optimistic, even utopian, terms. To this end, I would like to add to the features that Beezer identifies as characterising 'alternative' postmodern travel by drawing on Louis Marin's (1984) description of *utopics*. Utopics is a useful organising concept through which to analyse the spatial practices that may identify alternative travellers' values and the ways that they express them while travelling. I come to Marin following Kevin Hetherington (1998), who uses the concept to outline how new social movements translate their cultural politics into spatial practice, by searching out spaces where they can project utopian visions of good society. The idea that global travel offers a route to new hybrid identities and intercultural understandings is evidently a utopian outlook, since it demands the construction of certain sites and places within the travelled space as more perfect and authentic than the traveller is used to at home. Yet, as Hetherington notes (1998: 334), '[u]topias do not exist; what exist are the translations of ideas about the good life and about social and moral order onto social reality', so these authenticated, utopian spaces must be viewed as *contested* terrains where new meanings and associations may be attached onto older, more empowered certainties of representation.

The social geographer, Doreen Massey (1998: 126–7) makes an important point that addresses the limitations of attempting to access cultural hybridity through travel. She argues that territorialisation is an important component in any instance of intercultural exchange where the contested construction and production of identities takes place. Although alternative travel is organised around the liberal desire to experience cultural 'difference' through the process of travel, this doesn't stop participants from trying to carve out and control their own exclusive spaces across the globe. In one sense this means establishing categories of group membership and identification with other travellers (and excluding others). More specifically this has implications for the ways that travellers produce and consume other places as particular 'symbolic spaces' for the construction of new hybrid identities. Different countries and regions lend themselves to different utopian imaginings through prior expectation; this means that *where* 'alternative' travellers choose to enact their alternative adventures is significant, not the fact they travel at all.

India's popularity as an important site of overland and budget travel reflects back on the way that it has been framed historically within tourist literature, cinema, photography, colonial and literary texts as a very particular symbolic space. What is at stake is the extent to which those self-consciously alternative travel scenes that have emerged in India are implicated in a complex form of romanticism which taps into the global inequality between 'the West and the Rest'. The following sections examine a range of alternative travel positions, discourses and practices across some of India's popular budget arenas, to assess how travellers negotiate their relationships to India in ways that confirm or contest these received histories. It seeks to address how prior representations of Indian 'Otherness' frame the very *types* of transgressive identifications that can be enacted through spatial practice, and how these impact on travellers' desire for a transformation of the 'Self' and intercultural understanding.

Method and Data

This chapter is based on the findings of a broader ethnographic research project into contemporary travellers' production and consumption of India. The fieldwork extended observations of the traveller scene made during six visits to India between 1986 and 1997. A formal research strategy consisted of a period of participant observation in India's budget travel sites. This method was chosen on the grounds that while texts have an important role in shaping travellers' relationships to India, it is important not to lose the connection between the production and consumption of India through travel as a form of 'lived experience'. It is often 'on the road' that the discourse of alternative travel is revealed as budget travellers spatialise difference through their day-to-day encounters. Ethnography provides a way to understand the process of representation: the moments, contexts and situations through which India's meanings are decided by travellers in the geopolitical and discursive spaces of India's budget travel circuits. It also offers a framework to analyse how engaging with India's physical environments on a daily basis might destabilise the discourses through which travellers speak and how they represent themselves and 'difference' to themselves. In this sense ethnographic research helps to provide a sense of the new cultural subjects that emerge along the backpacker trails as new 'contact zones' of intercultural exchange.

Fieldwork sites were chosen from among a range of India's popular traveller stop-off points. Priority was given to locations that the *Travel Survival Kit* marked out as 'highlights': firstly, sites of interest for historical tourism, including former colonial stations; secondly, sites noted for the provision of facilities for spiritual development; thirdly, places that offer opportunities for travellers to engage in voluntary work. Lastly there were 'freak centres', areas known on the international dance culture circuit, those accommodating a semi-permanent traveller 'community', or where there is a concentrated drug culture. Already the 'Indian experience' for independent, budget travel is mapped in spatial terms as a series of overlapping 'scenes' that provide various alternative pleasures and activities.

Research began in New Delhi, the key international entry point to India. As Delhi was also the planned capital city of the former British colonial administration, it was an important site in which to study travellers' interest in historical tourism. A second site chosen was Dharamsala, of historical interest as a former hill station in the Himalayan foothills. This is, however, only one of the area's tourist 'attractions'. The geographical location has enabled a highly developed tourist infrastructure for trekking and other ventures. The nearby village of McLeod Ganj is the main settlement of India's 12,000 Tibetan refugees and home to the Dalai Lama and Tibetan government in exile. The community is dependent on international aid for infrastructural support and many foreign students and development workers are involved in fund-raising and political-humanitarian activity. This disenfranchised community is obliged to 'sell itself' for the annual influx of metropolitan tourists; therefore a significant service industry has grown to cater for the independent traveller market in yoga and meditational practice, alternative medicine and Tibetan language and history classes.

Equally important in identifying fieldwork sites was the issue of geography and aesthetics. Fieldwork centred on sites that could be said to incorporate the 'diversity' of India's urban and rural geography and to investigate how these aesthetic dimensions produced specific discourses about travelling and about India. As the imaginative aspects of pre-trip planning are a central component of global travel, it was also interesting to note how travellers' prior expectations of India, as framed by the representational strategies of Lonely Planet's promotional literature and other textual sources, were renegotiated as they travelled.

Individual travellers and groups were approached by casually hanging about in popular guesthouses and cafés and joining in a variety of classes and cultural events. I was interested in identifying a range of traveller-positions and therefore took up any opportunities presented to participate in the more visible traveller 'scenes'. The main body of research was conducted as participant-observer to their varied daily routines, experiences and travel practices, supplemented with in-depth research with 18 travellers who were identified as spanning a broad spectrum of traveller demographics. These informants were aged between 23 and 50 years; more than half were European (British, Scandinavian, Dutch, French, Italian, German), two were from Australia, three from North America, and two from Israel. Of the 18, nearly all were travelling alone; half were first-time visitors to India, while the others had a longer-term relationship with the independent travel scene there. Their educational and class backgrounds were diverse; subjects' occupations included teacher, filmmaker, small-time drug trafficker, university dropout, petty entrepreneurs and exporters, trustafarian, painter, ex-soldier, magico-anthropologist, charity worker, DJ, farm-worker, housewife, guitar-maker, goatherd and health-store worker. Evidently none fitted the category of 'gap-year' backpacker, although three did describe their trip as a career sabbatical. In fact, only four or five would have been happy to define their form of travel as backpacking; since this term now conjures up images of young, privileged gap-year students it has lost its cachet in budget travel circuits. Some would consider this term an insult to their status as travellers. Most participants define themselves as simply travellers, 'real' travellers or 'nomads' and while nearly every budget traveller in India is reliant on the *Travel Survival Kit* or *Rough Guide* to varying extents, a significant number are hostile to the idea of being perceived as consumers of an externally framed travel experience, rather than producers of their own unique experience.

Field notes taken from participant observation were produced as a 'thick description' (Geertz, 1973: 9), which included comprehensive information about travellers' day-to-day discussions and activities. This material was cross-referenced with verbal data, audio-recorded on an unobtrusive dictaphone, from a series of informal interviews with my 18 main respondents. The minimum length of interview was one and a half hours, but several informants allowed their casual conversations to be recorded regularly over an extended period. Interviews were non-directive; apart from prompting lines of enquiry about travellers' life histories, about the moment they decided to travel in India and about their prior familiarity with other texts about India, informants often set the agenda for conversation. While this sometimes produced inarticulate, fragmented and conflicting information, this material was welcomed as the 'creative potential of uncertainty' (Willis, 1997: 252) and used to open new areas of enquiry. This twin research strategy aimed to grasp travellers' key 'structures of signification' (Fabian, 1990: 5) in language and behaviour, to understand the personal and social investments that underpin their travel experience in India. Secondly, it aimed to address how the symbolic meanings and values they attach to India's diverse physical environments mediates their actual modes of participation, as they draw them into more locally inflected searches for identity.

Social Investments in Budget Travel

Within the culture of alternative budget travel in India we can identify a distinctly political element; significant numbers of participants consider their mode of travel to be a resisting, 'oppositional' practice that signifies an emergent form of cultural politics. At a local level, many travellers imagine and experience travel as a route to 'finding one's own space' outside of the social, political and economic contradictions of life at home. Travelling is conceived as a way to resist some of the profound impacts that broad global economic restructuring and other global processes have had on how people live and represent themselves more locally. Secondly, participants orientate themselves towards the ideal of the 'global village'. They take for granted a cultural fusion of references, from the popular sounds of 'World Music', international organisation of 'green' politics, media and fashion influences. It is this cross-fertilisation of eclectic political, social and cultural elements, and not the older, hegemonic framings of 'Self' and 'Other', that they claim have purchase on their self-identities, since they appear to provide space for the mobilisation and expression of new collective identifications, mythologies and 'imagined communities' (Anderson, 1983).

It can, of course, be difficult to carve out one's own space 'at home', amid the responsibilities and social ties that form the general background noise of our lives. This is why travel has a genuine appeal. By framing the world as an array of spatial encounters with difference, long-haul travel appears to provide more individual freedom to determine one's own space by participating as individuals in shared activities with other like-minded people, instead of as a representative of their race, social class or nationality. Further, by going 'on the road' and eschewing official tourist interventions, travellers generally view themselves as voluntary migrants who actively seek out the nomadic state through the process of the experiential encounter. In identifying themselves in this way, they imply that the important element of the alternative travel experience involves throwing off the shackles of rooted Western identities and learning about repressed and marginalised stories and histories via face-to-face encounters with different cultures and lived experience.

My fieldwork findings indicate, nevertheless, that so-called alternative travellers are not, as Munt (1994: 106) suggests, an undifferentiated mass of middle-class individuals. Those people who act out elements of this travel discourse within India's popular budget sites have often widely varying investments in the travel process, and in India itself, depending on their particular life histories, value-systems and self-conceptions. The oppositional aspect of alternative travelling is not characterised by any over-arching struggle against any single parent culture or source of power. There is no singular traveller identity in India *per se*; they can only be understood spatially as individuals participating within a series of overlapping local 'scenes' and identifications.

Travel as personal quest

Many people journey to India on a form of *pilgrimage*, motivated by a desire to reassess their life priorities or make significant career changes. Many are typical of Bourdieu's new intellectuals: professionals searching for a way to live 'humanely' within the contradictions of a restructured marketplace at home. Ann (46), a teacher from Ontario, admitted to feeling 'trapped in my life, with my friends and their expectations of me ... I just wanted to take a semester out. It seems like the students just remain the same year in, year out ... I'm just getting older'. A product of the baby-boom generation, Ann, like many other travellers, has grown up with strong sympathies for the liberalising ideals of the Sixties but is struggling to find any real form of social identification in the present:

> My friend said, out of the blue ... 'Why don't you go to India?' because of the fact there are a lot of ashrams and meditation centres where I could stay a while .... one guy that I knew ... had given me a trunk full of books written in and about India. So I sat down and ploughed my way through them ... I started to take it that there was something fatalistic about going to India. And of course, it fitted in with the meditation, the Buddhism and a lot of practices I was already involved in.

Similar feelings were expressed by Tamia, a Canadian filmmaker:

I was sick of a lot of things that were happening in my life ... of the work I was doing and its usefulness ... People travel for a lot of reasons and motivations and mine was definitely ... a personal journey ... a quest for internal development, something that I feel inside myself and not really experiencing anything external, like Indian culture, or about life in India.

For both women, travelling amounts to a 'romantic flight from the social world' (Bourdieu, 1989: 371). This desire resurfaces in their preoccupation with a 'cult of nature' (Barthes, 1973: 74), perceived to exist in India because of its long-standing association with natural therapies, ayurvedic medicines and a complementary blend of individualising spiritual influences. Their mode of travel on a meagre budget, living with the sparse facilities of cheap hotels and ashram accommodation, is that of the new ascetics, whose 'stripped down' lifestyle attests to their attempt to rid themselves of a 'Western' consumer identity (Beezer, 1993: 125). Participation in the discipline of meditational retreats implies that their travelling identities are produced through travel-as-labour, appropriate to sloughing off layers of Western Selfhood and discovering a more 'organic' Self. Their daily experience involves rising in the early morning, then devoting themselves to routine-bound meditation, yoga and Buddhist theology classes and cultural lectures. Yet, as Tamia insists:

I think in the West we put pressure on ourselves to ... force ourselves ahead, have a certain standard of material comforts. Since I've been travelling I've begun to take a lot from the way that Indian people live, more simplicity in their approach to living, their work.

The association between travel as *travail* is further grounded in the voluntary labour of those travellers who fall into charity and development work in India. Whereas pilgrim-types retreat from the social world into mental and spiritual contemplation, these people stretch out their local concerns about social and cultural inequality into the global arena through a form of travel that signifies a level of social commitment. Within minutes of meeting Martin, he pulls off his shirt to reveal 'my political affiliations on my body', tattoos of the Tibetan Snow Lion which signifies the Tibetan political struggle for *Rangzen* (freedom). Martin has worked as a volunteer with the Swiss Tibet Support Group for a few years, undertaking various public relations exercises and organising political lobbies. Annie travelled from Colorado to participate in a community development project in Rajasthan:

I've been saving for this trip for two years, after dropping out of journalism college ... In my teens, I was into saving the rainforest. I guess that's what everyone does once in their life ... It's a long story, how I came to be in India. I'd been searching a long time. The reason I chose this project is that it's involved with a lot of different schemes like schools, irrigation schemes ... they send two foreigners out together for three weeks to spend time in the villages and get an experience for the culture ... I didn't want to be your typical tourist. I knew I'd be bored.

The ideology of leisure

Against the orientating practices of these groups are the travellers who travel primarily for pleasure and for whom India symbolises the 'drifter' fantasy of 'dropping out' altogether from a normalised work-ethic. These travellers can be divided into broad sub-groups, brought together in travel through a shared ideology of leisure. Ralegh is a trustafarian whose private income enables a nomadic lifestyle:

> Travelling allows me to indulge myself in whatever I happen to be into at the time – throat singing, taking on epic projects like making an even-stringed Tibetan guitar, living in nomadic tents – then again, there's a long line of travellers and weird, offbeat people in my family, so I strongly identify with that ... Sir Francis Chichester ... an artist less well known, but a student of Gauguin ... my grandmother had gone around North America ... of course she'd really be on an extended tea party visit. But even so ...

Many other young people are taking time out from the rigid discipline of national military service, especially young Israelis who arrive in India fresh from the army to join their peers on the international club-culture circuit. While excess and hedonism characterises their orientating practices in India, they differ markedly from the 'hard-core' individuals whose longevity as travellers attests to a more 'dropped-out' and 'anti-establishment' status. Yardie Steve claims to be a 'freak' who 'freed myself from all sorts of attachments':

> I've spent thirty nine years at it so I do think I've remained quite outside all of the social structures ... most people I know have succumbed by now. They've got a mortgage and a job or some kind of bond, like a wife and kids, some kind of attachment.

Space and the temporality of identification

Although travelling subjectivities are produced in relation to individual travellers' social needs, they're also produced in transit as travellers shift identifications and form temporary affiliations on the road. Ben Malbon (1998: 279) has argued that immersing oneself in a particular 'symbolic space' may bring into play the 'significance of the moment', where the boundaries that structure travellers' normal identities are temporarily superseded by the *spaces* of their identifications. In other words, travellers' immediate environments often take paramount importance in shaping their temporary identifications. The Goan coastal state lends itself to the formation of an ephemeral transnational identity. As Ralegh points out: 'In Britain, there's been a lot of stuff in the press about Goa Trance coming back to the clubs in England. I was aware that Goa was really exploding.'

In Dinky's Bar in Calangute Beach, I meet Sonke (36), a Berliner who splits his time between trading specialist motorbikes and antiques in Europe and recording trance music for the Goan beach circuits. Dinky's is a cheap bar-restaurant in the village square, a spartan, Portuguese-styled building, with an open-fronted verandah. It is popular with independent travellers and clubbers; cheaper than other village restaurants, Dinky's stocks a vast range of bar products, the management don't set out to attract Calangute's extensive package-tourist market and they appear to turn a blind eye to the semi-regular foreign patrons' chillum consumption. The clientele are largely men in their 20s or 30s, dressed in baggy pyjama trousers, embroidered waistcoats (no shirts) and adorned with dreadlocks and 'New Age' tattoos. As with many Goan beach venues, a huge sound system dominates the bar, emanating base-heavy dub reggae and the psychedelic techno known as 'Goa Trance'. The layered sound and repetitive beat lends itself to the ecstasy-led dance rhythms of the transnational club culture; Sonke and other regulars use the bar to test out their own sounds, which they sell from the flea markets on the nearby beaches of Baga and Anjuna.

Goa is established as a very particular traveller space where young Europeans seek out a sense of affinity with others in a specific social situation. The beach setting and open-fronted bar shacks offer the promise of social proximity, a sense of unity and togetherness when the beaches come alive at night. The scene itself takes temporary priority over individual travellers' identities in producing a travelling subjectivity. Each evening, party-goers congregate at Dinky's to await the arrival of young men on motorbikes who circulate the flyers that announce that evening's main clubbing venue. The anticipation of a 'happening', of a coming together in shared pleasure culminates after midnight. The beaches fill with young clubbers, musicians, sub-culturalists, each both performer and spectator in a scene where their individual identities yield temporarily to the collective identifications produced in the ephemeral moment and space of the beach party and bound up in the tactile, bodily, emotional and chemical pleasures of Goan trance.

In many respects Goa's transnational club scene may be read as indistinguishable from Queensland's Doof parties, Glastonbury or Kuta Beach in the way that it invites particular travelling identities. The only specific 'Indian' aspects that might be distinguished within Goa's traveller scene are the surface visual signifiers of beach party backdrops – painted Shivas, Third Eyes and Oms or the psychedelic packaging of Goan trance music. Goa Trance itself is less of a unique musical sound than a generic term to conjure up 'the Scene' in popular cultural memory. However, in popular mythology Goa's status goes beyond that of other international clubbing sites because of the longevity of its associations with earlier traveller cultures. This gives it a particular form of authenticity for contemporary clubbers, who would claim that you haven't 'done' India if you haven't been to Goa.

Counter-cultural framings of travel mythologies

One of the problems that academic theory has come up against in studies of travel is the reluctance to examine the purchase that 'low' theory and popular culture have on the mythologies that inspire vast numbers of Western travellers to visit India. Since Cohen's (1973) work on 'drifter tourism', few studies have examined the significance of a counter-cultural residue in shaping the privileged metaphors and sensibilities of contemporary travellers in India, although passing reference has been made to travellers' investments in hippie-spiritual philosophy, sixties styles, music and drug-use (Hutnyk, 1996; Bhattacharyya, 1997; Wilson, 1997). India did, of course, provide a focus for the communitarian ideals of the 1960s counter-culture and is, therefore sedimented in a nostalgic gaze for older travellers. Savvo remembers:

> So many people in those days; many came overland across the Turkish and Afghanistan borders, walking or by bus. They were sometimes really amazing to look at ... If you went to Goa in those days and arrived at Chapora or Vagator you wouldn't be able to get near the water because there were hundreds of buses parked in rows. People would set up camp on the beach and stay for months. The English buses could carry twenty people, pick up hitchhikers along the way, sit inside and smoke and play guitars. It's sad that you don't see them now, because some were really beautiful.

Henning came to India in the 1970s 'to smoke, enjoy myself, listen to Pink Floyd, Keith Richards'. Steve's decision to visit was based on a chain of counter-cultural equivalences:

> I was listening to a lot of reggae and punk but was still more influenced by Indian things, mysticism mostly. I was taking a lot of LSD and there was that strong association with India, of collective ways of living and the whole drug culture was enmeshed with the idea of India ... religion and the spirit ... all the imagery is there anyway, even if you take Jimi Hendrix and Axis Bold as Love and the Mahavishnu Orchestra ... always a strong connection with that British alternative society.

India's longstanding relationship with counter-culture and the mythologies inspired by a popular knowledge of India's special place for subterranean practices have as much weight as colonial narratives in fixing India's symbolic value in travellers' cultural memory. As a site for contemporary alternative travel, India is constructed as a place where certain transgressive pleasures are on offer as travellers reorientate themselves within popular spaces on the former overland trails. The following section draws upon the issue of utopics to look at how India's urban and rural zones are constructed as utopian symbolic spaces that attest to this alternative heritage. It examines how the spatial construction of specific traveller scenes in India mediates travellers' modes of participation in the travelled space, as well as the types of traveller identity that are open to them. Some spaces and contexts have a greater appeal than others, as do the types of socialisation and identification that are perceived within them. This has important implications for the ways in which budget travellers seek out and project 'authenticity' onto Indian landscape and culture, as they draw them into their own narratives of self identity.

The Country and the City: The Utopics of Travellers' India

Independent budget travellers often 'frame' Indian space in a way that expresses the alternative values that mark their different planetary consciousness from colonial and neo-colonial travellers. They rarely express interest in the 'mastering of otherness' signified by heroic, discovery rhetoric, but are concerned with integrating themselves into their surrounding environments in India in the hope of transforming the 'Self' and their interpretations of the world. The romantic imagining that India is a powerful and life-changing 'experience without a code' does, of course, lend itself well to this spatial practice. As Lonely Planet's editorial (1993: 16) asserts, although 'nothing is ever quite the way you expect it to be', travelling in India is dependent on 'what you make of it and what you want it to be'. By perpetuating such myths, the handbook locates each traveller as both producer and consumer of India's authenticity and difference and in doing so, stitches over the gap between alternative travellers' desires to act and be acted upon in their surrounding Indian environment; to be an agent of their own destiny, yet remain open to new experiences.

Despite their internal differences, most travellers share utopian expectations of India's countryside and cityscapes that play an important part in the construction of their traveller-identities. While their utopic visions can borrow heavily from familiar and hegemonic Western mythologies of rural 'free space' and the 'oriental city', they simultaneously wrench the meanings of these sites from their older contexts and invest them with new significance. In this sense, they are actively engaged with a form of spatial politics. Carving their own space requires them to compete over the contested meanings of utopian social and moral orders with more privileged Western representations of India.

The utopics of the countryside

In the seasonal and transitory patterns that characterise independent travel in India, many groups congregate in and around India's mountain towns and hill stations during the summer months. As a consequence, a visible traveller 'scene' has built up in towns like Manali, Almora and Dharamsala in Northern India, and Hampi, and Kodai Kanal in South India. These places attract long-stay visitors, as well as a massive influx of backpackers arriving from the winter party season in Goa. Pilgrim-types form a significant proportion of the independent travel scene in these rural sites which exemplify the utopic of the imaginary, Indian 'past'. India's village life is represented via the trope of the 'noble savage', a benign cultural antidote to the traveller's own lived experience:

Annie: [India] has so much to offer, and education and discovery, whether it be internal or external, is a key part of that. History too, because America has no history. We just psssh the American Indians as if their history is not part of our history ... So it's really interesting to be exposed to a country that has those roots ... there is an innocence in this country, while so many Americans are capable of murder ... car-jacking is practically a native sport. So I wanted to come to a simple country and see what simplicity is and then you come here and you think, oh, there really is another way to live ... if I squint right now I'm in Denver or Beaver Creek in Aspen, but ... spending time with Rajindran's family, they don't let poverty get them down. They're living totally functional lives in an apartment the size of my bedroom and they have so few things, yet they're happy ... here's people that can live without a TV. To most Americans that is genuinely a revelation.

Tamia: There's definitely a calmer and more laid back attitude to life. I look around and see how middle-aged men are here. In the West, they're treated abominably because their labour is no longer worth anything; here they're given respect and greater status ... then there's the children! We tend to shoo them away and pretend they don't exist to make life more convenient ... here I see that children are an important part of family life ... They're allowed to develop at their own pace ... it's a much more natural life here in India. And I also feel like Indians and Tibetans have a more childlike quality ... something more innocent that I have no experience of in Canada.

Ann: I'd agree to a point. I don't know that its necessarily freer here; certainly there are social and cultural restrictions in people's lives ...

they certainly have to worry about money. But I'd agree in that we're trained to accumulate money and material things that feeds into a vicious cycle of respecting that type of consumption, whereas they seem to work for things they actually need and then that's enough for a while ... I was feeling at odds with myself and the world ... then on arriving in McLeod Ganj I felt I'd made a connection ... The countryside reminds me of Canada with the snow on the mountains and the peaks ... I thought, right, I'm staying, I've come home.

Within this discursive framework, India's rural landscape and cultural life is produced as a 'magical resource that can be used without actually possessing or diminishing it' (MacCannell, 1992: 28). Travellers' investment in the utopic of Indian countryside reveals a nostalgia for an imaginary past modelled on Third World rustic simplicity as a prototype for ideal living. In this sense it may be guilty of the 'salvage mentality' discussed by Clifford (1989: 74) when he argues that, 'in Western taxonomy and memory, the various non-Western "ethnographic presents" are actually pasts. They represent culturally distinct times ("tradition") always about to undergo the impact of disruptive changes.' Yet the utopian vision of many of these traveller-participants is grounded in the 'New Age', 'folkist' politics of small-scale communitarianism, which contests the familiar, picturesque authenticity of a tamed pastoral idyll that is favoured in more orthodox tourist literature.

Utopics and the alternative community

The loose and unbounded nature of backpacker identifications accommodates many people whose lifestyles outside of their experiences of India may be said to be already semi-nomadic. Among others, the Indian backpacker trail includes people from the Rainbow Village 'tribes', new age travellers and people who are involved in alternative lifestyles in their birth countries. Kay spent 10 years living in a self-built timber house in the Nimbin community, Australia. John lives on an organic Dorset farm commune. Henning moved into a self-financing communal living experiment in the Copenhagen suburb Christiana as a teenager during the mid-1970s. Today he deals in classic cars and motorbikes, with a lucrative sideline importing hashish and heroin from Nepal. Many more travellers claim to live in squatted buildings across Northern Europe and Australia and use derelict urban premises to create workshop space for artistic and creative ventures. A sense of marginality is at the centre of their orientating practices and values. In some cases this surfaces in a desire for identification with other social struggles and marginalised groups, both at home and more globally. Female travellers may seek out information on grassroots feminist organisations within India with the intention of expressing solidarity among the 'global sisterhood'; others orientate themselves towards anti-racist or class struggles (in India this means developing a rudimentary understanding of caste), or a concern for 'tribal' and other 'disappearing cultures'. It should be stressed, however, that solidarity takes on an explicitly cultural rather than political form in most instances, as revealed in many travellers' wholesale appropriation of the signs and signifiers of 'cultural difference': an aesthetic preference for mehndi-painted hands, tattoos featuring OM signs, native American sun symbols, bindhis and an ascetic preference for yoga and meditation and the works of the Dalai Lama, Deepak Chopra and Richard Bach.

A felt marginal status may equally be expressed as an affiliation with contemporary sub-cultural practices. Henning moves on the periphery of Bandito cultural milieus in Copenhagen, just as Slim claims to have played guitar for Sonny Barger, of the Oakland Hell's Angels. 'Yardie' Steve alternates his leisure time between Birmingham's (England) 'hard-core' Rasta and Yardie scenes and, like many such travellers, he also expresses an increased interest in Hindu theology. Steve is engrossed primarily in the idea that 'Western people don't really understand the concept of love as much as they do in the East' and immerses himself in the precepts of Hinduism's pantheistic system:

> I'm a bit of an idealist. Immortality is the realisation of the unification and reconciling, that a man or a woman is only half a being. That's a strong Hindu interpretation, that to complete the masculine and feminine means reconciling yourself to your other half, becoming one ... unfashionable in Birmingham, but then again I'm not quite a normal person ... I've got that feminine side but I don't like exposing it too often ... But where I'm at is saturating myself in Hindu mythology with a bit of Rasta thrown in. They're much the same type of consciousness – Chidananda, existence, knowledge, bliss.

Other travellers turn to 'nature religions and earth mysteries ... forms of rejected knowledge (which) ... seeks to find in the landscape forgotten practices of knowing and understanding, both natural and social' (Hetherington, 1998: 335). In June 1997, the nomadic 'Family of Light and Love' circulated hand-painted posters around traveller sites in northern India, inviting their 'brothers and sisters' to a 'gathering' close to the Kulu-Manali route:

> We are beyond the upraising 'spiritual materialism' of the New Age Scene. Our goal is to realise that humanity is one family beyond the illusions of Nationalism, Religion (ism), Politic (ism) and Sectarianism ... The Rainbow is made from Light of all colours, and the family is universal ... our Mother is the Earth and our Father is the Spirit of Bliss. Our God is within and not 'FarOut', our Goddess is fully manifest.

> There is the prophesy of the 13 Tribes and the Message of Unity ... We have no leaders and respect natural qualities seeing each of us as a Star. Love is our Law and Positive Development is the wish of all of us. May we join and fuse instead of being Lonely and Confused!

Elsewhere travellers congregate around Hindu pilgrimage sites and fetishise the idea of 'living like the locals': queuing for water and fuel, cooking 'simple' food on their lightweight brass stoves and washing in the mountain streams. This desire for identification can be read onto the ways in which they appropriate very particular spaces for their activities. Although there is a large market in budget accommodation for foreign visitors across Himachal Pradesh, the most down-at-heel, shabby village rooms, stables and neglected colonial chalets are highly sought after by long-stay travellers. Others reject outright this basic accommodation in favour of constructing tarpaulin 'benders' and tepees in forest clearings, impermanent and in close proximity to the earth. Instead of promoting rural India as a positional good, or as a site of leisure over which the traveller controls the view, they invest the landscape with mystical and spiritual connotations. As I was reminded by a Danish anthropologist, everyone believes in magic and most carry at least one lucky charm or religious symbolic object on their person. Their daily conversations are littered with references to the 'spiritual vibes' and 'positive energies' that they claim are perceptible in the Himalayan foothills; the earth is invested with a specifically magical quality and produced discursively by the travellers as an entity with the ability to act upon them and subject their deeply held convictions to strain.

The gathering of the tribes

Partying is central to the spatial practice of some traveller groups and a routine part of their seasonal lifestyle. This is not simply the excessive hedonism of Goan club-culture; as exemplified by the Family of Light and Love's workshops, celebration occurs in a carnivalesque atmosphere associated with earlier hippie ideals of the 'free festival'. Parties take place during times of astrological importance and celebration of events like solstice, full moon, and other earth festivals take priority over the arbitrary criteria of international rave culture. At other times travellers engage in quiet activities: playing the primordial sounds of the didgeridoo, dholak or Tibetan singing bowl. These activities, along with their joint participation in charas (hash) consumption, draws upon the spiritual rituals of Indian saddhus or the native American peace pipe and thus connotes communal identification with other marginalised earth rites. With this New Age focus on connecting the natural and the spiritual, it is hardly surprising the lure that Hinduism and Tibetan Buddhism hold for these voluntary nomads. Both religions incorporate a belief system that includes a potent element of occultism in which demons and spirits, mantras, reincarnation and prayer beads play an integral part; horoscopes are calculated on the movement of planetary constellations or, in the case of Tibetan Buddhism, on the traveller's individual humours. Gurus and Rinpoches protect individual seekers and steer them on their personal path towards 'ultimate Truth'.

Clearly, the travellers' utopian outlook on India's rural landscape ruptures its main representation within Western culture as a site of leisure or raw wilderness over which 'man' must exercise mastery. The Indian sites that hold an appeal for contemporary alternative travellers might be understood as heterotopic spaces (Foucault, 1986), an idea borrowed again from Hetherington (1998: 333–4) to define the tensions created by alternate orderings of the meanings that are projected onto certain spaces. Traveller 'scenes' created in rural towns like Dharamsala are represented by their difference from home and by their different moral and social ordering from other Western utopic representations of India. As Chambers (1994: 120) has observed, syncretic 'New Age' knowledge 'challenges and scrambles the binary certainties that pass for knowledge and truth' by juxtaposing other, more local reference points onto their representations of space. Although these travellers orientate themselves within rural India around the notion of re-engaging with a lost past, it is within the utopics of small-scale communitarianism, earth worship and ancient, tribal social orders.

Heterotopia in the Indian city

The spatial play of utopics is also relevant to travellers' representations and experiences of the Indian city, where aesthetic factors carry considerable weight in structuring travellers' expectations. Describing what have, through time and familiarity become perceived as 'typically' Indian streets is a generic expectation of the Euro-American travel writer and metropolitan audience; they, like documentary and fictional filmmakers, invariably turn away from the cultivated spaces of India's colonial cities towards the 'organic' old cities in search of an 'authentic' urban core. I have already noted that it is this 'spectacular' quality that attracts alternative budget travellers to the backstreets of urban India; in this sense their projections about the 'real' India are strongly subject to the power of the orientalist imagination. In Delhi, for example, most budget travellers stay halfway between the old and new cities in the Main Bazar of Pahar Ganj, a busy inner-city vegetable market full of cheap hotels, electronics workshops, jewellery and textiles exporters. While this arena offers the comforts and technological conveniences of the new city, these converge with the aesthetic qualities embodied by popularised images of Old Delhi and the pre-modern Indian city. In Main Bazar, cows, fortune-tellers and beggars roam among market crowds and the busy barter of trading and religious devotions takes place within a maze of 'labyrinthian' streets. As Annie remarks: 'This place is so crazy with so many little dark side streets … my whole sense of reality has taken its own holiday.'

This unfamiliar and spectacular *mise-en-scène* invokes the orientalist fantasy of stepping back in time into the medina, a site both mesmerising and dangerous for the unwary traveller.

For colonial travellers (and orthodox tourists today) the Indian city was imagined as a place to be feared, as represented in the trope of the Black Hole of Calcutta: a stifling invasion of one's physical and emotional space. For alternative travellers, these fearful representations of urban anarchy are appropriated and reworked for an anti-heroic, 'rites of passage' rhetoric. Confusion and claustrophobia are actively sought out, often with the aid of hallucinogenics.

> **Ralegh:** In Pushkar I got two bhang lassis for the journey … It was the maddest thing arriving in Jaisalmer. It seems to be regarded as one of the worst places to arrive in … there were tonnes of people at the train station, descending on you and trying to get you to their hotel. Everyone says Jaisalmer is unbelievable. So I'd been drinking the bhang lassi … I dropped unconscious in the train and woke up before six. I remember looking at myself in the mirror and it was just like one of those Ozric faces, completely bloodshot eyes … I was walking around like a zombie, out into this madness … all these people surrounding you, yelling, grabbing you and pulling you off balance. From time to time there would be a bit of a scuffle … they'd literally start punching each other and there was no escape from it … If I'd been there any longer I'd have lost it. I was like a trapped animal.

This delighted preoccupation with urban chaos is based on the notion that immersing oneself in India's 'otherness' and submitting the mind and body to poverty, disease and deformity will bring about a state of heightened sensory perception that crosses the boundaries of repressed Western perception. This popular outlook on the city reworks the mythologies of India as a particular symbolic space where 'beyond the boundaries' experimentations with structured 'Western' identities are effected. This paves the way for new forms of subterranean identity to emerge in the back streets as black market contacts and the underground flow of money, passports and drugs enable hard-core travellers to reaffirm their own more individualistic 'outlaw' status as travellers.

Heterotopic space and alternative heritage

It is within this framework that Main Bazar becomes another hetero-topic Indian space; what it represents to many alternative travellers disrupts other neatly ordered, hegemonic representations of the 'Oriental City'. Although the area's local businesses are thriving, Main Bazar is largely a tourist economy and is therefore open to contested debates about the extent of its 'authenticity'. In the ordering of traveller experience, Main Bazar is Delhi, yet not Delhi. 'Modern' Delhi appears to stand outside this traveller enclave, in the city centre and wealthy suburbs, yet travellers are too sophisticated not to notice that Main Bazar no longer bears much resemblance to the pre-modern oriental medina ('Come on! You've just come from the Internet café. We distort the local economy by being here'). In this area, it is another 'authentic' moment, that of the 'original' overlander experience, commodified for contemporary travellers via the recycling of 'hippie retro' fashions along the Bazar.

In one sense, it could be argued that the widespread consumption of traveller styles from the market traders is illustrative of the travellers' attempts to create a semiological fit between their own appearance and the local environment. Certainly, their preference for low-grade cotton and second-hand silk appears to consolidate the notion that alternative travellers are keen to moderate their consumption practices and use only basic amenities in accordance with the local economy. On arrival in India, Aviram made straight for a local tailor for roughly-woven kurta pyjamas, made from homespun khadi cloth. Yet Avi wasn't simply dressing to blend into Main Bazar's social and economic milieu; his attention to personal style is a significant factor in the production and consumption of a particular traveller identity. As Angela McRobbie (1989: 25) points out, within contemporary youth cultures, clothing is not bought because they are cheap and functional, but because they are culturally relevant. Buying and adorning throws 'emphasis on the wider social and historical factors which frame youth cultural expressions'. 'Traveller iconography' favoured around Pahar Ganj is simultaneously local and trans-cultural. It differs from that of Main Bazar's indigenous residents, and while some traveller styles bear a passing resemblance to the colourful, exotic dress of a neo-orientalist imagination, it is too simplistic to suggest that they are just attempting to enact this fantasy. Travellers are very aware that they don't 'fit' the local iconography. The romantic investments that they project onto Main Bazar suggests more than a simple nostalgia for an exotically imagined Indian 'past'. Their investments in experiencing the Indian city suggests a postmodern form of nostalgia for another hedonistic experience of travelling in India.

On the rooftop of the Navrang Hotel Avi and Shai spend an afternoon 'jamming' with other international travellers. Everyone sits around in a circle on the ground and Shai brings his guitar ('An Indian make, Givson. I couldn't resist it ... now I have to learn how to play like Jimmy Page'). A Swedish man accompanies him through a repertoire of Western progressive rock and folk music, interspersed with the fleeting melodies of Indian classical music; someone else bangs out the beat on a dholak. The Swede's girlfriend dances, two Australians sit, eyes closed, shaking their heads in appreciation of the music, and a German traveller silently sits in the lotus position, puts on his pebble sunglasses and opens a book on Buddhist philosophy. The musicians aren't accomplished, but enthusiastic to learn from each other. At intervals, someone makes up chillums and passes them around, each participant invoking the names of Lord Shiva, raising the chillum to their foreheads ('Boomshankar!') before they inhale. This act, partly expected convention in this context, signals an attempt to recreate an atmosphere of community and solidarity. The enactment of this spontaneous interchange evidently is dependent on ascribing an authenticity to the moment, one gauged from various intertextual images of India's popular-cultural past, and accessible to today's travellers only through this simulacrum of mediated images and commodified styles.

Conclusion: Consuming India in Search of New Self-identities

In this chapter, I have tried to redraw the boundaries of the alternative travel experience by suggesting that it is more than the material expression of new, middle-class identities that emerge in various hegemonic struggles over symbolic tastes and space. It is quite simply not the case, as Munt (1994: 106) argues, that these travellers are indistinguishable from each other, in terms of the international circuits they follow, their preferred travelling styles and modes of behaviour, and how they try to individuate their way of doing things against everyone else's ways. It is true that so-called alternative travellers do compete over the legitimacy and authenticity of their orientating practices and ways of relating to local Indian cultures (although these internal struggles are not dealt with here). However, the hegemonic struggles that they wage over the symbolic values and meanings of India's landscape and social and cultural life are not simply 'all in the mind'. The various rural and urban spaces that make up India's budget travel sites accommodate various traveller types who claim these spaces for very specific discourses and travel practices, which suggests that alternative travel locates a range of participants in multiple, complex 'scenes' across India.

My research findings do, however, indicate that there are equivalencies in how these travellers invest in the discourse of alternative travel. Most consider their mode of travel, and the travelling culture it enables, as a desirable way to seek out new self-identities and a sense of communitarian belonging with other like-minded people. Long-haul travel provides numbers of participants with the opportunity to reorientate themselves simultaneously towards the idea of global citizenship and to forge some new 'local' identifications through their spatial practice in India. On the one hand, the identities that they adopt through these relationships are bound up in practices that constitute a 'postmodernism of resistance' as boundaries of class and nationality are broken down in the contact zones of India's modest hotels, cafés and cultural arenas. Further, as they would argue, alternative travellers seek to break free of touristic excess by living on a budget, and integrating themselves within and among local, indigenous communities, learning from them forms of experience and knowledge rejected and repressed by the West. This is said to enable them to establish more honest cross-cultural relationships with the West's former 'Others'.

This focus on the encounter and on the interactive character of alternative travel does locate its participants as often genuinely self-reflexive about the nature of their relationships within India's travelled spaces. However, the limitations of the nomadic state they seek out is all too clear. The persuasive discourse of alternative travel and the ways that travellers orientate themselves within popular Indian sites is ideologically compromised since participants still bring prescribed cultural baggage with them along the budget trails. 'Finding your own space' continues to be shaped by the pursuit of India's absolute difference and authenticity against which these new, cross-cultural travelling identities may be formed. They continue to anticipate India as an encounter with exotica, chaos and spirituality and therefore a fascinating place to pursue a quest for spiritual and mental rejuvenation. The notion that this popular route towards cultural hybridity is a genuine alternative to ethnocentric 'Western' thinking breaks down in India's budget travelling zones; as the travellers' discussions and activities reveal, although they are preoccupied with the idea of travel as a route to overcoming constraining identities, they still think with concepts of 'home'.

References

Anderson, B. (1983) *Imagined Communities*. London: Verso.
Barthes, R. (1973) *Mythologies*. London: Paladin.
Beezer, A. (1993) Women and 'adventure travel' tourism. *New Formations* 21, 119–30.
Bhattacharyya, D. (1997) Mediating India: An analysis of a guidebook. *Annals of Tourism Research* 24, 371–89.
Bourdieu, P. (1989) *Distinction: A Social Critique of the Judgement of Taste*. Translated by Richard Nice. New York: Routledge.
Chambers, I. (1994) *Migrancy, Culture, Identity*. London: Routledge.
Clifford, J. (1989) The others: Beyond the salvage paradigm. *Third Text* 6, 73–94.

Cohen, E. (1973) A phenomenology of tourist types. *Sociology* 13, 179–201.
Crowther, G., Raj, P.A., Wheeler, T., Finlay, H. and Thomas, B. (eds) (1993) *India: A Travel Survival Kit*. Melbourne: Lonely Planet.
Desforges, L. (1998) Checking out the planet: Global representations/local identities and youth travel. In T. Skelton and G. Valentine (eds) *Cool Places: Geographies of Youth Cultures* (pp. 175–92). London: Routledge.
Desforges, L. (2000) Travelling the world: Identity and travel biography. *Annals of Tourism Research* 27, 926–45.
Fabian, J. (1990) *Power and Performance: Ethnographic Explorations through Proverbial Wisdom and Theatre in Shaba (Zaire)*. Wisconsin: University of Wisconsin.
Foucault, M. (1980) *Power/Knowledge: Selected Interviews and Other Writings 1972–1977*. Edited by C. Gordon, translated by C. Gordon, L. Marshall, J. Mepham and K. Soper. New York: Harvester Wheatsheaf.
Foucault, M. (1986) Of other spaces. *Diacritics* 16, 22–7.
Geertz, C. (1973) *The Interpretation of Cultures*. New York: Basic Books.
Hampton, M. (1998) Backpacker tourism and economic development. *Annals of Tourism Research* 25, 639–60.
Hetherington, K. (1998) Vanloads of uproarious humanity: New age travellers and the utopics of the countryside. In T. Skelton and G. Valentine (eds) *Cool Places: Geographies of Youth Cultures* (pp. 328–42). London: Routledge.
Hutnyk, J. (1996) *The Rumour of Calcutta: Tourism, Charity and the Poverty of Representation*. London: Zed.
MacCannell, D. (1992) *Empty Meeting Grounds: The Tourist Papers*. London: Routledge.
McRobbie, A. (ed.) (1989) *Zoot Suits and Second-Hand Dresses: An Anthology of Fashion and Music*. London: Macmillan.
Malbon, B. (1998) Clubbing: Consumption, identity and the spatial practices of every-night life. In T. Skelton and G. Valentine (eds) *Cool Places: Geographies of Youth Cultures* (pp. 266–88). London: Routledge.
Marin, L. (1984) *Utopics: Spatial Play*. London: Macmillan.
Massey, D. (1998) The spatial construction of youth cultures. In T. Skelton and G. Valentine (eds) *Cool Places: Geographies of Youth Cultures* (pp. 121–9). London: Routledge.
Mercer, K. (1994) *Welcome to the Jungle: New Positions in Black Cultural Studies*. London: Routledge.
Morgan, N. and Pritchard, A. (2001) *Advertising in Tourism and Leisure*. Oxford: Butterworth-Heinemann.
Munt, I. (1994) The 'other' postmodern tourism. *Theory, Culture, Society* 11, 101–23.
Pratt, M.L. (1992) *Imperial Eyes: Travel Writing and Transculturation*. London: Routledge.
Said, E. (1978) *Orientalism*. London: Routledge & Kegan Paul.
Said, E. (1984) *The World, The Text and The Critic*. London: Faber &Faber.
Said, E. (1994) *Culture and Imperialism*. London: Vintage.
Urry, J. (1995) *Consuming Places*. London: Routledge.
Urry, J. (2002) *The Tourist Gaze* (2nd edn). London: Sage. [First published in 1990.]
Venn, C. (1992) Subjectivity, ideology and difference: Recovering otherness. *New Formations* 16, 40–63.
Willis, P.E. (1997) Theoretical confessions and reflexive method. In K. Gelder and S. Thornton (eds) *The Subcultures Reader* (pp. 246–62). London: Routledge.
Wilson, D. (1997) Paradoxes of tourism in Goa. *Annals of Tourism Research* 24, 52–75.

Chapter 3

Representations of 'Ethnographic Knowledge': Early Comic Postcards of Wales

ANNETTE PRITCHARD and NIGEL MORGAN

Introduction

The question of identity, of how we define ourselves in relation to others and society has assumed an increasingly central role in today's rapidly changing cultural times (Hall, 1996, 1997). Paradoxically, despite the globalisation of economies, societies and cultural processes, notions of nationality and ethnicity retain their importance as everyday and theoretical constituents of identity (Edensor, 2002). Indeed, as previously centred social and national relations have become increasingly fractured, ethnicity, which implies an active cultural definition, has emerged as a key marker of self and others, defining how we see ourselves 'within the possible range of culturally constructed selves' (Osborne, 2002: 160). It is as much a marker of difference as of similarity – that which sets us apart as well as binds us together. Understanding any ethnicity, of course, involves not merely understanding the physical locations and movements of a people, but also the kinematics of their cultures, stories, myths and imaginings. Jonathan Rutherford also reminds us that our identities are not only constructions of culture and place, but also of time. They are formed where the past collides with today's social, cultural and economic structures – as Antonio Gramsci has put it: 'Each individual is the synthesis not only of existing relations but of the history of these relations. He [*sic*] is a précis of the past' (Gramsci, 1988, quoted in Rutherford, 1990: 20).

In this chapter, we take this historical perspective and explore how differences between identities were marked out and defined through linguistic and visual representation on early 20th-century postcards. In particular, we interrogate the comic postcard – a multimodal text – as an everyday cultural text that has both reflected and shaped particular discourses of place and identity. In doing so, we are attempting to further those analyses of representation that see 'tourism as a system of presencing and performance' (Franklin & Crang, 2001: 17), which, with reference to Hall's (1997) circuit of culture, consider tourism discourse as a key element in the circularity of knowledge and power (Morgan & Pritchard, 1998). Postcards, as a rich cultural reservoir of popular perceptions, play a similar role to tourism promotional material, travelogues and travel writing (Ateljevic & Doorne, 2003) in creating discourses of places and peoples (cf. Kennedy, this volume). Postcards imagine complicated, evocative places and several tourism scholars have examined the post-card within the discourse of the masculine, colonial gaze, which objecti-fies, stereotypes and romanticises notions of the exotic Other. Thus there is a particularly rich literature on the representation of indigenous peoples on postcards (e.g. Albers & James, 1983; Edwards, 1996). Such studies have explored how postcards have been seen to mark the cultur-al difference between the civilised and the uncivilised, between the colonial and the colonised, between 'us' and 'them'. However, whereas there have been many representational and theoretical analyses of picture postcards, specific explorations of comic postcards are rare – with some exceptions (see Gornall, 2003).

The particular focus of our study here is an investigation of the rela-tionship between identity, representation and discourses of Wales. We present a textual (visual and linguistic) analysis of a number of Edwardian comic postcards of Wales (drawn both by Welsh and other British cartoonists) and suggest that the cards' intended humour depends on ridiculing the Welsh language, including Welsh place names and formulaic expressions (e.g. greetings), stereotyping Welsh people and customs and, finally, from sexual innuendo to Welsh women and men. We argue that these comic narratives continued an established tradition of denigrating the Welsh as a marginal ethnic minority within the British Isles and, by presenting a brief analysis of 17th- and 18th-century wood-cuts and engravings demonstrate that the stereotypical representations of the Welsh seen in these early 20th-century comic cards have a long heritage. There is a strong parallel here with how other marginalised groups such as the Irish and the Boers were characterised in racist terms in cartoons, periodicals, guide books and the press of the 18th and 19th centuries (Lewes, 2000; Mackenzie, 2001), a tradition continued later in postcard depictions. In addition to discussing this hegemonically domi-nant reading of the postcards' meanings, we also suggest that there are potential oppositional readings to the cartoons, particularly those drawn by Welsh cartoonists. Thus, it is possible to discern alternative meanings and to see the cartoons as subverting the prevailing orthodoxy by poking fun at stereotypical representations of the English gentleman tourist. We begin our chapter by briefly contextualising the development of the postcard, before outlining our approach to examining this particular type of visual text. We then consider the socio-cultural constructions of Wales which these comic postcards continue, focusing particularly on the anti-Welsh iconography which runs throughout certain historical characterisations of Wales and the Welsh. The chapter then discusses the main sources of humour identified in the cards against the backcloth of this iconography, before briefly discussing the oppositional readings and concluding with a consideration of the study's implications.

The Development of the Postcard

The sample of postcards discussed in the chapter was produced during the golden era of the postcard. Evans & Richards (1980) describe the period between 1870 and 1930 in these terms and note that postcard sending in Britain peaked in 1914 when over 880 million cards were posted. This peak of postcard sending ended after the First World War, however, and when in 1918 the cost of postcard postage doubled to a penny, half the previous year's total of postcards was sent. In the years following the end of the war, the boom subsided as the growth of the telephone took much of the commercial business and the greater mobility provided by the motorcar led to a further decline in demand (Coysh, 1984). The emergent craze of popular snapshot photography also contributed to this decline as the price of the new cheap and convenient box camera fell progressively, so that by 1920 five times as many cameras were sold as in 1914 (Evans & Richards, 1980).

The world's first postcard was issued in Austria in 1869 – a plain card with a stamp on one side and space for a message on the other. The following year they were issued for the first time in Britain and were rapidly adopted by business so that soon all the major commercial companies were using them to acknowledge receipt of goods, confirm appointments, despatch price lists, etc. (Evans & Richards, 1980). Although when the first commercial firms began producing cards in 1872, they were not yet allowed to be sold to the general public, it was not long before everyone began using the postcard due to its speed of communication. Considerable concern about its lack of privacy was expressed in newspapers and periodicals, but its sheer convenience ensured its success and by 1879 the Post Office had an annual turnover of 50 million postcards (Evans & Richards, 1980; Coysh, 1984). A key development was the addition of pictures, with the first picture postcards appearing at the 1889 Paris Exhibition. By the time Edward VII ascended the British throne, picture postcards were an accepted part of national life, boosted by the Boer War and by the decision of the Postmaster-General in 1902 to authorise the divided back postcard, permitting both messages and an address on the back. This made it possible for publishers to use the whole of one side for a picture. The public welcomed this innovation and used them extensively as a new and cheap form of communication. They began to be sold everywhere and by 1903 some 600 million postcards were being sent annually, 10 times as many as were sent in 1871 (Evans & Richards, 1980).

With up to five postal deliveries each day, postcards became the telephone call or the email of the early 20th century and 'it is not uncommon to find messages written at lunchtime to say the writer will be late home for tea' (Phillips, 2000: 13).

Production companies multiplied to meet the growing demand and soon there were over 270 different firms all over Britain. Many photographers left their studios and started to photograph local landscapes and thousands of comic cards were produced by specialist publishers as the demand for designs became enormous. Artists and cartoonists were commissioned to paint landscapes and humorous subjects and existing pictures were reproduced from journals such as *Punch* and *The Bystander*, as well as from newspapers, books, and pictures in public galleries (Coysh, 1984). It is worth noting that postcards were not only used for personal communications but had several other functions. Advertising was a basic role of postcards from the outset, pin-up and glamour cards proliferated, as did immediate news photographs with photographers being despatched to fires, wrecks and disasters of all kinds. There was also a strong and continuous propaganda use, with picture postcards of the Royal Family and royal events, portraits of politicians and party slogans, and, during wars, anti-Boer and anti-German pictures, portraits of victorious British generals, and scenes of Allied victories. Postcards were also for collecting – nearly every middle class Victorian and Edwardian family had a postcard album in its parlor which 'served as entertainment, education and as tacit ways to claim status and identity' (Whittaker, 2000: 426).

The Postcard as Visual Text

Whilst almost every object, place and peoples have been the subject of a postcard, postcards themselves have been described as falling into several intersecting intellectual frames, including: colonialism, romanticism, liberal humanism, realism, postmodernism and the culture of the tourist industry (Whittaker, 2000). The postcard as a genre is a dynamic, context-sensitive narrative, which is a discursive expression of the popular culture of the time. Just like any cultural artefact, however, they are not a neutral medium and are more than ephemera, temporarily viewed and just as quickly disposed of. As a cultural text, postcards are representations of ethnographic knowledge, sites of cultural production and the output of both social interaction and individual experience (Pink, 2001). They can also be seen as repositories of stereotypical images, minimalist and simplistic representations, which mark and communicate cultural difference (Morgan & Pritchard, 1998) so that indigenous people are frequently 'identified only by costume or perhaps a single cultural artifact' (Whittaker, 2000: 426). Such analyses of postcards are firmly rooted in notions of the gendered gaze (developed by Mulvey (1989) in film studies) and of the 'archive' (developed by Sekula (1989) in photography). Advocates of both concepts suggest that women and the less powerful are oppressed by an objectifying masculine gaze that is implied by the manner in which they are visually represented. Adapting the ideas of Foucault, this approach has been extensively used to analyse visual representations of other cultures (Pinney, 1992) and several studies of colonial photography have characterised the 'colonial gaze' as an exploitative and objectifying project to catalogue and classify the colonised (Edwards, 1992).

Just as any visual representation, a comic postcard can be seen as part of the dominant ideology of a society, reproducing and enhancing its preferred values – indeed, 'At every historical turn, the everyday epistemology of the viewer, whatever that particular cultural literacy happens to be, is mapped onto the image' (Whittaker, 2000: 428). Of course, humour is a powerful carrier of cultural norms and whilst consumers of comic cards know that they do not attempt to present accurate representations, their comical stereotypes reinforce dominant ways of seeing the world, albeit as entertainment. Both authors and consumers (readers) 'respond to and refer to known visual forms, styles, discourses and meanings through the content and form of their visual images' (Pink, 2001: 27). Thus, in creating representations which reproduce or reference 'conventional compositions and iconographies individuals draw from personal and cultural resources of visual experience and knowledge' (Pink, 2001: 27). In this, there is no value free position from which to create or to consume – from the moment that they are drawn, paintings and illustrations define space and location and map position and situation, immediately suggesting social and spatial hierarchies and homologies. In fact, all such images 'are inextricably interwoven with our personal identities, narratives, lifestyles, cultures and societies as well as with definitions of history, space and truth' (Pink, 2001: 17).

In view of this, it is surprising that over the last three decades more qualitative researchers have not utilised images (such as films, photographs, drawings, cartoons, graffiti, maps, signs, symbols and diagrams) to enhance their understanding of the social world (Banks, 2001). This neglect ignores that: 'taken cumulatively images are signifiers of a culture; taken individually they are artefacts that provide us with very particular information about our existence' (Prosser, 1998: 1). This is especially so in the field of tourism research since the visual plays such a crucial role in the production, practice and performance of tourism (Crouch & Lubbren, 2003). However, understanding and interpreting any visual image is highly complex and the issues of 'representation', 'trustworthiness', 'interpretation', 'reflexivity' and 'sampling' are all highly contested in visual research. In the 1960s, 1970s and 1980s, the validity of the visual was heavily criticised on the basis of its subjectivity, bias and specificity and even today many sociologists continue to reject visual images, arguing that their subjectivity and specificity 'renders them invalid for the scientific project of sociology (Pink, 2001: 10). However, in the 1990s, sociologists such as Chaplin (1994) developed a more interdisciplinary approach to the visual, incorporating ideas from feminism, anthropology and cultural and critical studies – ideas which have influenced our approach here.

Sample and Method

Our focus in this chapter is a textual analysis of six 17th- and 18th-century woodcuts and engravings and 15 comic postcards dating between 1904 and 1915. All the material is held in the maps and photographs archive at the National Library of Wales and whilst the earlier material was exclusively produced in England, the postcards were produced both by Welsh cartoonists (including Lloyd Hughes, Llwyd Roberts and J.M. Stamforth) and by other British artists. The postcards under analysis were chosen to exemplify the series from which they are drawn, but no sample criteria was used and we make no attempt to address issues such as valid-ity or triangulation, as we believe this would be forcing our study to succumb to the agenda of a scientific orthodoxy. In the positivist tradition, validity refers to the extent to which the findings reveal the 'correct answer', a notion which is inappropriate when referring to approaches like discourse analysis which have different epistemological and ontolog-ical underpinnings (Tonkiss, 1998).

This, for example, is the position which has been advocated in Critical Linguistics (e.g. Hodge & Kress, 1993) and Critical Discourse Analysis (e.g. Fairclough, 1992, 2003). Both these (related) approaches reject the notion of an objective, complete and exhaustive interpretation of texts (including visual texts), which does not preclude a critical engagement with these texts, providing rigorous, though possibly multiple, descrip-tions and deriving theoretical insight out of them. More relevant to the discourse analyst than 'validity' are his or her abilities to gauge the results of the research against their own objectives, rather than some external 'reality'; in this, they must be open to the notion that there may be multi-ple, competing and conflicting interpretations of their analysis (Jamal & Hollinshead, 2001). Ultimately, any evaluation of the adequacy of our discourse analysis study will be pragmatic and it will be judged on the extent to which it 'makes possible new and meaningful interpretations of the social and political phenomena it investigates' (Howarth, 2000: 130). Nonetheless, all discourse research remains problematic and the multi-layered nature of texts such as comic postcards makes their analysis even more contested. Certainly, the notion that any visual text (especially comic postcards) portrays 'reality' is highly disputed and it is important to recognise that such cultural texts will be imbued with different and competing meanings as different people interpret them on the basis of their individual knowledge. As Louw (2001: 20) reminds us: 'Meaning(s) emerge out of relationships rooted in a particular place and time.... Ultimately, meaning(s) cannot be understood outside the power relationships and struggles of a specific context.' Thus, before we discuss the comic postcards themselves, we must first turn our attention to these power relationships.

Contextualising Visual Discourses of Wales

In addition to reading both 'with' and 'against' the text itself, a discourse analyst must also reinterpret social practices by situating their meanings in broader historical and structural contexts. Thus, we must consider the wider socio-historical context of Wales as a constituent part of the UK, before exploring the historical cultural, literary and artistic representations of Wales of which the comic postcards discussed here are a part. It is clear that, like any ethnicity, being Welsh revolves around the relationship between identity and subjectivity, between defining self and other, or inter-subjectivity and in defining the wider identity of what it means to be Welsh in terms of cultural, social and political solidarity. In saying this, we would strongly question the notion that identity must involve an essentialist idea such as 'Welshness', something that is immutably, naturally and essentially simply existing (see Pritchard & Morgan, 2003). Definitions of ethnicity and nationhood are always problematic, contested and multi-faceted; as Weber (1978) argued neither ethnicity nor nation can easily be precisely defined for sociological purposes. Interestingly, McCrone *et al.* (1995: 45) have commented how 'Ethnicity ... becomes a form of rhetoric read off a dominant white culture which is highly implicit. Hence there is a black but no white consciousness, female but no male ... Scottish but little English ... ethnicity helps to define the periphery to the centre rather than the other way round.'

This aptly describes the relationship between Wales and England which was and remains complex and variegated and requires a much wider exploration than we can provide here. Whilst this chapter focuses on historical visual representations, we have elsewhere (Pritchard & Morgan, 2001, 2003; Morgan & Pritchard, 2004) described how this relationship can be mapped across a series of discourses in terms of 'Othering' – conceptualised by Rose (1993: 116) as 'defining where you belong through a contrast with other places, or who you are through a contrast with other people'. People who differ from the majority (them as opposed to us) have traditionally tended to be represented in binary terms – bad as opposed to good; primitive in contrast to civilised; ugly rather than attractive. By exploring the historic Othering of Wales we can therefore begin to understand not only how Wales and the Welsh have been defined but also England and the English, since Othering:

> Sets up a symbolic frontier between the 'normal' and the 'deviant' ... the 'acceptable' and the 'unacceptable', what 'belongs' and what does not or is Other, between 'insiders' and 'outsiders', Us and them. (Hall, 1997: 258)

Clearly it is not possible to review here Wales' entire history; however, its historians have demonstrated that notions of conflict, foreignness and Otherness have historically defined Wales and the Welsh within the UK (Williams, 1985; Davies, 1993; Adams, 1996). Wales' relationship with England has been pivotal in this process and Jenkins (1997: 132) argues that ultimately one of the defining features of the Welsh is the 'sharing of a common ethnic boundary – with and against the English'. As Thomas (1992: 6) has pointed out, the very word *Cymru* (Wales in the Welsh language) '... was derived from *Combrogos*, a concept of an united people fighting against their enemies'. Similarly, the English word for the country – Wales – derives from *Wealas*, Anglo-Saxon for 'foreign' (Williams, 1985; Adams, 1996), whilst the term 'Celtic' served to distinguish non-Anglo-Saxons (Chapman, 1992). Lacking political independence since the 1536 Acts of Union, Wales has thus been termed as 'a classic example of an internal colony' (Davies, 1987: 60), and the 1536 Union with England described as marking:

> the beginning of a sustained campaign of cultural homogenization by the central state ... Welsh ... was banned for administrative and legal purposes ... [and] children were punished for speaking Welsh in schools. (Pitchford, 1994: 37)

This attempted cultural homogenisation of Wales accelerated in the 19th century in the belief that the Welsh 'like all natives were in need of instruction, conversion and control' (Adams, 1996: 28). This, of course, has to be set in the wider context of a 'fractured and ambiguous' transformation of 19th-century British society (Joyce, 1991: 3) in which articulate, middle-class Victorian reformers sought to 'forge more effective behavioural constraints' over the British working class (Bailey, 1987: 170). In Wales, this attempt at incorporation was highlighted by the desire of the English state to eradicate the Welsh language, the most obvious symbol of a culturally distinct group – a process which was repeated elsewhere in the British Isles with much greater success – as witnessed by the virtual eradication of Gaelic, Irish, Cornish and Manx (Thomas, 1992). Ironically, therefore, the Welsh language – the most visible element of 'Welshness' – remained the greatest remnant of 'difference' within the Union. The 1847 Report on the State of Education in Wales confirmed that the language was regarded by the English state as a 'barrier to moral progress'. The same report described the Welsh themselves as 'degenerate ... dirty, ignorant, bigoted and contented; promiscuous; wanting chastity; immoral; violent and vicious ...' (quoted in Adams, 1996: 28). Whilst the 1870 Education Act provided free education for children in Wales it also made English the compulsory language. At the same time as this sustained state-sponsored campaign (supported by many Welsh educators) was having a significant impact on the Welsh language and culture, the history of Wales was also deemed to be 'something primitive and contemptible and best forgotten' (Williams, 1985: 246). Such was the context of *The Times* editorial of 1866 which described the Welsh language as 'the curse of Wales', arguing that its prevalence and the ignorance of English excluded the Welsh people from the civilisation and material prosperity of their English neighbours. It concluded that:

> Their antiquated and semi-barbarous language ... shrouds them in darkness. If Wales and the Welsh are ... to share the material prosperity and ... we will add the culture and morality of England, they must forget their isolated language and learn to speak English and nothing else. For all purposes Welsh is a dead language. (cited in Morris, 1998)

These discourses are also echoed in visual representations and '[r]eference to the brutish, wild and animal characteristics of the Welsh, Scots and Irish is consistent in English representations of these peoples' (Cosgrove, 1993: 299). In fact, the Welsh, as seen through the lens of English history, have been construed as a most 'peculiar people' (see Stephens, 1992). Take *Geographical Fun* from 1869, a series of maps designed for middle- and upper-class British children discussed by Darby Lewes (2000). Here, England is represented as 'a classically beautiful, stately Britannia', yet the representations of the other UK countries are far less flattering. Ireland 'is a happy muscular peasant woman [and] ... Ireland is a nation of servants, happy in their work'. Scotland is 'a bespectacled figure who glares with befuddled rage', whilst Wales is presented as a country immured in the past. It is represented by Owen Glendower, who sings of past Welsh glory and 'other trivialities', of 'King Arthur's long, long pedigree, And cheese and leeks and knights of high degree' (Lewes, 2000: 140–2). In the same vein, Moira Dearnley (2001: xxi) has explored how English 18th-century fiction is riddled with stereotypes of Wales, arguing that the Welsh were 'viewed from afar as the romantic or ridiculous inhabitants of those "distant fields"'. She suggests that such representations were themselves rooted in the:

> satires of the Welsh [which] began to pour off the popular press in the 1640s.... The Welsh were ridiculed for being dishonest and stupid, credulous and superstitious ... abjectly poor but comically insistent on

their gentle birth.... They lived on mountains ... were addicted to cheese, ale and astrology ... were overrun by goats and cousins ... wore leeks in their hats ... [and] spoke gobbledegook. (Dearnley, 2001: xvi)

In such ways a particular strand within English popular culture created a Wales which was peopled by rustic characters – Wales 'was an "Other" that the English colonists romantically orientalized, racially denigrated or imperiously ignored' (Adams, 1996: 27). Whether ancient bard, noble savage or promiscuous deviant, the Welsh were the subject of racial stereotyping in political and cultural life. However, if we trace the antecedents of this stereotyping narrative to 18th- and 19th-century 'fictions' of Wales, we would only tell half the story. Instead, as Dearnley (2001) noted, our journey needs to begin even earlier with the popular and 'conventional Welsh person [who] first appeared in English literature, fully equipped with toasted cheese, leeks and a reputation for dirt and dishonesty in the early sixteenth century' (Lord, 1995: 33). We will argue below that the early 20th-century comic postcards of our study are the direct descendants of these caricatures of the Welsh which became popular from the 16th century. Of course, it is clearly possible to read the meanings of the postcards at several levels without any knowledge or discussion of this early anti-Welsh iconography. However, examining the postcards against the backcloth of this long tradition of symbology, allows a further, more complex level of analysis and thus, we begin our discussion with a detail look at some examples of woodcuts and engravings held in the National Library of Wales.

Hegemonic Readings of the Texts

The 1689 woodcut engraving of *The Welsh Fortune-Teller, Sheffrey Morgan* is an early example of the anti-Welsh symbology. As an astrologer who contemplates and distils the knowledge of the stars, *Morgan* characterises Wales's rich vein of associations with ancient, druidic magic and sits on a Welsh mountain surrounded by frolicking goats, echoing ancient associations with this mountain-bred animal, long seen as sexually licentious. The engraving also includes the stereotypical symbols which by this time were being used to denote Welsh people. *Morgan* wears a leek in his hat and is depicted cutting a piece of cheese – both foods symbolising the poor Welsh diet of the day. Such associations run as a thread throughout the discourses of similar 18th-century engravings. In *Shon ap Morgan – Shentleman of Wales'* and his wife *Unnafred Shones*, published by William Dicey of London in 1747, both characters are depicted riding goats instead of horses, have leeks in their hats and Shon has a herring tucked into his saddlebag – another contemporary symbol of poverty and a poor diet. Both *Shon* and *Unnafred* also speak 'Wenglish', a Welsh corruption of English, which, as we will see below, is also a major source of humour in the early 20th-century comic postcards. The inability of the Welsh to speak English had for centuries provided the English establishment with a source of fun and amusement: indeed, Wenglish 'provided the mainstay of literary satire against them' (Lord, 1995: 34). Wenglish encompassed not only this inability of the Welsh-speaking economic migrants to master a foreign tongue, but also encapsulated the particular style, cadence and rhythm which reflects a peculiarly Welsh intonation of English and which became synonymous with the supposed stupidity and backward nature of the Welsh.

Representations of Welshmen had also long associated them with goats – as we can see in *Sketches of National Character, Who says a Welshman is like a Billygoat?* published by Carrington Bowles in 1781. The Welshman here clutches his family tree which extends back before the creation of the world, and, whilst he is not seen astride a goat, his facial features have a distinctly goat-like quality. A couple of decades later, *A Welsh Tandem* published in 1801 by Hannah Humphrey of London strongly echoes the same iconography. This engraving depicts a carriage on its way to Wales, which can be seen in the background as a mountainous land inhabited by goats. The carriage is drawn by three ill-mannered, brutish, red-eyed goats, the leader of which can be seen to break wind in the others' faces. Astride the carriage are three Welshmen – denoted as such by the leeks which festoon their hats. Such representations of the Welsh not only depicted them as poverty-stricken, stupid and uncouth, but also as a people who were obsessively proud of their ancestry and thus backward, rather than forward-looking. This is particularly evident in Richard Newton's engraving of 1795, *On a Journey to a Courtship in Wales*, which depicts a grotesque Welsh suitor sitting astride a goat and carrying the (by now) obligatory leek. The suitor is accompanied by a similarly attired man-servant who carries his master's copy of *Pedigree before the Flood*. This engraving has many of the symbols found in stereotypical pictorial representations of the Welsh – as 'Taffy' was invariably shown as a poor man, raised on a diet of leeks, cheese and herrings, obsessed with his lineage, who spoke a strange, unintelligible language. 'Taffy' was also frequently accompanied by a goat which was seen in different guises, sometimes being ridden, sometimes pulling carriages and sometimes simply appearing in the background. Thus,

> [a]part from the peculiar language and the eating habits of its ill-odoured and hot headed inhabitants, the only other information about Wales was that it was mountainous and grazed by goats, both equally disagreeable. (Lord, 1995: 37)

Over 200 years after engravings such as *The Welsh Fortune-Teller, Sheffrey Morgan* first appeared, Edwardian comic postcards of the Welsh display remarkable similarities, demonstrating both the longevity of these associations and their strength in wider socio-cultural and political discourses. A set of postcards from *The Wrench Series* (printed in England and postmarked 1904) all derive humour from the Welsh obsession with lineage and use of 'Wenglish'. The Welsh women in each postcard are marked by their distinctive costumes and the men by their leeks – marking them by their dress and by a single cultural artefact as objects of the colonial gaze (Whittaker, 2000). In a card captioned, *Pedigree of the JONES family*, we see a woman in full Welsh costume with a knitting needle in each hand (see Figure 3.1).

She stands rather self-satisfied, in front of a chart which traces the Jones family history from before the time of *THE CREATION* through *THE FLOOD*, the *FOUNDING OF ROME*, the *DEATH OF J. CAESAR* and the *NORMAN CONQUEST*. The caption tells us *Oh! I atmit the Morgans are a ferry old ant ferry respectable family. But inteet the Joneses were already ancient at the time of the creation!* This is very similar to another card in the series which depicts a sombre-looking man in front of an ark which has a sign declaring *Ap-Morgan's Ark. Private.* The caption reads *For Look you, the Ap Morgans are a ferry ancient family, Inteet at the Floot They Chartered an ark of their ferry own!* In both cases, Mrs Jones and ap Morgan are ridiculed for their impossible ancestral claims, which are seen to be the only ways in which they can aspire to status and recognition.

Whilst these cards' use of a single cultural signifier (the leeks) and the Welsh costumes are an obvious form of stereotyping, their use of 'Wenglish' is also a powerful continuation of the earlier anti-Welsh imagery. At this time, postcards were occasionally published with dialect captions, particularly of Devon and Yorkshire (Coysch, 1984), often to poke fun at the speech of these regions and to associate them with backwardness. Indeed, the use of dialect, mispronunciation and malapropisms have traditionally defined the 'underclass', portraying them as stupid and naive – as discussed by Schulman (1995) in her study of comic portrayals of African-Americans. In our study, the cartoon characters' use of the Welsh language and 'Wenglish' perform the same function of ridicule and derision, confirming the stupidity of the Welsh by their inability and reluctance to speak 'proper' English. This together with a lampooning of the length of Welsh place-names, marks Wales as a different place, less civilised and liable to confuse the unsuspecting Englishman (for in the comic postcards, the tourist is exclusively male) venturing into wild Wales. In each case the English tourist is portrayed as a well-dressed, gentlemanly innocent abroad. Whether he is trying to catch a train, post a letter or ask directions, he is seen struggling to cope with the language spoken by his less than helpful hosts and ill-equipped to deal with the extremely long Welsh place names. Indeed, in one card, a rather well-dressed English gentleman raps on the ticket clerk's window and complains that it will take at least 10 minutes *to name the place I want to go to*, even though he is late for his train.

Figure 3.1 *Pedigree of the JONES family.* Reproduced by kind permission of the National Library of Wales

Such humour derived from the long Welsh places is seen in many comic postcards from this sample. For instance, *The Welsh Post Office* features a sorting room where both people and parcels are dwarfed by the enormous address tickets. Likewise, sending a letter or leaving a calling card is depicted as a hazardous and humorous activity, requiring several people to handle the immense envelopes and cards required for the place names. Perhaps the most well-known Welsh place name which appeared on countless comic postcards over the 20th century is Llanfairpwllgwyngyllgogerychwyrndrobllantysiliogogoch, a name artificially created in order to lay claim to be the world's longest railway station name. In one comic card in the Wrench Series, we see an English gentleman wearing tweeds, plus-fours and handle-bar moustaches, standing on a railway platform and admonishing a porter to *Hurry up with that label!* for this station. Struggling with a comically long luggage label which is at least three times the size of the tourist's suitcase is the *WELSH PORTER* who replies, *Dear Anwyl! I was thinking where to put it, syr.* The juxtaposing of the two figures is striking in this scene – the portly, well-dressed English tourist seems to exude authority, whereas the gaunt, shabbily-dressed Welsh porter stoops over the suitcase, with a decidedly goat-like face and unkempt hair (see Figure 3.2).

Such representations which link goats (symbolic of poor upland farming communities, but also associated with magic and sexuality) and Wales have, as we saw in our discussions above, a long history and

Figure 3.2 *Hurry up with that label, porter!* Reproduced by kind permission of the National Library of Wales

traverse a number of discourses. Not long after these postcards were produced John Maynard Keynes described the Welsh statesman Lloyd George (British Prime Minister 1916–1922) as a 'goat-footed bard, a half human visitor to our age from the hag ridden magic and enchanted woods of Celtic antiquity' (quoted in Adams, 1996: 30). In western wisdom traditions the goat has become primarily a symbol of Satan and magic but in ancient Greece its fecundity and cunning made it sacred to both Pan (half-man, half-goat, a rustic god and a symbol of man's raw instincts) and Artemis (the virgin goddess of nature and wildness) (Stassinopoulous & Beny, 1983). An interesting overlay to these associations with basic instincts and sexuality is provided by the numerous popular depictions of the notoriously licentious Prince of Wales (the future George IV) as a goat during the late 18th century. For example, *Taffy and Hus Wife, Shentleman of Wales*, published in 1786, not only caricatures the Prince, but also suggests the sexual availability and immorality of Welsh women. This characterisation was common across a range of discourses and in *Hoydens of Wild Wales*, Jane Aaron has explored how Welsh women were historically characterised as wild, immoral, sexual, uncontrolled and irresponsible creatures – exoticised and eroticised by the colonial, masculine English gaze. The 1786 engraving in which the Prince gallops towards Wales on a huge goat, typifies such characterisation. The goat symbolises not only his Welsh connections but also his libidinous nature. At his back rides an equally lusty and licentious Welsh woman – qualities which are indicated by her style of riding. Brazenly sitting aside the goat, she rides bareback, hugging the Prince as he urges the animal on into Wales. In case the reader misses the point, the caption tells us that this is not unusual as *The Welch women all ride cross legged and bare-backed.*

Clearly, such engravings in the late 18th century drew on contemporary popular views of the Prince of Wales and his relationships with those Welsh women who were regarded as sexually immoral. What is fascinating, however, is that we can discern clear connections to this iconography in comic postcards of the early 20th century. For instance, in one card a young, conventionally attractive woman in full Welsh costume drives a golden carriage, (signifying royal associations) which is drawn by two goats (signifying connections both to royalty and to Wales), whilst a red dragon sits behind her. In a similar postcard the same lady drives a motorcar and her headlamps are set in goats' heads while the Prince of Wales feathers figure prominently on the car's front grille. Taking our readings of these cards further, we can see that the sexual availability of Welsh women was also a key feature in the comic postcards. Various cards featured Welsh sweethearts and romantic scenes – many deriving their humour from a play on words. In *some charming bits of Welsh scenery* we see a young Welsh woman who poses arms akimbo and legs outstretched, showing a surprising length of calf for the day. A similar card, entitled

There are fine views in Wales, features a woman in full Welsh costume standing on a mountain peak (See Figure 3.3).

There are fine views in Wales.

Figure 3.3 *There are fine views in Wales.* Reproduced by kind permission of the National Library of Wales

She is similarly posed with her hands on her hips and her above-the-knee skirt floats seductively in the wind while two goats (whose sexual associations have been noted) gaze mischievously up it. As the young woman gazes out at the viewer, to read the meaning as an invitation to the masculine gaze needs little imagination. Again, another card in the same series features a well-dressed English gentleman with a woman in Welsh costume, literally reclining on the Isle of Anglesey. The island – the Mother of Wales (Mon Mam Cymru) has become a bed on which this English tourist dallies with the Welsh girl. It seems that the landscape of Wales has become entwined with the women of Wales and that both have been burdened with masculinist meaning, inviting interpretation by a colonial, male discourse (Pritchard & Morgan, 2000).

Anti-normative Textual Readings?

Until this point, whilst our analysis has revealed several layers of meanings in the postcards, it has read *with* the hegemonic meanings to examine the organisation of the drawings and text and to pay attention to how words and meanings are articulated. However, texts have no fixed or single meanings and whilst public, mass media texts such as postcards may seem to be closed – to generate only one meaning – there are of course many meanings to the drawings as different people will use their own subjective knowledge to interpret them (Pink, 2001). Meaning is social and communication takes place within a complex matrix of shifting power relationships, entwined within continuing struggles to establish, confirm or resist power relationships. Thus, Hall (1980) has argued that all messages have encoded into them a preferred meaning, which the hegemonically dominant would prefer decoders of the message to accept. However, it is possible for decoders, operating within 'an oppositional code' to reject the preferred message and negotiate their own individual understanding out of the multiple meanings available within the text (Fiske, 1987; Louw, 2001). Comic cards such as those we have discussed here are also full of puns whose meanings multiply, escape and overflow their context. Indeed, comedy's very focus on excess, vulgarity and the carnivalesque challenges the social control of 'taste' and offers opportunities for parody and subversion. Cartoons, as any popular texts, 'are inadequate in themselves – they are never self-sufficient structures of meanings ... they are provokers of meanings and pleasure, they are completed only when taken up by people and inserted into their popular culture' (Fiske, 1987: 6).

There are then also subversive readings of these cards – just as there are alternative readings to the 'saucy' seaside postcards of McGill which challenge rather than endorse hetero-patriachical norms (Gornall, 2003). The potential for such oppositional readings is also increased here since, as some of the comic cards were drawn by Welsh artists, they are auto-ethnographic; in other words they are the self-generated texts of a literate society capable of observing itself (Dorst, 1989). As such, there is a great opportunity here for resistance and for the disruption of normalised power relationships. Although it is impossible to ascertain the intentions of the cartoonist and we cannot know whether a subversion of the dominant orthodoxy was deliberately intended, the Lloyd Hughes cards (produced for the Valentine Series) do seem to offer such opportunities to 'foster ... group identity by widening the gap of those within and those outside the circle of laughter' (Levine, 1977: 359, cited in Abernathy-Lear, 1995). In one such card, a well-dressed young gentleman is staring perplexedly at a note and its Welsh message. The caption reads *Cholly (from Pimlico) receives a note from his Welsh sweetheart!* A grinning young boy (who presumably has delivered the note) stares out from the postcard directly at the viewer. We can guess that he knows what the note says but will he translate its contents for the young suitor? English-speaking readers can enjoy the joke and share in Cholly's predicament of courting a woman who only understands Welsh, but they are outside Levine's (1977) circle of laughter. In contrast, senders and recipients of the card who can read Welsh are within the circle of laughter and, knowing that the message says *wait for me tonight at eight o'clock, Gwladys*, they are able to appreciate another layer of humour.

Figure 3.4 *Courting under difficulties!* Reproduced by kind permission of the National Library of Wales

A similar theme runs through another card in the same series entitled *Courting under difficulties!* The same character – Cholly – is now seen seated next to Gwladys, a young woman dressed in full Welsh costume (see Figure 3.4).

Although he has his arm around her waist, Cholly looks extremely anxious. He is studying *How to Speak Welsh in 6 Volumes*. The remaining volumes (which include *Welsh Slang and How to Negotiate Welsh Place Names*) are scattered around his feet, but he is reading volume five – *Terms of Endearment*. It seems that time may be running out for Cholly, however, in more ways than one, for not only does his sweetheart look on bemused, but in the background a goat is eating his remaining volumes. Once again, whilst the card endorses the ideological apparatus, establishing and conforming to existing norms and values in seeing humour in the Welsh language, an anti-normative reading of the card sees Cholly as the butt of the joke. An alternative reading could suggest that his restless Gwladys, unable to communicate with her erstwhile suitor may soon look elsewhere, especially as Cholly's efforts to learn Welsh are being undermined (possibly deliberately) by the grazing Welsh goat that is never far away.

Conclusion: Welsh Comic Postcards as Visual Narratives of People and Place

In this chapter, we have explored the interrelationships between constructions of ethnic and national identities and postcard representations of place and people. Specifically, we have investigated how comic postcards can contribute to the cultural production, performance and consumption of ethnoscapes, places and identities, thus unravelling how 'postcards participate in the construction of particular collective identities ... [and] are engaged in the production of the nation' (Moors, 2003: 25). At the same time, we have seen how such mythologies of identity and ethnicity are continually contested and engaged in a process of becoming rather than simply existing in an essentialist form. We chose to spotlight this by focusing on comic postcards of Wales, demonstrating how these visual narratives form a long tradition of certain imaginings of place, culture and nationhood. There remains much scope for further historical and contemporary study of visual discourses of tourism and identity, ethnicity and nationhood – all of which are subject to continuous inventions and reinventions and which are journeys of being and becoming which invoke mythologies, memories and mythic geographies of place. In such processes today, repeated everyday visual images play an increasingly central role in the ongoing making and remaking of places and identities. Their constant privileging of certain stories and narratives contribute to particular definitions of identity, history and community. In the same way, of course, the occlusion of other stories and identities from the visual discourse silences these dissident voices and erases these alternative identities and readings from the emotional map of a nation.

The Edwardian comic cards which we have discussed here formed part of the popular culture of the day and popular culture is always in process. Hopefully, however, we have shown that such texts are much more than mere humorous ephemera and, since they were only made meaningful in social relations – as they were inserted into the fabric of everyday life (Fiske, 1987) – we have seen how they reflect early 20th-century definitions of self and other. As reservoirs of 'commonsense' understandings of peoples and places, they constitute a 'moment' in the circularity of knowledge and power and contribute to the tourism-representation dialectic. We are all engaged in the making of places through the telling of stories and myths and the promotion of images, whether from within or outside those places. Here we have argued that these postcards reflect the colonial mindset which characterised the English state's attitude to the Welsh at this time and how, as Wales was their immediate neighbour, the English could conveniently indulge their fascination for 'Otherness' on their own doorstep.

Whether representing the Welsh men as ancient bards and backward country folk or representing Welsh women as immoral and seductive, we have read how the Edwardian comic postcards continued a heritage of cultural and historical 'knowledge', constantly defining the periphery to the centre. Moreover, whilst this layer of the interpretation is clearly evident, the longevity and extent of this iconography is only apparent when the analysis goes deeper and moves beyond the particular cultural text to examine its context. Thus, we have seen how there is a long tradition of denigrating and deriding Wales and the Welsh in English art, literature and popular culture; indeed, following the footsteps of others (especially Lord, 1995; Adams, 1996) we have been able to trace such anti-Welsh iconography from the early 16th to the early 20th century in this chapter. Postcards such as these are sites of ethnographic knowledge, marking cultural difference, frequently by costume or by the representation of cultural artefacts – in this case, Wales' associations with leeks, goats and cheese. As minimalist and simplistic representations, they are repositories of stereotypes, firmly rooted in notions of the gendered gaze (Mulvey, 1989) and of the colonial archive (Sekula, 1989) and can be seen to fully endorse the hegemonic values of the day. At the same time, however, it is important in any discursive analysis to recognise the potential of alternative textual readings and we have also tried to do that here, particularly as our study deals with comic texts which rely heavily on parody, some of which are also ethnographic texts, which may have attempted to subvert the orthodoxy of the powerful by inviting the powerless to join in additional circles of laughter (Levine, 1977).

Acknowledgements

The authors would like to thank Adam Jaworski for his valuable comments on an earlier version of this chapter. We would also like to thank the University of Wales Institute, Cardiff for financing our fieldwork through its research opportunities fund.

References

Abernathy-Lear, G. (1995) His name was not on the list: The soap opera updates of Ti-Rone as resistance to symbolic annihilation. In G. Dines and J.M. Humez (eds) *Gender, Race and Class in Media: A Text Reader* (pp. 383–94). London: Sage.

Adams, D. (1996) *Stage Welsh. Nation, Nationalism and Theatre: The Search for Cultural Identity*. Llandysul, Dyfed: Gomer Press.

Albers, P. and James, W. (1983) Travel photography: A methodological approach. *Annals of Tourism Research* 15, 134–58.

Ateljevic, I. and Doorne, S. (2003) Representing New Zealand: Tourism imagery and ideology. *Annals of Tourism Research* 29, 648–67.

Bailey, P. (1987) *Leisure and Class in Victorian England: Rational Recreation and the Contest for Control 1830–1885* (2nd edn). London: Methuen.

Banks, M. (2001) *Visual Methods in Social Research*. London: Sage.

Chaplin, E. (1994) *Sociology and Visual Representations*. London: Routledge.

Chapman, M. (1992) *The Celts*. London: Macmillan.

Cosgrove, D. (1993) Landscapes and myths, gods and humans. In B. Bender (ed.) *Landscape: Politics and Perspectives*. Berg: Oxford.

Coysh, A.W. (1984) *The Dictionary of Picture Postcards in Britain 1894–1939*. Suffolk: Antique Collectors' Club Ltd.

Crouch, D. and Lubbren, N. (eds) (2003) *Visual Culture and Tourism*. Berg: Oxford.

Davies, C.A. (1987) *Welsh Nationalism in the Twentieth Century: The Ethnic Option and the Modern State*. New York: Praeger.

Davies, J. (1993) *A History of Wales*. Harmondsworth: Penguin.

Dearnley, M. (2001) *Distant Fields. Eighteenth Century Fictions of Wales*. Cardiff: University of Wales Press.

Dorst, J.D. (1989) *The Written Suburb: An American Site, an Ethnographic Dilemma*. Philadelphia: University of Pennsylvania Press.

Edensor, T. (2002) *National Identity, Popular Culture and Everyday Life*. Oxford: Berg.

Edwards, E. (ed.) (1992) *Anthropology and Photography*. New Haven, CT: Yale University Press.

Edwards, E. (1996) Postcards: Greetings from another world. In T. Selwyn (ed.) *The Tourist Image* (pp. 197–21). Chichester: John Wiley.

Evans, E.J. and Richards, J. (1980) *A Social History of Britain in Postcards 1870–1930*. London: Longman.

Fairclough, N. (1992) *Discourse and Social Change*. Cambridge: Polity Press.

Fairclough, N. (2003) *Analyzing Discourse: Textual Analysis for Social Research*. London: Routledge.

Fiske, J. (1987) *Television Culture*. London: Routledge.

Franklin, A.S. and Crang, M. (2001) The trouble with tourism and travel theory? *Tourist Studies* 1, 5–22.

Gornall, M. (2003) Knickerbocker glories and crushed nuts: Alternative masculinities in the saucy seaside postcard of the 1960s. Paper presented at Tourisms & Histories: Representations & Experiences Conference, 19–21 June, University of Central Lancashire, Preston.

Hall, S. (1980) Encoding/Decoding. In S. Hall, D. Hobson, A. Lowe and P. Willis (eds) *Culture, Media, Language* (pp. 128–38). London: Hutchinson.

Hall, S. (1996) New ethnicities. In D. Morley and K.H. Chen (eds) *Stuart Hall: Critical Dialogues in Cultural Studies*. London: Routledge.

Hall, S. (ed.) (1997) *Representation: Cultural Representations and Signifying Practices*. London: Sage.

Hodge, R. and Kress, G. (1993) *Language as Ideology* (2nd edn). London: Routledge.

Howarth, D. (2000) *Discourse*. Buckingham: Open University Press.

Jamal, T. and Hollinshead, K. (2001) Tourism and the forbidden zone: The under-served power of qualitative enquiry. *Tourism Management* 22, 63–82.

Jenkins, R. (1997) *Rethinking Ethnicity. Arguments and Explorations*. London: Sage.

Joyce, P. (1991) *Visions of the People. Industrial England and the Question of Class 1848–1914*. Cambridge: Cambridge University Press.

Levine, L. (1977) *Black Culture and Black Consciousness: Afro-American Folk Thought from Slavery to Freedom*. Oxford: Oxford University Press.

Lewes, D. (2000) *Nudes From Nowhere: Utopian Sexual Landscapes*. Lanham, MD: Rowman & Littlefield.

Lord, P. (1995) *Words with Pictures. Welsh Images and Images of Wales in the Popular Press, 1640–1860*. Aberystwyth: Planet.

Louw, E. (2001) *The Media and Cultural Production*. London: Sage.

Mackenzie, J. (2001) 'For the use of tourists, sportsmen, invalids and settlers': Imperial guide books and the tourism of empire. Paper presented at Tourisms & Histories: Representations & Experiences Conference, 19–21 June, University of Central Lancashire, Preston.

McCrone, D., Morris, A. and Kiely, R. (1995) *Scotland – the Brand. The Making of Scottish Heritage*. Edinburgh: Edinburgh University Press.

Moors, A. (2003) From 'Women's Lib' to 'Palestinian Women': The politics of picture postcards in Palestine/Israel. In D. Crouch and N. Lubbren (eds) *Visual Culture and Tourism* (pp. 23–40). Oxford: Berg.

Morgan, N.J. and Pritchard, A. (1998) *Tourism Promotion and Power*. Chichester: John Wiley.

Morgan, N.J. and Pritchard, A. (2004) Mae'n Bryd I Ddod Adref – It's time to come home: Exploring the contested emotional geographies of Wales. In T. Coles and D. Timothy (eds) *Travel to Promised Lands. Diaspora Tourism* (pp. 233–45). London: Routledge.

Morris, P.A. (1998) An evaluation of the brand 'Wales' in the North American context. Unpublished MA thesis, University of Wales Institute, Cardiff.

Mulvey, L. (1989) *Visual and Other Pleasures*. Basingstoke: Macmillan.

Osborne, R. (2002) *Megawords*. London: Sage.

Phillips, T. (2000) *The Postcard Century: 2000 Cards and the Messages*. London: Thames & Hudson.

Pink, S. (2001) *Doing Visual Ethnography. Images, Media and Representation in Research*. London: Sage.

Pinney, C. (1992) The parallel histories of anthropology and photography. In E. Edwards (ed.) *Anthropology and Photography*. New Haven, CT: Yale University Press.

Pitchford, S.R. (1994) Ethnic tourism and nationalism in Wales. *Annals of Tourism Research* 21, 35–50.

Pritchard, A. and Morgan, N.J. (2000) Privileging the male gaze. Gendered tourism landscapes. *Annals of Tourism Research* 27, 884–905.

Pritchard, A. and Morgan, N.J. (2001) Culture, identity and representation: Marketing Cymru or Wales? *Tourism Management* 22, 167–79.

Pritchard, A. and Morgan, N. (2003) Mythic geographies of representation and identity: Contemporary postcards of Wales. *Journal of Tourism and Cultural Change* 1 (2), 111–30.

Prosser, J. (1998) Introduction. In J. Prosser (ed.) *Image-based Research: A Sourcebook for Qualitative Researchers* (pp. 1–18). London: Falmer Press.

Rutherford, J. (1990) A place called home: Identity and the cultural politics of difference. In J. Rutherford (ed.) *Identity: Community, Culture, Difference* (pp. 9–28). London: Lawrence & Wishart Ltd.

Rose, G. (1993) *Feminism and Geography. The Limits of Geographical Knowledge.* Cambridge: Polity Press.

Sekula, A. (1989) The archive and the body. In R. Bolton (ed.) *The Contest of Meaning* (pp. 4–24). Cambridge, MA: MIT Press.

Schulman, N.M. (1995) Laughing across the color barrier in living color. In G. Dines and J.M. Humez (eds) *Gender, Race and Class in Media: A Text Reader* (pp. 438–44). London: Sage.

Stassinopoulous, A. and Beny, R. (1983) *The Gods of Greece.* New York: Abrams.

Stephens, M. (1992) *A Most Peculiar People: Quotations about Wales and the Welsh.* Cardiff: University of Wales Press.

Thomas, R.S. (1992) *Cymru or Wales?* Llandysul, Dyfed: Gomer Press.

Tonkiss, F. (1998) Analysing discourse. In C. Seale (ed.) *Researching Society and Culture* (pp. 245–60). London: Sage.

Tressider, R. (1999) Tourism and sacred landscapes. In D. Crouch (ed.) *Leisure/tourism Geographies: Practices and Geographical Knowledge* (pp. 137–48). London: Routledge.

Weber M. (1978) Economy and society. In G. Roth and C. Wittich (eds) Berkeley: University of California Press.

Whittaker, E. (2000) A century of indigenous images: The world according to the tourist postcard. In M. Robinson, P. Long, N. Evans, R. Sharply and J. Swarbrooke (eds) *Expressions of Culture, Identity and Meaning in Tourism* (pp. 425–37). Newcastle and Sheffield: Universities of Northumbria and Sheffield Hallam.

Williams, G.A. (1985) *When was Wales? A History of the Welsh.* London: Penguin.

Part 2

The Discursive Construction and Representation of the Tourist Experience

Chapter 4

Exclusive, Ethno and Eco: Representations of Culture and Nature in Tourism Discourses in Namibia

UTA PAPEN

Introduction

Tourism, as one of the so-called culture industries of post-modernity, is heavily involved not only in the economic but also in the 'cultural trans-formation of places' (Urry, 1995: 2). Tourists, as Urry (1995, this volume) argues, 'consume' the places and people they visit. In order to make places amenable to this consumption, geographical spaces have to be transformed into tourist destinations or tourist sites. Precisely what form the transformation of a place into a tourist site takes depends on a range of political, social and cultural factors, having to do with the immediate local context as well as with the currency of specific tourism products in the global tourism industry.

Tourism discourses can be defined as a set of expressions, words and behaviour as well as particular touristic structures and activities that describe a place and its inhabitants (see Lindknud, 1998). Tourism dis-courses are central to the creation of 'place-myths' (Lash & Urry, 1994: 265), and they do so by drawing on selected images, symbols and associ-ations, which characterise the particular site in question. Referring pri-marily to the tourists' own process of assembling different images and ideas received from various sources of information, Rojek (1997: 54) calls the process by which a tourist destination is created 'dragging'. Promotional tourism texts such as leaflets and brochures also 'drag' or draw on a range of discursive sources in order to construct the desired image of a place. In this chapter, I examine tourism discourses focusing on some texts used for tourism promotion in Namibia, a relatively recent entrant to the overseas tourism market.

Aim and Scope

In 1999 and 2000, while conducting ethnographic research on adult literacy in Namibia, I studied the reading and writing activities of local tourism workers, such as crafts vendors and tour guides. Starting from Katutura, a black township in Windhoek, the capital of Namibia, my research took me into various parts of the country, where I accompanied local guides on their tours, interviewed craft vendors and visited community-based tourism enterprises (CBTEs). These CBTEs, which are founded by local communities in urban and rural areas, struggle to establish themselves within the dense Namibian tourism market, where they face the competition of other well-established, privately owned tourism businesses.

Even a brief look at the world of tourists and tourism in Namibia is sufficient to draw one's attention to the importance of written communication in this economic sector, especially that of advertising and marketing materials. Flyers, brochures, posters and signposts tell the tourists where to go, what to do and what not to miss. Such texts can be found everywhere in Windhoek and in many other touristic 'hotspots'. They are displayed at the airport, in the lounges of hotels and guesthouses, arts and crafts centres, and at the Tourist Information Office in the centre of Windhoek. In this chapter, I discuss two examples of such promotional texts: a flyer and a small brochure that advertise the services of two CBTEs: the *Anmire Cultural Village* and *Face-to-Face Tours* (a small tour guiding service in Windhoek) both of which were set up by local communities in the summer of 1999. In fact, at the time of writing, *Face-to-Face Tours* is the only tourism business in Windhoek owned by black Namibians. They are also the only group offering township tours, a market that is much more developed in neighbouring South Africa.

I have chosen these two texts because they exemplify and represent two seemingly dominant strands within community-based tourism in Namibia: (1) 'ethno-tourism', which responds to the tourists' growing interest in Namibia's ethnic groups and their cultural traditions (*Face-to-Face Tours, Anmire Cultural Village*), and (2) 'eco-tourism', which aims to showcase the natural environment while also supporting local conservation projects (*Anmire Cultural Village*). In addition to these two leaflets, I analyse a page from the *Windhoek Tourist Info Guide*, which also describes Katutura, the black township of the capital and the place where *Face-to-Face Tours* take their clients; I also introduce some ethnographic data (see next section). Overall, I treat my data sources as sets of competing discourses (Lee, 1992), which are engaged in an ideological struggle of constructing strategically desirable versions of social reality.

In this chapter, I aim to develop three interrelated arguments. Firstly, I argue that the brochures, flyers and signboards of CBTEs, which represent a distinct but marginal sector of the Namibian tourism industry, are closely linked with the dominant tourism discourses of 'mainstream' tourism publicity (cf. Thurot & Thurot, 1983; Lindknud, 1998). Secondly, I demonstrate that tourism discourses, and accordingly the brochures and flyers in which they appear, are strongly shaped by the asymmetrical relationships of power that characterise the Namibian tourism sector. Finally, I postulate that Namibia's tourism discourses, although at first glance appearing to promote cultural diversity, in fact present a simplified and homogenised picture of local life and history.

Method

This research is informed by a number of earlier studies of language and advertising in tourism (e.g. Thurot & Thurot, 1983; Cohen & Cooper, 1986; Selwyn, 1996; Wai-Teng Leong, 1997; Omoniyi, 1998; Dann, 1996a, 1996b, 2000, 2001). Although my chapter is primarily concerned with a discourse analytic approach to the study of promotional texts of CBTEs, I supplement it with ethnographic data obtained in the course of participant observation and interviews. Over a period of 10 months between 1999 and 2000, I visited seven different CBTEs, and interviewed their members. As I took on the role of a tourist, I participated in guided tours, stayed on campsites, visited museum villages and crafts centres. In all the CBTEs I visited, I interviewed at least one of its members, often the person who had initiated it or who was acting as its manager. In several cases, these interviews took on the form of group discussions with several members of the CBTE.

In the case of *Face-to-Face Tours*, my initial contact led to a long-term engagement with the group, which stretched over a period of five months. During this time, I accompanied the group repeatedly on their tours and conducted additional interviews. Many of the insights about the situation of CBTEs in Namibia, their attempts to attract tourists and their advertising practices stem from my close contact with *Face-to-Face Tours*. After our initial contact, they soon drew me into their business as an informal adviser. In this capacity, I accompanied them on several visits to the Namibian Community-Based Tourism Association (NACOBTA), a local umbrella organisation for CBTEs, and to the Windhoek Municipality, who had offered to support them with training and publicity.

I also conducted several interviews with independent tourism workers (i.e. those who did not belong to a CBTE): a crafts vendor in Windhoek and two guides in Kaokoveld, in the northwest of the country, who accompany tourists on visits to the homesteads of the local Himba population, as well as with staff from NACOBTA, with an officer in the Ministry of Environment and Tourism (MET) and with the manager of a private training agency for tour guides. Finally, I consulted a range of research publications, policy documents and promotional materials pertaining to tourism in Namibia.

Background: Tourism in Namibia

Previously governed by South Africa, Namibia achieved independence in 1990. With the final abolition of apartheid and its homeland structure, which had been implemented in Namibia in much the same way as in South Africa, in 1990 almost the entire country was opened to tourism. What followed was a slow but steady growth in the number of foreign visitors. Early on in the 1990s, the discovery of ethnic or ethno-tourism (Vorlauefer, 1996; Chambers, 2000) or indigenous tourism (Smith, 1996) began. As a result, Namibia's ethnic population slowly became part of the tourist gaze.

Namibia's small population (approximately 1.8 million) is ethnically and racially highly diverse. There are 11 recognised ethnic groups in Namibia and about 15 languages are spoken in the country (Maho, 1998; Puetz, 1995). Until recently, the society has been divided between the Afrikaans-, German- and English-speaking white minority and the black majority. At independence, English was made the official language of the country, and it is also the main language of tourism, although German as well as Afrikaans play a significant role.

At present, tourism is the fastest growing sector of the Namibian economy. By 1995, it had become the third largest sector of the economy, contributing 5% to GNP (Ashley, 1995). The potential of tourism for the country's economy has been recognised by the government and the industry profits from a favourable policy environment (see Ministry of Environment and Tourism, 1994). This includes community-based tourism, earmarked as a promising endeavour to support local development and to redress the inequalities inherited from the apartheid era (Ministry of Environment and Tourism, 1995, 1996). The latest tourist statistics released by the Ministry of Environment and Tourism in 1997 give an overall figure of 502,000 tourists visiting the country, compared to 250,000 tourists visiting Namibia in 1993 (http://www.met.gov.na). The majority of tourists come from South Africa, Germany and other European countries and from North America (Brits & Wiig, 1998).

Its colonial past has left Namibia with a highly divided economy and a highly unequal distribution of land. Although at independence, political power was turned over to the former black liberation movement, today much of the economy is still in the hands of white Namibians. The strong divisions that exist in the Namibian economy and society are mirrored in the country's tourism industry. In the commercial areas, covering 44% of the country's territory, the overwhelming majority of approximately 4300 farms are owned by white Namibians. Many of these farms have turned to guest-farming, hunting and safari tourism as additional income. Former homelands have been turned into communal lands and constitute 41% of the territory, with an estimated 150,000 black farmers striving to make a living (Schade, 2000). Many of Namibia's natural and cultural attractions are located in the communal lands, but only 10% of all tourism facilities can be found there. Private tour operators (see further below), who are mostly based in Windhoek and in the other major cities, profit from touring the communal lands; however, except for the sites deemed as *conservancies*, no clear and legally binding regulations exist regarding the redistribution of the tourism income.

Tourism in Namibia reflects the hierarchies and inequalities inherited from the colonial and apartheid past. The lion's share of the income derived from tourism goes to privately owned hotels, lodges, guest-farms and tour operators remaining in the hands of the predominantly German-, Afrikaans- and English-speaking, white Namibians (Rothfuss, 2000). The lodges and campsites situated in Namibia's Game Parks are owned by the state, but they are in the process of privatisation. Many of the private companies and lodges have links with tour operators abroad, in particular in Germany, England, France and South Africa. By contrast, the sector of community-based tourism is much smaller and most of the CBTEs have been set up only in the years since 1999. The majority of the CBTEs are not registered as private businesses, but as community-managed enterprises operating in communal lands. A community that wants to establish a CBTE applies to the Ministry of Environment and Tourism for a 'Permission to Occupy' (PTO), which grants them the right to establish a tourism business in the area specified in the PTO. Other CBTEs have been established in conjunction with the introduction of conservancies (see Ministry of Environment and Tourism, 1996).

The mainstay of Namibian tourism is safari holidays. However, in terms of wildlife numbers, Namibia cannot compete with other African countries, which attract a much larger share of overseas visitors. Therefore, government and private tour operators aim to diversify the Namibian tourism product by emphasising the country's many cultural assets and its colonial history. By doing so, they have opened the door for CBTEs to enter the Namibian tourism market. While some CBTEs have accepted partnerships with private tour operators who seek to develop ethno-tourism, others, such as the CBTEs that I discuss in this paper, have remained independent and stand in direct competition to private tourism businesses.

Face-to-Face Tours and Anmire Cultural Village

Simon, Anna and Elisabeth, the three *Face-to-Face Tours* guides, grew up and went to school in the township of Katutura. As many others in

Katutura, on leaving school they could only find occasional employment. Simon, the founder of the group, worked as a taxi driver, taking tourists from the airport situated about 30 miles outside Windhoek to their hotels and guesthouses in the city centre. It was while he was working as a taxi driver that he first got the idea to set up a tour guiding business. His passengers often asked him about the city and about Katutura. Some showed interest in the township and wanted to hire him and his car to take them to the township. The tour of Katutura, which is only one of several offered by *Face-to-Face Tours*, includes visits to a community-based recycling project, local markets and bars and an 'authentic' Namibian homestead.

The *Anmire Cultural Village* is a museum village in the former Damara homeland, situated in northwestern Namibia. *Anmire* is run by a group of local people from the nearby Khowarib community. At *Anmire*, several guides show the visitors around the village, while explaining and staging different cultural events and customs. Visitors can see rebuilt huts, watch a 'traditional healer' prepare a herbal remedy, admire the Damara people's dances and assist in the proceedings of a local court.

Competing discourses (I): Windhoek versus Katutura or (White) colonial history versus contemporary African life

Experience Katutura Face to Face (see Figure 4.1) is the main source of publicity for the *Face-to-Face Tours* operation in Katutura.

The flyer is dominated by the oversized letters in which the group's slogan is printed. The large font and the central position of the word 'experience' suggest that tourists who accept the group's offer can expect a multi-sensory encounter with something unknown and exotic. The name 'Katutura', which is probably new to the majority of tourists visiting Namibia for the first time, is likely to sound sufficiently novel to suggest an appealing and intriguing strangeness of the place to be visited. This is reinforced by the promise of an 'exclusive adventure' when visiting Katutura. The offer to 'experience' the township is expressed in what Omoniyi (1998) calls 'an invitational imperative', which is frequently used in tourism texts. The directness and multi-sensory character of the experience is further emphasised by the use of the phrase 'face-to-face', which is printed in a 'hand-drawn' font suggesting sensuality, informality and authenticity. The phrase is repeated twice on the leaflet, in the logo on the right-hand side of the main slogan, and further below in the name of the group, giving additional emphasis to the message of direct contact between tourists and hosts, which it aims to convey.

The group's logo, positioned on the right-hand side of the slogan, contains a message that the viewer is unlikely to miss: *Face-to-Face Tours* are a group of black guides who take white tourists to the black township of Katutura. The logo – two heads, one white and one black, facing each

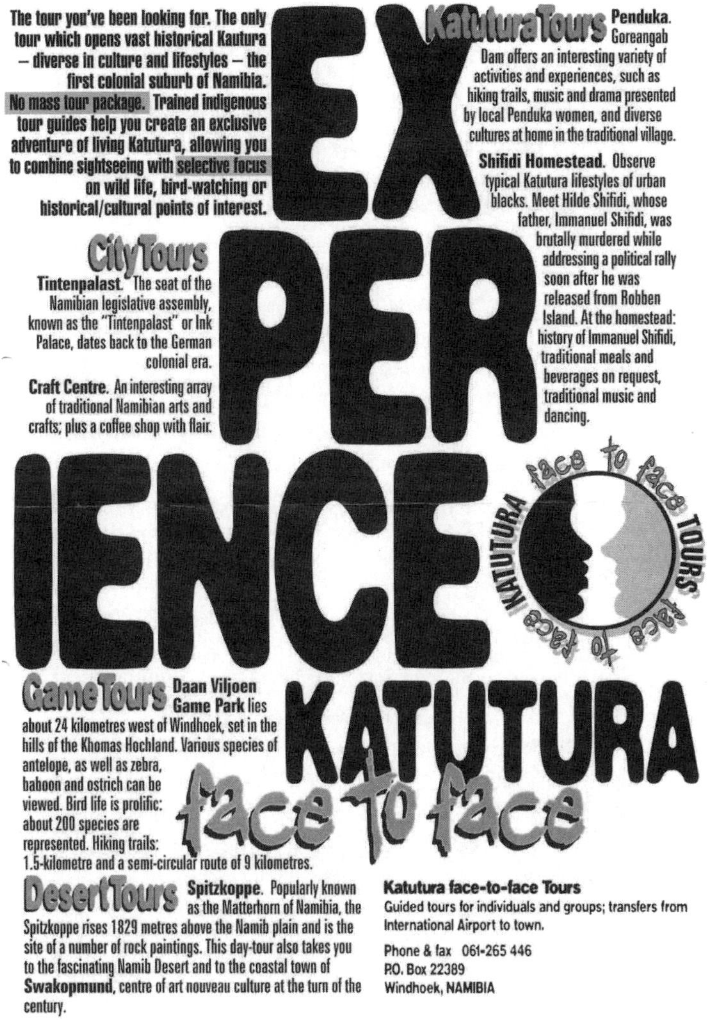

The tour you've been looking for. The only tour which opens vast historical Kautura – diverse in culture and lifestyles – the first colonial suburb of Namibia. No mass tour package. Trained indigenous tour guides help you create an exclusive adventure of living Katutura, allowing you to combine sightseeing with selective focus on wild life, bird-watching or historical/cultural points of interest.

City Tours

Tintenpalast. The seat of the Namibian legislative assembly, known as the "Tintenpalast" or Ink Palace, dates back to the German colonial era.

Craft Centre. An interesting array of traditional Namibian arts and crafts; plus a coffee shop with flair.

Katutura Tours Penduka. Goreangab Dam offers an interesting variety of activities and experiences, such as hiking trails, music and drama presented by local Penduka women, and diverse cultures at home in the traditional village.

Shifidi Homestead. Observe typical Katutura lifestyles of urban blacks. Meet Hilde Shifidi, whose father, Immanuel Shifidi, was brutally murdered while addressing a political rally soon after he was released from Robben Island. At the homestead: history of Immanuel Shifidi, traditional meals and beverages on request, traditional music and dancing.

EXPERIENCE KATUTURA face to face

KATUTURA face to face TOURS

Game Tours Daan Viljoen Game Park lies about 24 kilometres west of Windhoek, set in the hills of the Khomas Hochland. Various species of antelope, as well as zebra, baboon and ostrich can be viewed. Bird life is prolific: about 200 species are represented. Hiking trails: 1.5-kilometre and a semi-circular route of 9 kilometres.

Desert Tours Spitzkoppe. Popularly known as the Matterhorn of Namibia, the Spitzkoppe rises 1829 metres above the Namib plain and is the site of a number of rock paintings. This day-tour also takes you to the fascinating Namib Desert and to the coastal town of **Swakopmund**, centre of art nouveau culture at the turn of the century.

Katutura face-to-face Tours
Guided tours for individuals and groups; transfers from International Airport to town.

Phone & fax 061-265 446
P.O. Box 22389
Windhoek, NAMIBIA

Figure 4.1 Flyer for the Katutura Face-to-Face Tours

other – suggests the racial identity of hosts and guests, which is not direct-ly revealed in the text, except in the reference to the lifestyle of urban blacks. The most striking aspect of the logo, i.e. the way the two heads face each other, echoes the slogan of the group: 'Katutura face-to-face'. Furthermore, the closeness of the two faces suggests to the (white) tourists a promise of a close, direct encounter with the (black) hosts. Thus, the leaflet seems to address predominantly the tourists who are interested in the 'ethnic' Namibia.

THE SPIRIT OF KATUTURA
– THE PULSE OF WINDHOEK,
THE HEART OF NAMIBIA
(Cont. from Pg. 59)

Protest

Most Main Location residents opposed the planned closure of the Main Location and refused to consider moving to the proposed new location which was ultimately names Katutura. Opposition to the move reached climax in December 1959. A group of Herero women made a protest march to the Administrator's residence on 3 December. Five days later saw an effective boycott against municipally operated facilities such as buses, the beer hall and the cinema. On the night of 10 December, a protest meeting held in the Main Location developed into a confrontation with the police.

The police shot and killed 11 people and some 44 required medical attention (Goldblatt: 1971; 262,Hall: 1961; 3).Immediately after the confrontation, between 3 000 and 4 000 people fled the location and refused to return because they were afraid of further trouble. It was a time of great turmoil. The Old Location was officially closed on 31 August 1968. Eventually all people in the Old Location, with the exception of about 300 people who decided to go to their reserves (communal areas), moved to the new location, Katutura, without further incident.

A changed Windhoek

The rich history of Namibia's freedom struggle is well known. And Windhoek today is a different picture all together. Of course, Katutura is still there but the circumstances have changed drastically. It all started changing in 1990 when Namibia became an independent sovereign state led by His Excellency Dr Sam Nujoma, President of the Republic of Namibia. In 1992 the Local Authority Act 23 of 1992 was promulgated which ushered in new blood and an enlightened city leadership for Windhoek. The first ever democratically elected SWAPO-led Windhoek City Council immediately set about putting matter right in the previously neglected areas Council set about their mandate to improve the quality of life for its

inhabitants. Their focus lay on providing much needed municipal services to the previously neglected communities and unemployment was still rampant at that time. The City of Windhoek set about addressing the unemployment issue in line with the national policy of employment creation. This was the catalyst for the creation of the now bustling Soweto Market.

62 Windhoek Tourism Guide

Figure 4.2 Page from the Windhoek Tourist Info Guide

'Katutura' means 'the place where we do not have any permanent habitation'. This is the name given to Katutura by its black inhabitants in 1959, when they were forcefully moved from their homes in the so-called 'Old Location' to the new township that was located further away from the city centre and the growing white neighbourhoods of Windhoek (Pendleton, 1996). The township soon became a symbol of the struggle against apartheid and South African occupation. Nevertheless, over the years, and in particular since independence, Katutura slowly turned into what could be called 'Matutura' or 'a place where we stay' (Pendleton, 1996), highlighting its inhabitants' acceptance of their new home, if only for want of a better place where to go. In *Face-to-Face Tours'* flyer and in the *Windhoek Tourist Info Guide* (see Figure 4.2), the township is once again transformed: this time into the 'Pulse of Windhoek' and a place of 'vibrant' (*Windhoek Tourist Info Guide*) and 'diverse' (*Face-to-Face Tours*) culture, highlighting the city's 'diversity' as well as the 'development' and 'freedom' that were achieved after independence.

Both the tour guides' flyer and the Municipality's Tourist Info Guide appeal to a new trend in Namibian tourism: many tourists' interest in 'indigenous' life. Yet, despite this growing interest in ethnic tourism, the guides' position within Windhoek's tourism market is far from secure. Windhoek's private tour operators offer a range of 'city tours' with white Namibians or Europeans as guides focusing on 'white' Windhoek and its colonial history. Some of these city tours drive through Katutura's main road, but they do not stop in the township.

Therefore, for Simon, Anna and Elisabeth it is important that their leaflet highlights what is special about their tours and what sets them apart from the city tours of the other agencies. The phrases 'no mass tour package' and 'selective focus' are aimed to draw the reader's attention to the specific features of the group's tours. No mass tour package is an indirect hint at the other tour agencies that take groups of between 30 and 40 tourists in large coaches along pre-determined routes through Windhoek. By contrast, *Face-to-Face Tours* cater for groups between two to eight travellers offering what they describe as a 'selective focus' on different aspects of the country's history, culture, flora and fauna.

Although several other destinations are offered in the leaflet, it strongly focuses on Katutura. This is the first theme introduced on the top left side of the page and it is continued throughout the centre (with its large slogan) and over the entire right side of the page.

When Simon, Anna and Elisabeth first started their business, they wanted to offer not only the township tours, but also trips through the city of Windhoek, to a game park near the city and into the Namib Desert. In the leaflet, these are offered as 'City', 'Game' and 'Desert' tours. The parts of the leaflet that describe these tours orient predominantly to the large group of German tourists visiting Namibia. This can be seen, for example, in the use of the original German word for the colonial administration's headquarters 'Tintenpalast', and in the description of the 'Spitzkoppe', a sharply formed mountain southwest of Windhoek, as the 'Matterhorn' of Namibia. However, despite the leaflet's exploitation of Namibia's colonial past and its post-colonial language legacy, a resource commonly used by other, private tourism operators in their publicity materials, the 'City', 'Game' and 'Desert' tours have not been successful in drawing many tourists.

As the above discussion suggests, there are two sets of tourism discourses, which accentuate different aspects of Windhoek's past and present and compete with each other for the largest share of visitors to Namibia's capital: the 'white' colonial Namibia of the capital city, and the 'black' Namibia of the capital's township. Both occupy different fractions of the tourism sector. The first attracts primarily package safari tourists, whose itinerary, in addition to Namibia's wildlife, includes a dose of heritage and cultural tourism. Amongst these, German tourists are a prominent group, attracted by the lively German-Namibian culture (which is particularly present in Windhoek) and bringing with them a special interest in German colonial history. The second discourse of 'African', i.e. black Namibian culture, speaks mostly to younger travellers, independent tourists and backpackers. However, the relationship between these two discourses is far from equal with the discourse of colonial Windhoek receiving a much larger share of visitors. In their flyer, *Face-to-Face Tours* take up both discourses, attempting to attract both sets of customers, and although the Katutura tours seem to attract a steady stream of visitors, their City, Game and Desert tours seem to lose out to the dominant, 'mainstream' operators and their promotional discourses.

While much has changed in Katutura since the gaining of independence, the reality of this growing suburb, at least for my informants, is different from the generalising and simplifying picture of the tourism discourses. Although apartheid and colonialism finally ended in 1990, Namibia remains racially divided. An urban black middle class has emerged, but many coloured and black Namibians still suffer from the poverty, unemployment and bad housing. Katutura remains a testimony to this racial and economic divide as it is a site of vast squatter and informal settlement areas with substandard living conditions. However, none of this is mentioned in *Face-to-Face Tours'* flyer or in the Municipality's brochure, as this would unduly draw the visitors' attention to the inequalities that persist in the new Namibia, in contrast to the official discourses of reconciliation and development strongly promoted by the government. Instead, in the *Face-to-Face* flyer, the history of Katutura is emphasised and a rather (self-)stereotyping image of 'typical' lifestyle is mentioned briefly, while the Municipality brochure seems to celebrate contemporary culture of the area. Thus culture is turned into folklore and history becomes 'heritage', a past that is 'dead and safe' (Urry, 2002: 99), thereby not only hampering the development of more diversified and nuanced tourism discourses, but also supporting the government in its rejection of any public debate about the country's recent past.

Beneath the presentation of the township as a place where tourists can experience the diversity of Namibia's history and present cultures is a common dilemma of 'Third World' tourism. Tourists who come to visit the township want to 'experience' Katutura 'face to face', but this does not mean that they necessarily want to look inside its shacks and houses. Poverty, malnutrition, sickness and death, all phenomena that even an ephemeral glance at Katutura reveals, do not lend themselves to the beatifying tourist gaze.

Necessarily, then, tourism discourses are simplifying. In its *Tourist Info Guide*, the Windhoek Municipality carefully constructs a view of the township's present that says very little about the social and spatial inequalities its inhabitants continue to experience, well over a decade after the end of the South African rule. Instead, it celebrates the township's 'African spirit' (*Windhoek Tourist Info Guide*, pp. 59 and 64) by highlighting the government's recent achievements in 'improving the quality of life' and tackling unemployment (p. 64) in the area. For example, the guide mentions the newly built and 'now bustling Soweto Market' (p. 64) in the centre of Katutura. As most visitors will not fail to notice, however, the Soweto Market is anything but bustling: many of the shops and stalls are closed or not even occupied, with only a few customers milling around, one reason for this stalemate being high rent unaffordable to most of Katutura's small entrepreneurs.

One may wonder why *Face-to-Face Tours* have also chosen to portray a rather simplified image of the township, which certainly differs from their own view of Katutura. Talking to the tour guides, it became obvious that the making of Katutura into a tourist destination for them required a major change in their own perceptions of the suburb. For Elisabeth, Anna and Simon, Katutura is essentially a boring and derelict place, where there is nothing to see except for endless rows of run-down houses and shacks. For them, Katutura is a place that offers little formal employment and a future that is more than uncertain. Their own view of the township stands in striking contrast to how they describe Katutura in their flyer as a place of 'diverse culture and lifestyle'.

Competing discourses (II): Safari- versus eco-tourism

The *Anmire Cultural Village* is one of the new CBTEs, which in recent years have been founded in communal areas. It is located in Damaraland, the former homeland of the Damara people. Most of the big tour operators and safari companies, who take tourists throughout the country, drive their clients to Damaraland where they visit the famous rock-paintings and rock-engravings. However, relatively few tourists stop at *Anmire*.

The village of *Anmire*, however, tries to attract tourists outside of the 'mainstream' channels by targeting a relatively new breed of tourists engaged in eco-tourism. Eco-tourism provides a counter-discourse to the safari-theme that dominates Namibian tourism. In its leaflet, *Anmire* speaks to this new consumer identity. Central themes in the leaflet are environment protection and community development. Farming in Damaraland, as in many other parts of Namibia, suffers from frequent droughts, erosion and growing soil degradation. The Namibian government has introduced a range of legislative measures to support wildlife and soil conservation while at the same time supporting rural development. Through the 'conservancy' these efforts are combined with attempts to promote community-based tourism schemes (Ministry of Environment and Tourism, 1995, 1996). The conservancy scheme lends itself ideally to the idea of eco-tourism, a new trend in European and Third World tourism, which responds to the growing environmental awareness among tourists, and to the 'back to nature' movement of western late-modern societies.

Indeed, *Anmire* attracts a specific clientele of tourists: independent travellers who see themselves as 'beyond' the photo-hunts of safari lovers, and who are interested in environmental issues, in local culture and history. *Anmire's* leaflet (see Figures 4.3 and 4.4) takes up a range of discourses that are likely to appeal to tourists who think of themselves not only as 'nature lovers' (an identity the safari tourists would also claim for themselves), but as 'conservationists'. It speaks about *Anmire* as 'an initiative of a local woman', and as a 'community-based enterprise'. In the leaflet, *Anmire* expresses its gratitude to the visitors for their contribution to the 'conservation of the environment' and explains that part of the enterprise's profit is distributed to the community. The tourists are invited to 'witness traditional fire making' and 'rituals of the hunt'. With phrases such as 'traditional knowledge', 'cultural heritage' and 'natural resources', the leaflet uses a vocabulary that responds to many tourists' desire to be both 'responsible tourists' and to experience 'authentic', pre-modern village life. By doing so, *Anmire* combines the discourses of eco-tourism and ethno-tourism. Not unlike *Face-to-Face Tours* present Katutura, *Anmire's* leaflet draws the reader's attention to the history of the Damara people. The focus is on the ancient history, and on what are called 'traditions', rather than on the more recent or even the present-day situation of the Damara. This is reinforced by the image of an old man shown on the front page. Although the leaflet claims that visitors to *Anmire* can get a glimpse at 'ancient *and* present ways of Damara living' (emphasis added), my own experience when joining a tour through the village is that tourists are told very little about 'modern' Damara life.

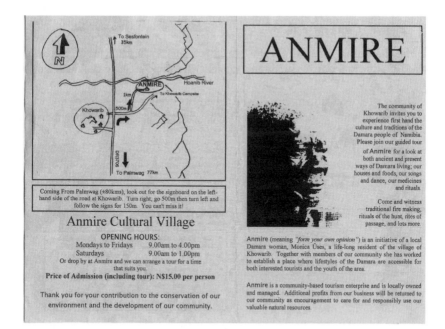

Figure 4.3 Brochure for the Anmire Cultural Village, pp. 1 and 4

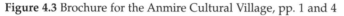

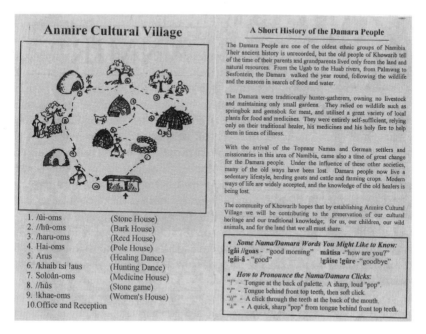

Figure 4.4 Brochure for the Anmire Cultural Village, pp. 2 and 3

The leaflet serves several functions. It explains the origin and nature of this museum; it offers a short history of the Damara people and some Nama/Damara words the visitor might want to learn; and it features a hand-drawn map of the village and instructions on how to get there by car.

The leaflet uses a range of key words and images. These are important semiotic markers, which embody the discourses that inform specific texts. The reference to 'traditional knowledge' in *Anmire*'s leaflet reflects, for example, the discourses of nostalgia and cultural diversity. 'Conservation' refers to the fashionable 'green' discourses of sustainable development and reflects *Anmire*'s attempts to find a niche in the growing eco-and ethno-tourism markets. In this context, the image of the old man on the front of the leaflet stands in a metonymic relationship to the Damara and their culture: the image of a token old man signifies the whole of the 'traditional' Damara culture.

Just as *Face-to-Face Tours*, *Anmire* promises its visitors a direct encounter with local traditions and culture. This is most directly expressed in the invitation to 'experience first hand' the ways of living of the Damara people. Again, this promises not only a sufficiently exotic experience (indicated by the foreign sounding name of the village 'Anmire'), but also suggests *authenticity*. From the first paragraph on, the leaflet talks about the people who have built *Anmire* in the first person plural, implying a degree of familiarity between 'you' (the tourist and reader of the leaflet) and 'us', the people of *Anmire*. This again highlights the authenticity of the experience on offer: the visitors will get to know 'real' people from a local community. This is further emphasised by including the founder's full name in the text, which indicates that the visit will not be an anonymous experience, but a personal encounter with a group of Damara people. As in *Face-to-Face Tours*' leaflet, the invitational imperative is used, for example, in 'Come and witness traditional fire making'. The style of the text, however, changes on the back of the leaflet. The history of the Damara people is presented in a much more academic style that signals 'expertise' based on historical and ethnographic research. Such pseudo-academic accounts, which can frequently be found in travel guides, aim to lend credibility and authority to the information these provide.

The suggested directness and authenticity of the experience on offer and the focus on indigenous life need again be interpreted in relation to the structures of the Namibian tourism industry and the niche CBTEs try to find within it. *Anmire* tries to benefit from the growth of eco- and ethno-tourism and to capitalise on its strategic advantage over the established tour companies in Namibia. At present, very few of these have developed links with local communities and can offer visits to local villages. Although a reconstructed village, *Anmire* can offer a glimpse of rural Namibian life and an encounter with Damara people.

The materiality and colour of the leaflet reinforce the image of the village as a local enterprise that uses locally available material and aims to contribute to the protection of the natural environment. The leaflet is printed on plain matt paper and it exists in two versions: a light green and a light yellow or sand colour version, both likely to be easily associated with the colours of the Namibian landscape itself.

According to Kress and van Leeuwen (1996), hand-drawn maps, such as the map that indicates the way to *Anmire* and the plan of the village, refer to low visual modality. They do not represent the observable 'reality' as directly as photographs do. The drawings in *Anmire*'s leaflet do not offer much in terms of naturalistic modality, i.e. in terms of a reality value that is based on the highest possible congruence between what you can see of an object in 'reality' and how it is represented in an image. While it can be assumed that the choice of drawings instead of photographs was at least in part motivated by economic reasons, other considerations may have been important. Hand-drawn maps are likely to appeal to the tourists who *Anmire* tries to address. In this particular case, it may be more appropriate to think about the viewer's assessment of the image in terms of a sensory modality (Jewitt & Oyama, 2001), associating hand-drawn maps with greater authenticity. The map of the village that almost looks as if one of the guides from the village had sketched it, suggests to the reader closeness with the producers of the leaflet, the people from *Anmire*. Hand-drawn images such as those used on the leaflet may even have the effect on the viewer to be associated with 'primitive' forms of art. In this way, by choosing hand-drawn maps, the leaflet aims to appeal to the romantic views of many Western tourists who come to Namibia in search of the 'primitive' but 'happy' life of the 'noble savage'.

The textbox on the inside of the brochure, containing some Nama/ Damara phrases and a short guide to the clicks, is an instance of commodification of a local language in the service of tourism. The box invites the tourists to a playful use of the language in what could be an attempt by a tourist to act like a local person. This offers the possibility of a symbolic suspension of the tourist identity and a momentary linguistic crossing to the host population (cf. Rampton, 1998; Jaworski *et al.*, 2003). This offer is again restated for visitors as they are invited to learn a few Damara words and phrases during their visit to the village.

Conclusion: Local and Global Discourses in Tourism – What is the Role of Local People in the New Ethno- and Eco-tourism Discourses?

Despite ethno- and eco-tourism, exemplified by *Face-to-Face Tours* and *Anmire*, having recently become quite visible in Namibia, the country's CBTEs' initiatives and workers occupy a marginal position. Inevitably, their future prospects depend on their ability to compete with the private sector in Namibia and on other forces in global tourism industry.

Tourism illustrates well the increasing globalisation of the world's economy, its high level of international connections and the presence of multinational tour operators that have the power to impose the same uniform standards wherever they work (Burns, 1999). Most travellers who come to Namibia are likely to have booked a pre-arranged trip through a travel agency in their home country. These agencies, many of which are part of multinational tourism companies, have links with tour operators in Windhoek who, in turn, work with a set number of lodges, hotels and campsites, thereby making it very difficult for other local companies to attract tourists to their own services.

In this context, CBTEs like *Face-to-Face Tours* and *Anmire* often do not have a role to play in the production of tourism discourses, much of which takes place in the home countries of the tourists and in the marketing centres of the global tourism industry. Because international tour operators and their local counterparts distribute their own promotional materials to their customers, prior and during their journey, they have considerable leeway in channelling the tourist gaze towards the destinations and services that are part of their intended itinerary. Brochures, travel guides and websites available to tourists shape their expectations long before they arrive at their destination. Thus, the representations of local life presented in those texts become the codified and authorised versions of local culture and history. In this structural context, CBTEs occupy the least powerful position, as they are compelled to take up and replicate the dominant tourism discourses created by Namibia's tourism industry and its international partners.

Given the hierarchical structures of tourism, an important question to ask is whether local tourism workers such as those involved in Namibian CBTEs have the power to influence and change tourism discourses. The examples I have presented in this chapter demonstrate that although CBTEs create their own brochures and leaflets to attract tourists to their businesses, the content of their PR material is largely defined by the dominant discourses of mainstream tourism. Although emphasising difference, e.g. eco- rather than safari-tourism, and 'black' Namibia rather than 'white' colonial history, they still remain within the boundaries set by the main discourse configurations that dominate global tourism.

CBTEs often have little choice but to accept and to adapt to the identities and cultural views that are created for them by the tourism industry. There is a significant difference between the skills to reproduce dominant tourism discourses, which many CBTEs and local tourism workers acquire, and the ability to define what forms local tourism in Namibia will take, for example by deciding how local people and local history are to be presented in a tourism brochure.

A further difficulty for local groups like *Face-to-Face Tours* and *Anmire* is that in order to influence tourism discourses, they need to understand the currency of specific tourism products in a market that is highly unstable and influenced by continuous changes in the consumer culture of Western tourists (Lash & Urry, 1994; Urry, 1995). Tourism – like any other service industry – requires its employees to 'continuously invent and market' their services as well as to 'vary' and 'customise' them (Gee *et al.*, 1996: 5). But with the limited capital, infrastructure and experience available, most CBTEs are not necessarily in a position to successfully explore the semiotic resources of their destinations and to continuously monitor their position within the discursive order of global tourism.

At present, *Anmire*'s leaflet skilfully addresses the growing eco- and ethno-tourism market. It's the selective picture of the past, framed in the discourses of folklore and nostalgia, which show striking similarities with the 'heritage' discourse of English tourism (Urry, 2002 [1990]), which appeals to tourists. Whether eco- and ethno-tourism catches on, however, depends on what is happening in the marketing centres of the global tourism industry where new tourism products are continuously being invented and discovered.

Yet, despite their fragile position, local tourism workers and community-based tourism groups are not totally without a stake in the creation and promotion of fashionable tourism discourses. In their attempts to secure for themselves a niche in Namibia's competitive tourism market, local tourism enterprises like *Face-to-Face Tours* and *Anmire* capitalise on the fashionable idea of 'community' development and the government's eagerness to promote black empowerment. The community label, much promoted by governments and NGOs alike, is a good example of how local groups effectively subvert some of the dominant tourism discourses. The ideology of community-based tourism resonates well with many Westerners' idea of the 'African' community as a group of people who share the benefits of their work.

Acknowledgements

This research was supported by a King's College London Association (KCLA) research studentship and by the University of London's Central Research Fund. I thank both institutions for their support. I would also like to thank Adam Jaworski and Annette Pritchard for their editorial comments and support.

References

Ashley, C. (1995) *Tourism, Communities and the Potential Impacts on Local Incomes and Conservation*. Research discussion paper No. 10, Windhoek: Ministry of Environment and Tourism.

Brits, A.M. and Wiig, A. (1998) Regional integration in Southern Africa: the tourism sector. In The Namibian Economic Policy Research Unit (NEPRU) *In Search of Research. Approaches to Socio-Economic Issues in Contemporary Namibia* (pp. 141–71). Windhoek: NEPRU Publications No. 6.

Burns, P. (1999) *Anthropology and Tourism*. London: Routledge.

Cohen, E. and Cooper, R.L. (1986) Language and tourism. *Annals of Tourism Research* 12, 5–29.

Chambers, E. (2000) *Native Tours. The Anthropology of Travel and Tourism*. Waveland Press: Prospect Heights, IL.

Dann, G. (1996a) *The Language of Tourism. A Sociolinguistic Perspective*. Oxford: CAB International.

Dann, G. (1996b) The people of tourist brochures. In T. Selwyn (ed.) *The Tourist Image* (pp. 61–83). Chichester: John Wiley and Sons.

Dann, G. (2000) Differentiating destinations in the language of tourism: Harmless hype or promotional irresponsibility? *Tourism Recreation Research* 25, 63–75.

Dann, G. (2001) The self-admitted use of cliché in the language of tourism. *Tourism, Culture and Communication* 3, 1–14.

Gee, J.P., Hull, G. and Lanksheer, C. (1996) *The New Work Order*. St. Leonards: Allen & Unwin.

Jaworski, A., Thurlow, C., Lawson, S. and Ylanne-McEwan, V. (2003) The uses and representations of local languages in tourism destinations: A view from British television holiday programmes. *Language Awareness* 12, 5–29.

Jewitt, C. and Oyama, R. (2001) Visual meaning: A social semiotic approach. In T. van Leeuwen and C. Jewitt (eds) *Handbook of Visual Analysis* (pp. 134–57). London: Sage.

Kress, G. and van Leeuwen, T. (1996) *Reading Images. The Grammar of Visual Design*. London: Routledge.

Lash, S. and Urry, J. (1994) *Economies of Signs and Space*. Sage: London.

Lee, D. (1992) *Competing Discourses*. London: Longman.

Lindknud, C. (1998) When opposite worldviews attract: A case of tourism and local development in Southern France. In S. Abram and J.Waldren (eds) *Anthropological Perspectives on Local Development Knowledge and Sentiments in Conflict* (pp. 141–60). London: Routledge.

Maho, J.F. (1998) *Few People, Many Tongues. The Languages of Namibia*. Windhoek: Gamsberg Macmillan.

Ministry of Environment and Tourism (1994) *White Paper on Tourism*. Windhoek: Ministry of Environment and Tourism.

Ministry of Environment and Tourism (1995) Promotion of Community-Based Tourism. *Policy Document*. Windhoek: Ministry of Environment and Tourism.

Ministry of Environment and Tourism (1996) Nature Conservation Amendment Act. Windhoek: Ministry of Environment and Tourism, Government Gazette (June).

Omoniyi, T. (1998) The discourse of tourism advertisements: Packaging nation and ideology in Singapore. *Working Papers in Applied Linguistics (4)*. London: Thames Valley University.

Pendleton, W.C. (1996) *Katutura: A Place Where We Stay*. Athens, Ohio: Ohio University Centre for International Studies.

Puetz, M. (1995) Official monolingualism in Africa: A sociolinguistic assessment of linguistic and cultural pluralism in Namibia. In his (ed.) *Discrimination through Language in Africa? Perspectives on the Namibian Experience* (pp. 156–73). Berlin: Mouton de Gruyter.

Rampton, B. (1998) Language crossing and the redefinition of reality. In P. Auer (ed.) *Codeswitching in Conversation* (pp. 290–317). London: Routledge.

Rojek, C. (1997) Indexing, dragging and the social construction of tourist sights. In C. Rojek and J. Urry (eds) *Touring Cultures* (pp. 52–75). London: Routledge.

Rothfuss, E. (2000) Ethnic tourism in Kaoko: Expectations, frustrations and trends in post-colonial business. In G. Miescher and D. Henrichsen (eds) *New Notes on Kaoko* (pp. 133–59). Basel: Basler Afrika Bibliographien.

Schade, K. (2000) Poverty. In H. Melber (ed.) *Namibia: A Decade of Independence: 1999–2003*. 1990-2000 (pp. 111–25). Windhoek: NEPRU (The Namibian Economic Policy Research Unit).

Selwyn, T. (1996) Peter Pan in South-East Asia: Views from the brochures. In M. Hitchcock, V.T. King and M.J.G. Parnwell (eds) *Tourism in South-East Asia* (pp.117–137). London: Routledge.

Smith, V.L. (1996) 'Indigenous tourism: The four Hs'. In R. Butler and T. Hinch (eds) *Tourism and Indigenous Peoples* (pp. 283–308). London: International Thompson Business Press.

Thurot, J.M. and Thurot, G. (1983) The ideology of class and tourism: Facing the discourses of advertising. *Annals of Tourism Research* 10, 173–89.

Urry, J. (1995) *Consuming Places*. London: Routledge.

Urry, J. (2002) *The Tourist Gaze* (2nd edn). London: Sage. [First published in 1990.]

Vorlauefer, K. (1996) Tourismus in Entwicklungslaendern. Darmstadt: Wissenschaftliche Buchgesellschaft.

Wai-Teng Leong, L. (1997) Commodifiying ethnicity: State and ethnic tourism in Singapore. In M. Picard and R.E. Wood (eds) *Tourism, Ethnicity and the State in Asian and Pacific Societies* (pp. 71–79). Honolulu: University of Hawai'i Press.

Chapter 5

Venice Observed: The Traveller, The Tourist, The Post-Tourist and British Television

DAVID DUNN

> *Ay, because the sea's the street there; and 'tis arched by ... what you call*
> *... Shylock's bridge with houses on it, where they kept the carnival;*
> *I was never out of England – it's as if I saw it all.*
> Robert Browning, *A Toccata of Galuppi's*

Introduction

This chapter offers a snapshot of what three television features about one destination reveal about the conventions of British television holiday programmes. The destination is Venice, a 'typical' television destination in terms of its recognisable images and familiar sights, but one with a uniqueness of setting which increases its potential to offer the camera a variety of meanings. The first is a 'conventional' documentary, *Venice: the Vanishing Lady*, made by the journalist James Cameron, and originally shown in 1969 on BBC2 with a subsequent repeat in 1993; the remaining two were shown in 1993 and 1996 respectively as reports on BBC2's *The Travel Show* and C4's *Travelog*. In each of the three films the convergence between touristic practice and the camera's gaze is evidenced by the different discursive roles, traveller, tourist, post-tourist, constructed for the presenters and their cameras as they encounter and mediate a foreign place. Although Cameron's documentary predates most holiday programmes, it represents a type of documentary film making which subsequently informed the genre. In his patriarchal way he acts as a traveller, observing and categorising from a distance, concerning himself with Venice's struggle with the elements, filming in a sunless and almost monochromatic winter. By contrast, Carole Smillie's report for *The Travel Show* is an account of sightseeing, shopping and a cruise in a gondola. Its tourist discourse makes no attempt at any empathic involvement with Venice or with its people, her hosts. Post-tourism underpins Pete McCarthy's account of Carnival in Venice for *Travelog* which uses irony and performance to foreground the illusory nature of the city while at the same time subverting the conventions of holiday programmes.

In each of these reports, the role of the presenter as mediator of a touristic experience is paramount, but the destination and the presenter share, as it were, an equal, if occasionally uneasy, billing. Since these reports were transmitted, the genre has continued to evolve, showing increasingly less concern for place, and foregrounding in its stead consumption and celebrity in more or less equal measure. So the snapshot which this chapter offers is a snapshot in time, a signifier of how holiday programmes, influenced in part by those traditions of documentary on which Cameron draws, represented the tourist destination in the last years of the 20th century. Given the importance to tourism studies of the scopic it is not inappropriate to use the image of the snapshot. Yet the camera's gaze involves not only reproduction but is also discursive, informed by the touristic ideologies and discourses of the time, the saying and doing of tourism and tourists, and informed too by the institutional practices of programme makers and their engagement with specifically British principles of public service broadcasting. The democratisation of tourism has created its own divisions and tensions between popular tourist practice and a mythical ideal of travel, between the pursuit of pleasure and the moral purpose of travail. That tension has been reflected in the editorial and signifying practices of television programmes, resulting in the creation of ambivalent responses to the purposes, pleasurable or improving, to which the tourist destination is put.

Television and Tourism

Crawshaw and Urry (1997) draw attention to the collusion between tourists and photographers in the construction and reinforcement of place as touristic resource, while Osborne (2000: 79) suggests a direct relationship between a resort's photogenic qualities and its attractiveness. Television's visual language is derived in part from still photography, and there are consequent parallels between the gaze of the television camera and the gaze of the tourist, not least in their reliance on and recycling of familiar images. Boorstin's (1961) patrician lament for the demise of the traveller may have over-exercised a generation of critics, but his accompanying identification of the increasing importance of the image and of its voracious consumption in contemporary culture remains relevant. Critical both of the rise of popular tourism and of the growth of influence of media industries, he argued that a world constructed increasingly of familiar images could mean only superficiality of response.

People go to see what they already know is there. The only thing to record, the only possible source of surprise, is their own reaction ... [W]e look into a mirror instead of out a window, and we see only ourselves. (Boorstin, 1961: 116–17)

MacCannell (1976: 111) countered this, claiming that tourists were active constructors of meaning, seeing not a city but a succession of sights each of which was a symbolic marker of that city and which contributed to a cumulative narrative. Yet both he and Urry (2002 [1990]) recognised that graphic and electronic revolutions in the field of communications have meant that such sights have become increasingly familiar, not least through their reproduction and recirculation in photograph albums or on television. Crang (1999: 252), reflecting the performative nature of leisure activities (see also, amongst others, Goffman, 1959; Rojek, 2000), writes of such tourist photography as 'the capitalising of experience', adding that constructing pictorial narratives 'is a form of self-creation that is based around a fractured and presentational existence'. In a world in which television programmes offer viewers surrogate sightseeing, however, that self-creation is increasingly undertaken by television presenters. They assume touristic roles which inform their, and their camera's, narratives and their performance, while their celebrity and consequent, if solipsistic, televisual authority have power over their viewers. As Rojek suggests, '[t]he domestication of the medium meant that messages from television had equivalent power to the messages from parental authority figures in the socialisation of children' (Rojek, 2000: 137). In this context Marshall's (1997: 121) identification of 'the close affinity of the celebrity with the organisation and perpetuation of consumer capitalism' has its own resonance.

MacCannell (2001: 26) suggests that Urry's (2002 [1990]) tourist gaze, in which the extraordinary gazed upon should not be too extraordinary, is a gaze which 'makes sightseeing closer than it need be to television'. MacCannell's claim that tourists reject the institutionalised gaze for some-thing less visible and more empathic might owe as much to tourist *angst* as to empiricism, but Urry's (2002) own revision of *The Tourist Gaze* recog-nises the variety of other senses involved in contemporary tourism, and in addition suggests that television travel programmes play their part in the discursive construction of the gaze between *gazer* and *gazee* (p. 145), and in the consumption of place. Tourism is not just about visual con-sumption, and in the critical debate about the primacy of the scopic (see, amongst others, Franklin & Crang, 2001), Cronin (2000) has suggested that most tourists gaze because they do not understand the language of the object of their gaze, adding that in any process of translation there remains an imbalance between the tourist and the toured since 'speakers of major languages are more likely to expect others to speak their lan-guage … In other words, for powerful languages, the Other is always already translated' (Cronin, 2000: 95).

Television holiday programmes reflect the difficulty of, and the imbal-ance implicit in, such translations. Jaworski *et al.*'s (2003b) sociolinguistic analysis of the very limited interactions between presenters and local people, conventionally 'cast' in the brief supporting roles of guides, helpers or servants, emphasises the problematic relationship between tourist and toured, not least when local language and culture have to be made meaningful by the presenter *in situ* for camera and viewer. The genre is more at ease with visual consumption of place and its facilities, and the evidence of its conventions (Dunn, 1998) suggests that television's signifying processes continue to rely heavily on the scopic at the expense of the empathic, and that the role of its presenters in effecting and projecting their own discursive translations is paramount. That scopic discourse is, of course, verbal as well as visual, television remaining highly reliant, as Ellis (1992) argues, on the words of the mediating 'talking head' to attract the attention of the domestic viewer.

Broadcasting institutions and their ideology, their practitioners, and their audiences have had an occasionally uneasy relationship. The broadcasting chain which begins with the institutions and ends with the viewers reflects wider hegemonic struggles, and, as Corner (1999: 19–20) suggests, television is both a political and a cultural agency, and is thus subject to controls. Hall (1981), writing before the deregulation of British broadcasting, argued that broadcasting institutions set the agenda for their audience, and were reactive to establishments rather than proactive (see also Fiske, 1987, 1992; Corner, 1995, 1996). He further claimed that in the communication of events there was an inequality in a relationship where broadcasters 'not only manage and monopolise the *means* (technical, social, financial) for finding out *and* for transmitting information. They must also constantly *select*' (Hall, 1981: 274 [emphasis in the original]).

Hall was writing here in the context of news, but his argument reflects the realities of the wider structure of broadcasting. Elsewhere (Hall, 1986), he suggested that popular media may have reflected popular culture but that as part of the establishment they made no commitment to it. Less than a decade on, however, Tunstall (1993) identified marginal differences between ITV and BBC1; the former more concerned with a populism which would be reflected in enhanced viewing figures, the latter with public service. Of holiday programmes he wrote that:

> ITV's leading travel/holiday programme, *Wish You Were Here?*, adopted a popular mix of useful holiday advice for people on average incomes, plus an element of glossy fantasy (sunny beach holidays) during the January and February evenings. The BBC's *Holiday* programme had similar popular/fantasy ingredients, but covered also more expensive and ambitious holidays and did more documentary-style film reports. (Tunstall, 1993: 83)

These are subtle distinctions perhaps, distinctions of aspirational consumption rather than of moral purpose, and they are being eroded as the BBC makes itself more commercial in order to justify its continuing funding by licence fee. Holiday programmes, however, have tended in their 'glossy fantasies' to remain detached from outright celebration of popular culture, preferring to reflect the ideological discourse identified by many as anti-tourism (see, amongst others, Boorstin, 1961; Fussell, 1980; Brendon, 1991; Buzard, 1993). Buzard (1993) argues from history that anti-tourism has allowed individuals to parade their superiority by travelling 'off the beaten track' of the tourist, while Munt's (1994) study of contemporary postmodern tourism follows the same path, suggesting that contemporary tourists seek 'alternative' destinations not for their perceived intrinsic value but as a way of self-projection. The tourist destination on television has thus been a potential site of conflict in which the 'improving' model of a combination of information, education and entertainment enshrined in the BBC's Charter, and historically also informing commercial broadcasters, has often privileged the ideology of anti-tourism over the celebration of popular tourist activity. The 'improving' myth of the traveller has existed in tension with the myth of the tourist destination as a place for excess, and the 'pleasurable instruction' of the Grand Tour (Batten, 1978) has been, however dimly, reflected well into the 1990s in television's holiday reports. Fulfilling high cultural obligations with the breviary of the guidebook, it was implied, was the penance to be paid for less cerebral pleasures enjoyed beside the pool or on the beach.

Before considering the specific film reports about Venice a brief summary of the genre is appropriate. Television holiday programmes are those like BBC1's *Holiday* and ITV1's *Wish You Were Here?* which offer reports and information about the tourist product and the tourist destination. Historically they have reflected the similarities between the scopic practices of the television camera and those of the tourist in their construction of narratives of place. They use power/knowledge strategies to their own discursive advantage but often, through linguistic or other inadequacy, fail to effect an adequate translation of cultures beyond a gazing upon and recycling of familiar images. They are informed by discourses of consumption and of cultural capital, belonging to the category known as 'lifestyle' and reflecting the link between consumerism and tourism. They are presenter led, and reflect in their reports not only the generality of celebrity culture foregrounded over place but also the specific ideologies of broadcasters as embodied in the touristic persona adopted by the presenter.

Venice: The Vanishing Lady

The first of the three film reports, *Venice: The Vanishing Lady* (1967 [1993]), is a 'conventional' documentary which was made by the journalist James Cameron and was originally shown in 1967 on BBC2 but subsequently repeated in 1993. If, as Morgan and Pritchard (1998) suggest, holiday programmes owe something to the promotional, they draw too on television's traditions of documentary making. This film was, therefore, selected as representing that tradition. It is concerned with the fragility of a city under the onslaught of natural forces. Given its choice of subject matter, and the image which Cameron presents of himself as the solitary traveller, this film engages implicitly with the tourist/traveller debate. It also raises issues of the balance between the scopic and the empathic. Limitations of space allow discussion here only of two key sequences.

The film starts not with familiar tourist sights but with images of Venice under flood.

Extract 1. *Venice: The Vanishing Lady*[1]

Cameron V/O

Colonnades under water	At high water the wintry Venetians must
Child taken by hand by	trudge and trip their way to work across
woman	their little catwalks above the flood.
Procession on boardwalk,	They've long since got used to this.
umbrellas up, *San Marco* **b/g**	They're vaguely aware that the old
Similar, *San Giorgio* **b/g**	wooden foundations beneath their feet
	are rotting and subsiding …
	[...]
Young boy picked up and	It looks amusing enough but what a bore
carried on shoulder by	it must be, year after year this tedious
woman	splashing about, worse every winter.
	How demoralising ...
Pan off roof statues to	Venice could compromise with the
facades of *Riva degli*	twentieth century, pave the canals,
Schiavoni, water lapping	admit the cars, accept new values.
Gondolas moored, strongly	Or will she shamble away as a tourist
backlit	sanctuary, splendid, serene, and
	stagnant?

In his encounter with 'the wintry Venetians' Cameron is an invisible observer, describing them as a quasi-amphibious race who 'trudge and trip their way' in a state of semi-awareness of the rotting nature of their city. Coping with the water is a 'bore'. The discourse, at once observational and patronising, with its dismissive reference to 'little catwalks' and to 'splashing about' is one which Victorian explorers might have used when encountering an interesting new tribe of child-like sensibilities and behaviour.[2] It is not the self-referential discourse of democratised tourism. Cameron's film was made before *Death in Venice* (1971) or *Don't Look Now* (1973) made representations of a city where crumbling facades hid much that was sinister and malign familiar to many. For Cameron's original audience, at least, such representations would have been less familiar. The historical connection which Buzard (1993) makes between anti-tourism and the need to avoid 'the beaten track' is underpinned by the way in which Cameron chooses to portray Venice. These are scenes that are off the beaten track both geographically and seasonally. It is left to the viewer to identify them, or not. The aspirational traveller might, the ludic tourist might not.

The image of Venice as an old woman[3] shambling off, fit only to provide sterile comfort for a breed of tourists who, by definition, must be almost as feeble as their sought-after protectress is not one of elegance, nor one which magnifies tourists and their works. Cameron, or his director, chooses to illustrate this metaphor with what is the most conventional and recognisable image of Venice, but in this case the gondolas which are seen bobbing are empty of tourists and are moored on a wintry Grand Canal where there is no sun to take the chill off waters better known as a site of summer pleasures. This deviation from the normal is significant and allows for some complex underpinning of meaning. The words denote an image of impotent old age and faded gentility while the pictures denote a familiar tourist sight in an unfamiliar light. The gondola is a metonym for the city, a city which is set here in the winter of its days. So, in a televisually sophisticated text, there is metaphor as well as metonym in these pictures. The connotations of the coldness and emptiness of death are implicit for those who choose to read them. Most importantly the rich counterpoint of word and picture, metaphor in the one, metaphor and metonym in the other, makes even stronger the prevailing mood. In this discourse of decay the implication is that to become a tourist site is a fate at least as bad as death. Cameron is arguing from a high cultural standpoint, but his words parallel the theory of the lifecycle of the tourist destination (see Butler, 1980; Ryan, 1991) from exploration to decline or rejuvenation.

The shot cuts to an interior, as Cameron, until this point a disembodied voice, is seen at a café table.

Extract 2. *Venice: The Vanishing Lady*
CU Cameron, only one side   **Music**: *Adagio: Albinoni*, 0.30"
of his face lit, background
unlit; **widen** as he lifts
spoon from saucer, puts
sugar lump into it and dips
it into coffee in cup; it soaks
up the coffee

Superimpose lapping water Cameron stirs the crumbling sugar in, looks pensive, lifts spoon out and watches the drips, continuing to look pensive

Cameron V/O
When Napoleon at last handed Venice over to the Austrians like a gratuity he said, 'Dust and ashes, dead and done for, Venice spent what Venice earned.'

High shot of water; prow of funeral gondola comes up from bottom of frame and reveals coffin draped in black with gold cross, and crew of four in black with black *birette*. Gondola is poled past pile in Lagoon towards *San Michele*, cemetery island

Music: *Adagio: Albinoni*, 0.30"

Cameron's appearance marks a contrast to what precedes it. Unlike his wintry Venetians he is foregrounded in close up. The café is associated with people watching, but the people whom Cameron is watching, recording, are elsewhere. For 30 seconds he gazes past the camera, presented as a traveller, an observer, and the audience is held by this pause, encouraged to read in his face the sensibilities of his solitary gaze. The technique is borrowed from drama, and blurs the distinction between Cameron as documentarist and Cameron as performer. He begins with a visual metaphor, encouraging the viewer by the absence of commentary to make the connection between the business of the crumbling, dissolving sugar lump in his coffee and the crumbling of those sodden and rotting piles on which the city is founded. He extends the image with a sequence of shots of a funeral gondola, its cargo of ceremony, a metaphor of the impending death of the city, as it heads out towards the cemetery island of *San Michele*. Although shot on colour film, there is virtually no colour in these images where sky and sea meet in a dull blur, save for the rich gold set against the black of the funerary trappings. The light is the monochrome grey of winter, the faces of the gondoliers, shown in profile, are timeless, the formality of their framing on screen reflecting an aspirational centuries old painterly tradition.

When Beloff (1985: 92–3) argued that serious photographers often chose the light and dark of monochrome to underpin the seriousness of their intention, that their aim was to strip off the surface gloss and to go beyond mere description to show the underlying essence, she was, perhaps, reflecting an older high cultural discourse, one in which she saw no need to offer a definition of 'serious'. Yet colour television was still a comparative novelty when this film was first transmitted in 1969, and in such a context her belief that colour photography, by virtue of its 'realism', richness and opulence, was best suited to being deployed in the popular of advertising, in the portrayal of the upbeat, of the successful, of commodity is one which may also have informed Cameron's camera and his original viewers. For more recent viewers there may, perhaps, be issues of perceived credibility in an image so desaturated of colour (see Kress & van Leeuwen, 1996: 163ff.), yet in a recent study of the motifs of literary representations of Venice, Dann (2002: 268) has identified in most references to death and decay a verbal imagery that is monochrome. Such imagery, he contends, maintains a counterpart in tourist photography, while Boddy (1999: 237) has argued that tourists no longer seek verisimilitude in their photographs but, in a world where everything has been explored and recorded, aspire to take shots which resonate with existing images. And Osborne (2000) suggests, on the evidence of promotional images of Papua New Guinea, that while the connotations of colour photography articulate with the mainstream tourist the use of 'ethno-doc-monochrome' is intended to attract the independent traveller or 'culture tourist clutching, one supposes, if not a Leica then at least a serious Nikon' (Osborne, 2000: 86).

Filming in the monochromatic winter light of the Venetian lagoon thus allows Cameron to assume a similar seriousness of high cultural intention, and his images, resonant with a painterly familiarity for at least some viewers, are counterpoint to a musing commentary which manages both another metaphor and another metonym, for this is the televisual equivalent of a writerly text (Barthes, 1975b), one which requires the viewer to provide meanings and make connections. He likens the city to a gratuity, handed over by Napoleon as a spoil of war, and that image is counterpointed by the visual action of the consumption of coffee, itself worthy of a gratuity to the person who served it. In Napoleon's valediction, 'Dust and ashes, dead and done for, Venice spent what Venice earned',[4] there is no reference to the people who live in Venice. Instead the name of the city stands metonymically for her inhabitants.

As elsewhere in this film so here, the Venetians are given no voice, and as the object of Cameron's gaze they are reduced metaphorically to the occupants of a funerary gondola and its defunct contents. If travel films' representations of locals conventionally offer glimpses of waiters and service providers other than undertakers, here even the café where Cameron sits musing is an abstract moodily lit *locus* devoid of waiters or commercial exchange. If his Venetian hosts are consumed in a touristic sense (Urry, 1995) it is not material consumption. They and their city are there to offer Cameron the traveller/presenter a little world weary *schadenfreude*. For in his traveller's baggage, along with the instruments of observation and recording, he carries that great prophylactic, the sum of his cultural experience, which protects him from foreign parts.

The Travel Show

The Travel Show was BBC2's prime time holiday programme until it ceased transmission in 1999. In Carol Smillie's 1993 report (*The Travel Show*, 1993) she too is foregrounded over place, but unlike Cameron she is represented as a tourist who makes excursions to Venice from the neighbouring Lido di Jesolo. In this the developing genre reflects a new democratisation of holidaymaking. Reports for holiday programmes are not personal essays but are made to a lifestyle-oriented format, presented by a variety of members of a team who, according to their availability, are allocated destinations. Reports, usually three per half hour programme, are self-contained and offer their own closure, but the series format is open-ended, encouraging viewers to watch the following week. To that extent the sum of each programme's parts may be less than the whole. The uniqueness or otherwise of a destination is only one element in a viewing experience which combines tourist activity with escapism, surrogate sightseeing and the intertextuality of their show business *personae* which many presenters, amongst them Smillie, bring to their reports.

Despite the foregrounding of popular tourist activity in this feature, there is an implicit narrative tension between the limited opportunities for licence and the carnivalesque (Thompson, 1983; Stallybrass & White, 1986) and the obligations to high culture. This, although scarcely made explicit, forms the main thrust of Smillie's piece, and gives it its underpinning of anti-tourism. Again space precludes consideration of every sequence. It begins in the familiar of the touristic.

Extract 3: *The Travel Show*

	Smillie V/O
GVs of *Piazetta* and Doge's Palace; *San Giorgio* and its Island; Canal	In Venice nothing will strike you as mundane. There are very few great cities in the world which are so free of modern buildings, and none where there are no cars in the streets.
Bell Tower with figures striking bell	
Tilt down off *Campanile* to WS *Piazza San Marco* full of (?) tourists; facade of Basilica	However every tourist comes to St Mark's Square, so it does get incredibly crowded.
GVs Basilica; *San Giorgio*; City and Lagoon behind Basilica'sDomes	Geographically, Venice is unique: built on more than 100 islands and linked by 400 bridges the buildings are supported by billions of stakes driven into the mud.

WS Causeway	On the north side of the island is the only bridge to mainland Italy.
WS looking down on *Piazza* Pan pigeons through tourists' feet	The *Piazza San Marco* is the focus of Venetian life.
Café orchestra; waiter foreground, tourist crosses	**Music**: *Café Orchestra*
WS Smillie in midi-length orange dress open to thigh, walking through *Piazza*	**Smillie to Cam** (**Music** continues under ...) A lot of the bars and cafés around here provide live entertainment, so if you do have time to sit down for a coffee don't be surprised if that's included in your bill. Having said that, it is a small price to pay for such a magnificent setting.
WS to *San Giorgio* from *Piazzetta* Figures on Column and Rooftop Mosaics on **CU**s Sculpture **WS** Doge's Palace	**Smillie V/O** Surrounding the *Piazza* are some of the greatest buildings of Europe including the Gothic style *Palazzo Ducale*, or Doge's Palace, the seat of Venetian power for 800 years ...

As with Cameron, Smillie is foregrounded, and is not seen interacting with (fellow) tourists. She is a part of the tourist scene but she is apart from it. By addressing the camera she becomes an intermediary. That the report begins in a style which the audience might associate with the words of a guide book before shifting focus away from sightseeing to consumer advice and back again it underpins the narrative and discursive tensions between the obligations of sightseeing and the less cerebral pleasures of holidaymaking. Despite the anti-tourism implicit in the former, the shots of sights to be seen are firmly on 'the beaten track', illustrative after the fashion of postcards or the already familiar. The commentary refers to an extraordinary place devoid of the 'mundane', emphasising its antiquity and the absence of modernity, and offering a series of statistics. Since Smillie's script is filled with the mundane it can, however, scarcely be said to rise to the challenge of describing a city supposedly devoid of the same. Barthes' (1972 [1957]) deconstruction of the myth of the *Blue Guide* suggests that such a museum guidebook approach was already inappropriate by the 1950s for contemporary travellers encountering people and landscapes, but in this report due regard continues to be paid to the past and to information which validates and marks the site in question. In the reduction of Venice to a place comprising a particular number of islands linked by a greater number of bridges and supported by an even greater number of stakes there may be a geophysical truth, but, as Barthes suggests, a consequence of the discourse of the guidebook is that 'the human life of a country disappears to the exclusive benefit of its monuments' (Barthes, 1972: 75).

To redress the balance would require a less overtly mediated production technique, and the overheard dialogue of passing Venetians would need to be made meaningful to an Anglophone audience as might the cultural references. The *communitas* of others implies the exclusion, or at least the liminality, of the onlooker (Turner, 1974; Nash, 1996), especially when those others are foreign. The scopic of the holiday programme and the holidaymaker alike is performed at the expense of the empathic. This is perhaps why, for the tourist in search of place, such importance is given to sights and markers, each of which, *pace* MacCannell (1976), is perceived to contribute to an imagined or constructed whole. It can, of course, never *fully* be understood or *totally* constructed, since new signs will constantly present themselves. One result is that many visitors to Venice, including television presenters and their cameras, who would not in the normal run look at buildings and sculpture, possessing neither the eye nor the interest of the art historian, are required to look at such artefacts rather than attempting to make contact with local people. For that reason alone it is unsurprising that Smillie's script should, in a dutiful but somehow halfhearted way which makes few demands on an audience echo the phrases of *The Blue Guide* rather than transgress, as did generations of travel writers (Porter, 1991) with the foreign body.

The relationship between tourist and toured is often referred to as one of 'guests and hosts'. In this sequence, however, Smillie's hosts are reduced to one waiter whose role is to signify the high cost of the Venetian tourist infrastructure. Such service providers are described by Smith (1978: 4) as 'marginal men' (*sic*) whose function suggests a more complex interaction than the binary opposition of hosts and guests; and Edensor's (2001) subsequent use of the metaphor of performance to describe the role of cultural go-betweens further tests what is, perhaps, an over simplistic model. In a television report, of course, the presenter is already the key performer within a *tourist* space which leaves little *screen* space for the performance of others, hosts or intermediaries, save in supporting roles. The waiter does not appear in shot with Smillie. In the sequence which follows, however, presenter and intermediary, in this case an unnamed gondolier, are involved together, albeit without any acknowledged interaction on her part, in a performance both for the camera and for other tourists.

Extract 4: *The Travel Show*

	Smillie V/O
'Lovers' sitting on wall	To see Venice at its most serene take a trip in the most famous boat of all.

| Gondolas moored, *San Giorgio* in background | **Music**: *Violin Concerto, Vivaldi*, 0.20" |

Gondolas moored, *San Giorgio* in background
Shot from water of *Palazzo*
Gondolas pass
CU Sign *Fondamenta S Caterina*
Rialto Bridge
Shots from water of Canals and oncoming Gondolas

| **2S** Smillie and Gondolier sailing down Grand Canal | **Smillie to Cam** Venice is a very well preserved masterpiece. The best way I can think of to describe it would be like eating a whole box of your favourite chocolates and then still wanting more. |

Words give way to a mix of music and pictures, cerebral *plaisir* gives way to physical *jouissance* (Barthes, 1975a). Unlike Cameron's funeral gondola sequence where the combination of heavy-laden music and the black-clad appearance of the gondoliers laid emphasis on the signified metaphor, here there is no meaning except for pleasure in the signifiers themselves, in the shape of the gondolas, in the water, in a half-seen street sign, in buildings glimpsed from the water, and perhaps greatest pleasure of all, of being translated from the pavements of the cultural to the gentle shallows of the natural. Ironically, Smillie is not only drawn by the spectacle of others being propelled down a canal by a gondolier, a standard tourist icon, she also becomes the spectacle itself, observed in turn by other tourists and continuing a self-fulfilling cycle of signifying tourist practices. This vindicates MacCannell's (1992: 241ff.) argument that the icon subordinates both those who appear to create it and those who view it. Just as Cameron performed for the camera so Smillie performs both for the camera and for the tourists.

Like the sightseeing which precedes it, however, it is a surrogate experience for viewers, conveyed by a medium which cannot touch all of their senses, and supported not by the song of the gondolier but by the safe and predictable sound of Vivaldi whose gentle chords offer little that is subversive but much that is aspirational. Nor does the screen time allowed to this sequence of 20 seconds in a piece lasting around eight minutes over-privilege physical pleasure. Even the sensual reference to chocolates may be a little disingenuous. Truman Capote (*Observer*, 1961: 25) is quoted as saying, 'Venice is like eating an entire box of chocolate liqueurs in one go.' In this controlled and weakly articulated moment of *jouissance* the implicit anti-touristic ideology of the film is that the all too brief climax of a Venetian gondola cruise is heightened by the lengthy foreplay of dutifully appreciative sightseeing.

Travelog

C4's series *Travelog* offered the televisual equivalent of the travel essay and aimed to provide imaginative and often quirky or subversive responses to place. It did not feature holiday products *per se* or use cost free 'facility trips', and that, given increasing budgetary constraints, may have brought about its demise in 1997.[5] Pete McCarthy's 1996 film (*Travelog*, 1996), engages with the irony of the post-tourist, representing Venice as a place of shifting and fragmented illusions, a setting for the playing of parts, where the costumed and masked players of Carnival are often glimpsed through a CCTV monitor or a distorting mirror. It begins in the West Midlands, establishing Venice as the Birmingham of the south, but one endowed with fewer canals than Birmingham.

Extract 5: *Travelog*

	McCarthy to Cam
Signpost/Glass Frontage/ Cars on Flyover McCarthy in from **rt** in **Silhouette** **MCU** Flips coin over shoulder	Birmingham has far more canals than Venice, yet somehow it never quite made it as a world famous city full of gondolas.
Reflection of Signpost in Water Coin in and ripples Surface	As an international byword for romance and fragile beauty Birmingham missed out and Venice cleaned up.
WS under Bridge McCarthy in **LS** from behind Piping McCarthy disappears behind Pipes	And of course there's the history. In the ninth century Venetian agents stole the body of their patron saint, St Mark, from Alexandria and are said to have made good their escape by wrapping the cadaver in pickled pork to keep their Muslim pursuers at bay.

WS Canal and Bridges Over McCarthy leans over Parapet almost invisible	In the twelfth century false beards and moustaches were made illegal because so many assassins were wearing them.
L/A WS under Motorway McCarthy in to **LS**/Traffic Cone **f/g**	On the downside, well, even if you think it's going to be expensive it's always more expensive than you think. The price of a cup of coffee in the *Piazza San Marco* in August would buy a family of four a two week camping holiday in Romania. And the food's a disappointment too. Say what you like about Birmingham, but you'll never find a decent Balti in Venice.
H/A WS Same Location Constant Traffic **b/g**	But hang the expense and forget the food. If you only ever visit one city in your life then it should be this one … Venice, I mean.

There are echoes of *film noir* in McCarthy's appearance in silhouette with coat collar turned up and hat pulled low. Emerging from and returning to the shadows cast by the concrete piers and piping of a motorway flyover he inhabits a liminal space of which the people who travel, literally, over his head are barely aware. There are implicit, if ironic, allusions to Venice's own liminality and to her sinister past in this location perhaps more suited to a television crime series car chase or gangland slaying than to the promotion of a tourist destination. Yet any sense of a threatening sub-world is quickly subverted by the irony of a script in which high cultural historical references to a patron saint, false beards and assassins jostle with the contemporary of Romanian caravan holidays and Balti cooking. If the post-tourist as defined by Feifer (1985) and elaborated by Urry (2002 [1990]) is marked by postmodern 'playfulness' in an eclectic consumption of signs, by the belief that the old divisions between high and low are no more, and that the kitsch is worth the same as contemplation of a work of art, then McCarthy's range of cultural references suggests a vigorous engagement with post-tourism.

This report from a place represented as a city of illusions treads, in addition, a continuous path between the comedic and the grave, now pausing beside a tank of shellfish in the Rialto fish market with the observation that 'in the middle ages this marketplace was the banking capital of Europe; today the prawn is a safer bet on the international currency market than the lira', now leading his viewers post-touristically to a place 'whose name originally meant iron foundry; the ghetto'. This latter sequence includes shots of a memorial to Venetian Jews who died at the hands of the fascists in World War Two, of ancient tenements 'which stacked people in' and turned blind windowless walls to the rest of Venice, and of empty squares silent except for the sound of pigeons and a distantly heard song played on an old gramophone. The subversiveness of *Travelog*, prepared to show that Venice is a city of illusions not all of which are of a kind to put people in a holiday mood, sets it apart from the mainstream. The intertextuality of death in Venice, does not, by and large, extend to information about the ghetto. Thus in McCarthy's film what had been Cameron's painterly monochromatic cemetery island of *San Michele* is revealed as another place of illusion where JCB earth movers hover behind graves in which coffins are allowed 12 years before being removed to make way for the next intake. An island bursting at the seams with cadavers has to do what it can to meet demand, to keep up with the present.

Extract 6: *Travelog*

	McCarthy V/O
WS Graves and Flowers	At first the profusion of fresh flowers is
LS Woman placing Flowers	dazzling. But there's a catch. It's terribly
on Grave	impressive and it makes you think that
	these people really do know how to
CUs Graves	treat their dead.
	McCarthy to Cam
LS McCarthy walking	But then it occurs to you that it's an
through Graves	island, and sooner or later I suppose it
	must fill up.
Pan him to JCBs	And then you come across a row of JCBs
	– industrial digging machines – and you
	think, 'Oh no, they wouldn't would
He kicks one	they; not with one of these…'.

Pemble's (1995) study of the city suggests that Venice increasingly resembled a stage set, deserted by its own great and good as it drifted from sovereign autonomy to provincial status, but appropriated by outsiders and brought back to historic life when the film crews of the 20th century arrived. He quotes the Italian writer Ojetti as he watched the filming of *I Due Foscari* in 1922:

The worst of it is, that by watching for half an hour this masquerade in the sun, we ourselves lose the sense of solid reality, and instead of the walls of the [Ducal] Palace making the actors seem real, it is the actors who make the place seem fake. (Pemble, 1995: 2)

That sense of shifting reality is compounded by the urban vistas unspoilt by traffic and modern building and by the annual celebration of Carnival when Venetians and visitors blur together disguised in fancy dress, their faces hidden by masks, creating a city of illusion, a setting for the playing of parts. At a Carnival reception, in which one reveller wearing a priapic phallus has it draped on camera with a napkin while fellow guests sing madrigals and drink nothing stronger than hot chocolate, McCarthy plays his own knowing part, costumed as an 18th century grandee and glimpsed first on the monochrome CCTV screen of security camera and then in the circular convex mirror of another security system, the fleeting 20th century image of a fleeting 18th century ghost. Yet whereas Smillie's performance was an essentially solo one, *Travelog* subverts the genre conventions of its time by giving equal screen status to the performances of the revelling Venetians and by including snippets of conversation between McCarthy and his hosts. The term hosts is apposite here since he is an invited guest, albeit one whose presence may owe something to his status as a visiting television presenter. His hosts speak English as they advise him on costume. The Italian of the madrigals is subtitled. It is, however, significant that this transgression into foreign tongues takes place during Carnival, a time for transgression and the inversion of the everyday, a time in which the city becomes a public space for public performances.

The party over, McCarthy, still in costume, observes the moonlit city.

Extract 7: *Travelog*

	McCarthy V/O
Gondola on moonlit Canal	Outside there may just be a chance to take in a quick cliché, then it's time for bed.
	…
	McCarthy V/O
McCarthy in **C18 Costume** walks down Lamp lit Street	You can feel that you're wandering the biggest opera set in the world on a night when there isn't a show. You'll believe
Fountain	that you've stepped back in time and
Lamp lit Building/Canal	that this magical place exists only for you.

WS empty Courtyard/
Rubbish Skips
McCarthy **A/B** walking
away from Camera

Present Day McCarthy's   **McCarthy to Cam**
hand then face appears   But of course it's just an illusion
f/g from round Pillar

McCarthy's reference to the gondola as a cliché reflects the city's most familiar image (Dunn, 1998). Yet if the gondola is the most recognisable signifier of the city, McCarthy's ironic and knowing dismissal of it as a cliché threatens to unravel a discursive conspiracy between the travel industry and programme makers. The instrument of Smillie's *jouissance* is here given little more than five seconds of screen time in which McCarthy subverts both touristic activity and a genre. A consumer of simulacra he presents himself as a simulacrum haunting empty streets. At the climax of his film he walks through a square full of rubbish, of the debris of a party which has moved on. The camera makes no attempt to clean up the shot, but it does have its final moment of electronic irony, a deconstructive, post-touristic conclusion which places a 20th century McCarthy in the same frame as his 18th century doppelgänger. On the word 'illusion' the 18th century McCarthy walks out of frame, and immediately in the foreground, an effect engineered in video editing, the 20th century McCarthy appears from behind a pillar and smiles knowingly. Nothing is real, it is suggested. The authentic and the once in a lifetime experience are chimeras.

Conclusion: The Traveller, the Tourist and the Post-tourist in Venice

Each of the three film reports has its own (tele)visual style. Cameron uses the symbolic images of crumbling sugar lump and funerary gondola as visual metaphor, adopting what Corner (1996: 27–30) terms an *associative* mode of representation and creating a film sophisticated in its use of a painterly tradition, while Smillie's shots of tourist Venice are essentially *illustrative*, their references limited to the familiar of the travel brochure. McCarthy's piece is both *associative* and *illustrative*, now offering the visual counterpoint of a motorway flyover or the electronic images of lives long gone, now offering visual evidence of how Venice actually copes with its dead. Yet despite television's need for the visual, it is, as already remarked, strongly informed by radio and by journalism and thus has traditionally privileged the verbal (Ellis, 1992). Thus it is the presenters' words and the discursive touristic roles which inform them which have occupied most of the discussion. Each reflects too the scopic conventions of representation of the genre throughout the 1990s, and each illustrates its limitations; the convergence between the camera's gaze and touristic practice highlighting another of the problems of translation which Cronin (2000), as noted above, has identified as follows:

[T]he experience of travel in a country where the language is unknown to the traveller will be heavily informed by the visual. If you cannot speak, you can at least look. Sightseeing is the world with the sound turned off. (Cronin, 2000: 82)

Yet tourists-as-sightseers hear a variety of sounds in the tourist destination, and even those foreign voices which cannot be understood play their part in the multi-sensory experience of being abroad, serving to mark and to authenticate its Otherness. Television is, by its nature, less multi-sensory. Although holiday programmes' soundtracks make use of the ambient sounds of the destination, their privileging of the presenter's voice means that in the main local voices speaking local languages, what Jaworski *et al.* (2003a: 20) term the 'linguascape' of the tourist destination, feature little, and contribute only in small measure to the totality of a general, and generally low level, background ambience. In consequence the presenters and their cameras are required to operate within the familiar of the scopic, foregrounding their performance in assumed roles, traveller, tourist, post-tourist, as they encounter and mediate a place foreign to them. Cameron the traveller is concerned with Venice's struggle with the elements, filming with a painterly eye, observing and categorising from a distance. Placing the inhabitants of a dying city figuratively under a microscope and grieving for them, he projects his own high cultural sensibilities while remaining remote from them, waiterless at his solitary café table. Smillie does a round of dutiful sightseeing in order to enjoy the rewards of shopping and a cruise in a gondola. Such implicit anti-tourism makes no attempt at any empathic involvement with Venice or its people, reducing them to the status of silent 'walk ons' and offering instead self-referential televisual picture postcards. In addition Smillie is isolated from the fellow tourists whose discursive role she shares, and is, perhaps, *pace* Smith (1978) the holiday programme's equivalent of that cultural intermediary of the tourist destination, the 'marginal [wo]man'. Post-tourism underpins McCarthy's subversive account. The significance of his film lies not only in its rare originality in upsetting the self-referentiality of the genre, but also in its ironic representation of the city as a place of illusion, illusion illustrated by electronic visual trickery. Ostensibly about Venice, the subject of this televisual text is in equal part the city and the illusory nature of the text itself. In addition, McCarthy presents himself as one of a new breed of tourist, detached, ironic, in awe of nothing and with an awareness of the importance of the performative in the tourist destination which allows him to share the screen with at least some of the Venetians on whose city he is reporting, and to whose performances he adds his own.

Whatever the discourse which informs their reports, each of these presenters is trying to make sense of an experience for the viewers. That they do it with differing kinds of enjoyment and with differing approaches to understanding is evidence of the range of touristic discourses reflected within the genre of holiday programmes. Yet whether Cameron, Smillie and McCarthy are presented as travellers, tourists or post-tourists they are, like all who travel, foreigners in a foreign country, struggling with the familiar and the unfamiliar, and with issues of language and translation. When Boorstin (1961: 117) writes so contemptuously of the contemporary ranks of tourists of which he is an unwilling member that 'we look into a mirror instead of out a window, and see only ourselves' he tells only half the story. Travellers, tourists and television presenters alike can look through the window. But often enough in the process they scarcely register the half heard voices and, catching sight of their reflection in the glass which separates them from the object of their attention, they concentrate on that reflection, turning everything else into a background of soft focus.

Notes

1. The transcripts, all made by the author, follow common television practice in detailing the visual in the left column and the sound in the right (Millerson, 1993: 128). These cannot convey totally the effect of what they denote. Pictures can be 'read' in different ways, their elements, even if unconsciously, occasionally rearranged to omit or give undue prominence to certain details. Tone of voice, timing of delivery, and the stressing of particular words go untranscribed and are subject to 'interpretation'. No system which does not allow every reader of this chapter equal access to the programmes as transmitted can be perfect, and even then the viewing conditions of the academic viewer, watching *in vacuo* without the surrounding flow of an evening's programmes, might alter perceptions and readings. Definitions of all technical terms used in this chapter follow.

    B/G or **Background**.
    CU or **Close Up**: term to describe a head and shoulders shot of one person.
    F/G or **Foreground**.
    Floating: in this case a shot taken from a moving boat.
    GV or **General View**: term to describe conventional shots of places, buildings or people.
    H/A or **High Angle**.
    L/A or **Low Angle**.
    LS or **Long Shot**: full length shot.
    MCU or **Mid Close Up**: wider than **Close Up**.
    Pan: term to describe movement when a camera pivots horizontally.
    Tilt: term to describe movement when a camera pivots vertically.
    To Cam: the presenter addresses the camera.
    V/O or **Voice Over**: where the words form a commentary and people are not seen speaking those words.
    WS or **Wide Shot**: self-explanatory
    2S or **2 Shot**: term to describe two people in shot simultaneously.

2. Schwarzbach (1982: 61–84), tracing images of English cities in mid-19th century English literature, finds parallels between the *terra incognita* of the explorers of continents and the similarly named *locus* of the new urban

explorers, who were often doctors or engineers working, with altruistic motives, in the slums of industrial cities. Like their colonial counterparts their role was to lead and to govern, while the duty of the explored, tribal native or poor inhabitant of the inner city, was to follow and be led.

3. The common assumption is that Venice's gender is feminine, her Italian sobriquet, *La Serenissima*, most serene [sc woman], under-pinning that assumption.

4. The same words appear in Stanza XII of Browning's (1855) *A Toccata of Galuppi's* where they are those of the old musician Galuppi himself, addressing the poet. This writer has been unable to trace the attribution of the words to Napoleon, either in commentaries on Browning's poem or in studies of Napoleon and Venice, and Cameron may stand guilty of poetic licence in shifting a quotation from one source to another. Even so, his use of the words is apposite.

5. Conversation between the writer and *Travelog*'s editor Jenny Mallinson Duff in April 1992 indicates that even then the series' budget was being reduced by C4.

References

Barthes, R. (1972) The *Blue Guide*. In R. Barthes *Mythologies* (pp. 74–6). Translated by A. Lavers. London: Cape: [Originally published in 1957].

Barthes, R. (1975a) *The Pleasure of the Text*. New York: Hill & Wang.

Barthes, R. (1975b) *S/Z*. London: Cape.

Batten, C.L. (1978) *Pleasurable Instruction*. Berkeley, CA: University of California Press.

Beloff, H. (1985) *Camera Culture*. Oxford: Blackwell.

Bennett, T. (1986) Hegemony, ideology, pleasure: Blackpool pleasure beach. In T. Bennett, C. Mercer and J. Woollacott (eds) *Popular Culture and Social Relations* (pp. 135–54). Milton Keynes: Open University Press.

Boddy, K. (1999) The European journey in postwar American fiction. In J. Elsner and J-P. Rubies (eds) *Voyages and Visions: Towards a Cultural History of Travel* (pp. 232–51). London: Reaktion Press.

Boorstin, D.J. (1961) *The Image*. London: Weidenfeld & Nicolson.

Brendon, P. (1991) *Thomas Cook: 150 Years of Popular Tourism*. London: Secker & Warburg.

Butler, R. (1980) The concept of a tourism area cycle of evolution. *Canadian Geographer* 24, 5–12.

Buzard, J. (1993) *The Beaten Track: European Tourism, Literature, and the Ways to 'Culture'*. Oxford: Clarendon Press.

Corner, J. (1995) *Television Form and Public Address*. London: Edward Arnold.

Corner, J. (1996) *The Art of Record*. Manchester, Manchester University Press.

Corner, J. (1999) *Critical Ideas in Television Studies*. Oxford: Oxford University Press.

Crang, M. (1999) Knowing, tourism and practices of vision. In D. Crouch (ed.) *Leisure/Tourism Geographies: Practices and Geographical Knowledge* (pp. 238–56). London: Routledge.

Crawshaw, C. and Urry, J. (1997) Tourism and the photographic eye. In C. Rojek and J. Urry (eds) *Touring Cultures: Transformations of Travel and Theory* (pp. 176–95). London: Routledge.

Cronin, M. (2000) *Across the Lines: Travel, Language, Translation*. Cork: Cork University Press.

Death in Venice (1971) Film directed by L. Visconti, Italy.

Don't Look Now (1973) Film directed by N. Roeg, UK.

Dann, G. (2002) La Serenissima: Dreams, love and death in Venice. In M. Robinson and H.C. Andersen (eds) *Literature and Tourism* (pp. 239–78). London: Continuum.

Dunn, D. (1998) Home truths from abroad: Television representations of the tourist destination. Unpublished PhD thesis, University of Birmingham.

Edensor, T. (2001) Performing tourism, staging tourism: (Re)producing tourist space and practice. *Tourist Studies* 1, 59–81.

Ellis, J. (1992) *Visible Fictions*. London: Routledge.

Feifer, M. (1985) *Going Places*. London: Macmillan.

Fiske, J. (1987) *Television Culture*. London: Methuen.

Fiske, J. (1992) British cultural studies and television. In R. Allen (ed.) *Channels of Discourse, Reassembled* (pp. 284–326). London: Routledge.

Franklin, A. and M. Crang (2001) The trouble with tourism and travel theory? *Tourist Studies* 1, 5–22.

Fussell, P. (1980) *Abroad: British Literary Travel Between the Wars*. New York: Oxford University Press.

Goffman, E. (1959) *Presentation of Self in Everyday Life*. New York: Doubleday.

Hall, S. (1981) The structured communication of events. In D.C. Potter and J. Anderson (eds) *Society and The Social Sciences: An Introduction* (pp. 269–89). London: Routledge in association with Open University Press.

Hall, S. (1986) Popular culture and the state. In T. Bennett, C. Mercer, and J. Woollacott (eds) *Popular Culture and Social Relations* (pp. 22–49). Milton Keynes: Open University Press.

Jaworski, A., Thurlow, C., Lawson, S. and Ylänne-McEwen, V. (2003a) The uses and representations of local languages in tourist destinations: A view from British television holiday programmes. *Language Awareness* 12, 5–29.

Jaworski, A., Ylänne-McEwen, V., Thurlow, C. and Lawson, S. (2003b) Social roles and negotiation of status in host–tourist interaction: A view from British television holiday programmes. *Journal of Sociolinguistics* 7, 135–63.

Kress, G. and van Leeuwen, T. (1996) *Reading Images: The Grammar of Visual Design*. London: Routledge.

MacCannell, D. (1976) *The Tourist: A New Theory of the Leisure Class*. New York: Shocken Books.

MacCannell, D. (1992) *Empty Meeting Grounds: The Tourist Papers*. London: Routledge.

MacCannell, D. (2001) Tourist agency. *Tourist Studies* 1, 23–37.

Marshall, P.D. (1997) *Celebrity and Power: Fame in Contemporary Culture*. Minneapolis, MN: University of Minnesota Press.

Millerson, G. (1993) *Effective TV Production*. Oxford: Focal Press.

Morgan, N.J. and Pritchard, A. (1998) *Tourism Promotion and Power: Creating Images, Creating Identities*. Chichester: John Wiley.

Munt, I. (1994) The 'other' postmodern tourism: Culture, travel and the new middle classes. *Theory, Culture & Society* 11, 101–23.

Nash, D. (1996) *Anthropology of Tourism*. Oxford: Pergamon.

Observer (1961) Sayings of the week. 26 October 1961, 25.

Osborne, P. (2000) *Travelling Light: Photography, Travel and Visual Culture*. Manchester: Manchester University Press.

Pemble, J. (1995) *Venice Rediscovered*. Oxford: Clarendon Press.

Porter, D. (1991) *Haunted Journeys: Desire and Transgression in European Travel Writing*. Princeton, NJ: University of Princeton Press.

Rojek, C. (2000) *Leisure and Culture*. London: Macmillan.

Ryan, C. (1991) *Recreational Tourism: A Social Science Perspective*. London: Routledge.

Schwarzbach, F.S. (1982) Terra incognita: An image of the city in English literature, 1820–1855. In P. Dodd (ed.) *The Art of Travel: Essays on Travel Writing* (pp. 61–84). London: Frank Cass.

Smith, V. (1978) Introduction. In V. Smith (ed.) *Hosts and Guests: The Anthropology of Tourism* (pp. 1–14). Oxford: Blackwell.

Stallybrass, P. and White, A. (1986) *The Politics and Poetics of Transgression*. London: Methuen.

The Travel Show (1993) The Venetian Riviera. Presenter C. Smillie. BBC2: 12 August 1993.

Thompson, G. (1983) Carnival and the calculable. In Formations Editorial Collective (ed.) *Formations of Pleasure* (pp. 124–37). London: Routledge.

Travelog (1995) New Zealand. Presenter P. McCarthy. Channel 4: 15 February 1995.

Travelog (1996) Venice. Presenter P. McCarthy. Channel 4: 13 March 1996.

Tunstall, J. (1993) *Television Producers*. London: Routledge.

Turner, V. (1974) *The Ritual Process*. Harmondsworth: Penguin.

Urry, J. (1994) Cultural change and contemporary tourism. *Leisure Studies* 13, 233–8.

Urry, J. (1995) *Consuming Places*. London: Routledge.

Urry, J. (2002) *The Tourist Gaze* (2nd edn). London: Sage. [Originally published in 1990.]

Venice: The Vanishing Lady (1967/1993) Written and presented by J. Cameron, directed by R. Marquand. [Second transmission, BBC2: 30 July 1993.]

Part 3

Identities on the Move

Chapter 6
Discourses of Polish Agritourism: Global, Local, Pragmatic

ADAM JAWORSKI and SARAH LAWSON

Introduction

This chapter examines some of the discourses surrounding Polish agri-tourism – a form of tourism which could be perceived as very localised – within the framework of the discourses of globalisation. Our aim is to unravel the tension between the global positioning of tourism in general, and the largely local consumption of Polish agritourism.

Agritourism comes under the umbrella of 'ecotourism', which is currently tapping into the discourses of global environmental concern and responsibility. As Mühlhäusler and Peace (2001) demonstrate with regard to the discourses of ecotourism on Queensland's Fraser Island, however, the primary concerns of the tour operators and tourists visiting this particular site are not to do with the educational, interpretative and awareness-raising issues surrounding the interrelationship between an ecology and its inhabitants. Mühlhäusler and Peace are therefore inclined to adopt the label 'nature-based tourism' (p. 378), which may be lacking in the sophistication and loftiness of the designation 'ecotourism', but, as in the case of Polish agritourism, better reflects the consumption-oriented stance of tourists and profit-generating stance of hosts towards the environment.

In this chapter, we begin our discussion of the global–local dialectic of Polish agritourism with a general discussion of tourism as a manifestation and an agent of globalisation. Then, we overview the positioning of Polish agritourism in some of its promotional materials as an exemplification of the industry's tapping into the global discourses of 'ecotourism'. In the main part of the chapter, we discuss agritourism hosts' accounts of their contacts and interactions with their visitors, and their perceptions of themselves and their visitors, whether global or local, as 'same' or 'different'. This is followed by an interpretation of the global ideology of agritourism and its largely local relevance.

Global Framing of Tourism

One of the dominant metaphors of globalisation is that of *flow*. According to Appadurai (1990), global cultural flows take place in five dimensions or *scapes*: movements of people (*ethnoscapes*), of technologies (*technoscapes*), of finance (*finanscapes*), of images and information (*mediascapes*), and of ideologies (*ideoscapes*) (see also Lash & Urry, 1994) Although when talking about tourism, we are primarily interested in ethnoscapes, as Appadurai points out, all of these flows are closely interlinked. They are, moreover, characterised by growing disjunctures, i.e. asymmetries, paradoxes and contradictions evidenced, for example, by the unequal distribution of goods, processes of deterritorialisation, the hegemony of and challenge to the nation-state (often leading to the creation of new nation-states as in the case of the former Soviet Union and Yugoslavia). Furthermore, Appadurai argues that, in contrast to popular belief, the globalisation of culture is not synonymous with homogenisation. Rather, globalisation involves various instruments of homogenisation such as the widespread use of certain types of armaments, advertising techniques, dominant languages, clothing styles, and so on, all of which are 'absorbed into local political and cultural economies, only to be repatriated as heterogeneous dialogues of national sovereignty, free enterprise, fundamentalism, etc. in which the state plays an increasingly delicate role ...' (Appadurai, 1990: 307). Finally, Appadurai postulates that contemporary global cultural processes 'are products of the infinitely varied mutual contest of sameness and difference on a stage characterised by radical disjunctures between different sorts of global flows and the uncertain landscapes created in and through these disjunctures' (Appadurai, 1990: 308).

One of the inevitable corollaries to the world conceived of flows and disjunctures is the unequal participation of different geographical areas and social groups in the patterns of production and consumption. In tourism, just as in any other sector of travel, the contrasts and disproportions across the world remain vast. For example, international travel is dominated by the big four touring nations: USA, UK, Japan and Germany accounting for 37.5% of world tourism expenditure (WTO, 2003). Equally, whereas approximately 100,000 overseas visitors (mostly from Britain) visit The Gambia annually, it is clear that a similar proportion of The Gambian population (approx 1.5 million) is not able to enjoy international (and especially intercontinental) travel.

Due to such disproportions and asymmetries, individual and group experiences of globalisation will vary depending on one's role in the global flows – whether one is part of the flow (i.e. 'tourist'), or a recipient of such flows (i.e. 'host'). The tourist–host dichotomy forms a mini implicational scale. Other things being equal, upon their return 'home', all tourists become potential or actual hosts to other visitors, but the reverse does not necessarily hold true, i.e. not all hosts become tourists (cf. Smith, 1989: 3; Urry, 2002: 52).

However, the unequal distribution of goods, services and resources globally does not mean that anyone in the world actually 'functions' outside of globalisation. In fact, many patterns of cultural or economic *exclusion* are commonly attributed to globalisation, especially as it is linked to the development of modern capitalism (e.g. Jameson & Miyoshi, 1999).

A typical example is the media (Appadurai's *mediascape*); they no doubt have a global reach in disseminating information and images, but at the same time demonstrate huge disproportions in terms of the sources and directions of flows as well as patterns of access and uptake (Thompson, 2000). Yet, most people around the globe live (or grow up) sharing a sense of a globalised world, whether they actively engage in the activities deemed to be 'global' (e.g. international travel), or only aspire to do so (cf. Lawson & Jaworski, 2006). This is in line with Meethan's (2001: 35) observation, following Hoogvelt (1997) and Robertson (1995) about the emergence of a 'global consciousness', or a shared conceptualisation of social, cultural, political and environmental relations on a global scale.

Thus, globalisation can be said to *frame* the social lives of people, regardless of their degree or type of participation (actual or perceived) in the processes of globalisation. Urry (2002: 142) argues that '[w]hile clearly most people across the world are not global tourists *qua* visitors, this does not mean that the places that they live in and the associated images of nature, nation, colonialism, sacrifice, community, heritage and so on, are not powerful constituents of a rapacious global tourism' (see also Bauman, 1998 on the metaphor of the 'tourist' for the modern global). The somewhat paradoxical reaction to globalisation seen in the resurgence of local 'heritage' sites and the exploitation of 'nostalgia' as a dominant tourist theme (e.g. Hewison, 1987; MacCannell, 1989; Wright, 1995; Macdonald, 1997; Coupland *et al.*, this volume) is paralleled by the development of different forms of 'alternative', 'niche' tourism such as 'eco-tourism' or 'agritourism', which, apart from targeting and attracting international tourists, are very often geared towards the domestic market. Such processes are probably what Appadurai (1990; cf. above) meant by the sense-making absorption of the homogenising trends and production of dialogues of globalisation of local relevance.

Present-day mass tourism is thought of as one of the hallmarks of globalisation (e.g. Bauman, 1998; Held & McGrew, 2000) because it is usually thought of as *international* tourism. But mass tourism originated as, and quite importantly continues to be, greatly a domestic affair. At the beginning of mass tourism in the modernist era, placed somewhere between the two world wars, domestic travel was the norm, apart from the continued tradition of the 18th century Grand Tour or spa trips enjoyed only by the super-rich. Such was the origin and the sharp rise of the British seaside resorts, when one- or two-week holidays became accessible to British city dwellers on a mass scale. It was not until the 1960s and the beginning of jet air travel that these resorts came to be superseded by the Mediterranean ones, while the holiday camps in the USA gave way to Americans' holidays in the Caribbean and Latin America. The meaning of 'home' and 'away' seems to have changed from 'home' and 'seaside resort/holiday camp' to 'home' and 'abroad' (see Urry, 2002 [1990]; Meethan, 2001).

The difference between domestic tourism of the 1920s and today is that when contemporary tourists decide to spend their holiday in their own country, they do so against the idea of travelling abroad. International travel with the nearly unlimited choice of global destinations is the default point of reference for contemporary travel (whether actual or aspirational). Likewise, tourist destinations all over the world depend on international tourism for survival. Despite these changes, domestic tourism continues to be as important for many local economies as before (Urry, 2002 links it to the sharp rise in car ownership in Britain in the last quarter of the 20th century) although its connotation seems to have changed from a sign of newly acquired affluence to an impoverished relative of foreign travel; from taking a 'holiday' to going on a 'short break', or just making a 'day trip'. Having said that, tourists taking a day trip to a local destination may well seek the symbolic capital of a positive identity and high moral ground by activating discourses of belonging, shared local knowledge, tradition, and so on (McCabe & Stokoe, 2004).

As mentioned above, recent developments in heritage tourism, agritourism, etc. seem to stand in direct response to the forces of globalisation. With every tourist site being potentially a global/international destination, local people in such destinations seem to develop new levels of self- and place-awareness – a renewed sense of self-worth, community identity, positive re-alignment with local landscape and history. This is at least in part due to the appropriation and appreciation of the tourist discourses of romanticisation and commodification of local people, traditions, countryside, and so on. As Casey (2003) states in her study of the impact of tourism on a small Irish village: 'Faced with a pluralisation of value systems and lifestyles, the locals in Ballygannieve adopt a self-reflexive attitude which differentiates between their indigenous culture and a globalisation of cultures' (Casey, 2003: 55).

The present study of the discourses of Polish agritourism examines this dichotomy through the reflections of Polish agritourism operators on their interactions and relationships with their tourist clients, both domestic and international. Our approach is broadly speaking sociolinguistic, by which we mean here analysing spoken (interview) data pertaining to other aspects of interpersonal communication. In this sense, the focus of the chapter is on the metalinguistic actions of our informants, i.e. their accounts of their own and others' language use.

Metalinguistics has long been recognised as a fruitful area for the study of ideology, social structure, identity, and so on (e.g. Silverstein, 2001/1981; Schieffelin *et al.*, 1998; Jaworski *et al.*, 2004) as it is through our more or less explicit conceptualisation of language, language varieties, language structures and language use that we inevitably make manifest our subject positions, allegiances and patterns of power and dominance. As we demonstrate below, it is precisely through their metalinguistic comments elicited in the course of our fieldwork that our informants allow us an insight into their underlying conceptions of 'community' and 'identity' (for a related study of representation of language and communication in tourism see Jaworski *et al.*, 2003).

Furthermore, social actors' ideologies, or their social, political and cultural worldviews, which are motivated at least in part by their interpretations of linguistic diversity, have a knock-on effect on language itself. Woolard (1998: 12) argues that linguistic '[s]tructure conditions ideology, which then reinforces and expands the original structure, distorting language in the name of making it more like itself (cf. Bourdieu, 1991). In a move that joins the conceptual to the active side of ideology ..., this approach shows that to "understand" one's own linguistic usage is potentially to change it (Silverstein, 1979: 233).' In this line of our work, for example (see Jaworski & Lawson, forthcoming), we demonstrate how the 'new' international identities of the operators running Polish agritourist businesses embracing cross-European *differences* may be a contributing factor to their increasing bilingualism. This is in contrast to the more traditional, 'old' nationals, whose primary point of reference lies in their indexing their *sameness* with other Poles, and whose linguistic competence remains largely monolingual.

Polish Agritourism as 'Ecotourism'

As a first step, approximately 30 Polish tourist publications with English as one of the featured languages were surveyed for information about agritourism. Seven publications were chosen to form an initial view of how agritourism in Poland is marketed for a non-Polish audience (see Appendix 1; the numbers in brackets after the material quoted in this section correspond to the numbers in the Appendix). These include catalogues with addresses and short descriptions of the farms nationally, regional maps and brochures advertising whole regions, several farms or just one farm.

As evidenced in the promotional materials surveyed here, the main images used for marketing Polish agritourism are of unspoilt environment, peace and quiet. The prospective tourists are enticed by the idea of going back to basics, nature and history. This turn to 'ecotourism' is part of what has been identified above as one of the trends of globalisation to turn to the more grass-roots concerns of the 'local'. Thus, the imagery of locally driven concern for the environment also has connotations of responsibility towards the planet, while tourism money is supposed to go back into the local community.

Polish agritourism is marketed as a way to experience traditional Polish life: 'Folk traditions are cultivated in everyday life' [5]; natural environment: 'Peace and quiet and a primeval natural environment await guests at the picturesque Marciniak family farm' [5]; but also in comfort: 'Separated entry and a bathroom make guests feel comfortable and not embarrassed' [6].

Much emphasis is placed on tasty, organic, regional home cooking: 'meals prepared by Gertruda include Silesian dumplings and apple pie' [5], 'home-made herb liqueurs can be purchased' [5], 'home-made lard with cranberries is a favourite snack' [5], 'home-made cake for tea' [5], 'There are goats in the farm so you can drink health goats' milk' [4]. 'All the produce has an Ekoland certificate' [5].

Outdoor activities include a mixture of traditional (riding, hiking, tennis, fishing, hunting, and so on) and modern pursuits (hang-gliding, helicopter rides). Working farms offer tourists the possibility of experiencing tending farm animals or helping in the fields: 'The hosts are grateful for help during the hay mowing season' [5]; 'Visitors can help feeding calves and pigeons' [6]. Much is made of activities which may seem somewhat archaic but appealing through their past charm: 'cart rides to Brodnica are another attraction' [5], themed festivals focused on the past and folklore, e.g. jousting tournaments, folk and archaeology festivals, summer blacksmithy shows, and historical and ethnographic museums. The area of Nowy Tomyśl, for example, promotes itself as using 'natural' resources by being a centre for traditional wickerwork, even boasting the largest wicker basket in the world [2].

Much of the discourse in the brochures is geared towards making the potential visitor feel 'at home'. Tourists are referred to predominantly as 'guests', e.g. 'Guests are welcomed anytime of the year' [6], and the notions of hospitality are emphasised in self-reference of hosts as 'hosts' extending a warm welcome to their homes, as in: 'The host family can organise bonfire, attractive excursions also with a boat' [6]. Hosts are usually identified by name, as part of the practical information about how to make a reservation, but also as a way of personalising the description of the prospective destination, e.g. 'Hosts offer incredible home-made meal made by Mrs Ula' ('Ula' being the hostess' first name, which signals informality and familiarity) [4]; 'another attraction of a stay at Wiesława Krupa's house is ...' [5].

Apart from the practical visual imagery depicting the holiday homes, selected brochures also feature photographs (or drawings) of the countryside and nature (fields, rivers, lakes, mountains, etc.), historical monuments, as well as people wearing traditional costumes or doing traditional activities (e.g. farming, lace-making, feather plucking, performing in 'medieval' or 'Viking' festivals), tourists pursuing local attractions (e.g. horse-riding, mushroom picking, walking), traditionally decorated houses, 'historic' buildings (e.g. windmills, thatched houses, half-timbered houses). Probably to enhance the image of agritourism holidays, the brochures are almost completely devoid of images of cars, promising walking, cycling and horse-riding as the three main modes of transport (cf. Crashaw & Urry, 1997 on the idealised, people- and object-free tourist images of the Lake District).

In sum, Polish agritourism is predominantly marketed as a form of escapism for busy townsfolk to find true 'peace and quiet'; 'The surrounding silence makes it difficult to believe that our house is situated only 60 km from overcrowded Poznań' [7]. Additionally, agritourism offers the experience of traditional rural life, the main attractions being home cooking, country walks, mushroom picking, fishing, horse-riding, and so on, as well as engaging in 'typical' farming activities. However, although tourists are enticed by exotic images of a 'different' way of life and indulging in the unspoilt, they are also reassured that they will find a home-from-home, with comfortable facilities and welcoming hosts. This seems to be a characteristic of ecotourism, where the guest is offered both the promise of raw earthy authenticity, and the security of a flushing toilet and a hot shower. This tension between 'traditional/rural' and 'modern/safe' representations of agritourism is also reflected in the interviews discussed below, as an important aspect of the interviewees' self-image and their way of managing relations with their visitors.

Think Globally, Act Locally

In a series of open-ended interviews, we gathered meta-discursive commentary of Polish agritourism operators on their contacts and forms of interactions with their visitors. As mentioned above, we believe that the study of locally managed interaction between hosts and tourists affords us the best way of accessing and theorising such basic notions as *identity, difference, otherness,* and *community.*

Seven open-ended interviews with agritourism 'farmers' were conducted in the Poznań area in western Poland between April and July 2001 and in June 2002. They lasted between 40 and 80 minutes and were audio-recorded. Some interviewees were interviewed individually, others with their partners and/or (adult) children. On some occasions the composition of the interviewed groups changed as different family members attended to their daily business around the house and farm.

The interviewees were informed at the beginning of each interview that the main focus of the research was on 'language, communication and globalisation' in order to justify the detailed questioning about their personal contacts with visitors and other language-related issues.

The interviewees were selected from a national agritourism directory for 2000/2001 bought in a tourist office in Poznań, and a smaller national directory published in English, obtained from the Polish Tourism Centre in London. The latter publication features more upmarket country homes, villas and manor houses, in contrast to the more modest, and sometimes rather basic farm houses predominantly listed in the directory oriented towards the home market. The English-language publication contains many colour photographs of the advertised holiday homes and various tourist attractions, unlike the other directory, which contains no such illustrations.

The places visited during fieldwork varied greatly as far as the occupation of the interviewees, types of 'farms', location, quality of the accommodation and activities offered to tourists. The following is a brief summary of the interviewees and sites:

- GD – housewife on a working farm; guest rooms in the old farmhouse and the newly built family house (24 April 2001);
- AD1, AD2 – couple on a working farm; guest rooms in an adjacent old farmhouse (24 April 2001);
- CB, LB, JB – couple and their (elder) son on a non-working farm; guest rooms, dining hall, cafeteria and micro-market in converted farm buildings (25 April 2001);
- JP, SP – retired father and son running a working farm; guestrooms upstairs in the family house and dining hall in a converted farm building adjacent to the house (22 July 2002);
- BW – housewife in a country house converted from an old farmhouse; guestrooms in one wing of the family house (5 June 2002);
- MM – housewife on a working farm; guest rooms in the family house (7 June 2002);
- GP – businessman, lives and works in the city of Poznań; bought a ruined farm and built two new country homes for tourists there (7 June 2002).

All the interviews were conducted in Polish but are reported in the text in their English translation following standard orthographic conventions. The Polish transcripts are included in Appendix 2. All the translations are ours, and take the form of glosses rather than polished translations, to retain the flavour of the original words of our interviewees.

Domestic tourists

Most interviewees declare that the majority of their visitors are domestic, predominantly from Poznań, the closest large city and the region's capital, with only a few tourists coming from Warsaw, Łódź and the industrial region of Silesia. According to some interviewees (especially JP), tourists' choice of a nearby holiday destination is dictated predominantly by economic factors – according to JP, 'society' is increasingly worse off and tourists seek to reduce the cost of transportation. Short distance encourages also short weekend visits to the farms. MM reinforces the expectation of agritourism farms receiving visitors from the predominantly local area by stating how surprised she was that a family from Gdynia (a port city on the Baltic coast in the north of the country) come on holiday to her house:

Extract 1

MM: A family from Gdynia will now come [here] for the second season. I was completely surprised, I said, 'What are they looking for here?' From the seaside to, well, also to [a place] on the water because there are many lakes around here, so I thought of their booking as rather odd, why is it like that?

Implied here is the assumption that tourists opting for agritourism holidays will seek the most attractive places 'close to home', and that the proximity of the Baltic will preclude anyone from choosing a holiday inland. Interestingly, the possible motivation of the tourists to explore a different region of their country does not occur to MM at this point, and the only explanation she can find is that her region abounds in lakes, which must compensate the family from Gdynia for the absence of the sea.

The clear advantage of the predominantly Polish tourists visiting the farms is that they are perceived by the farmers as 'same'. In a business run by families where hosts and guests live in close proximity, the barrier of letting strangers into one's house can be a significant one. In fact, many of our interlocutors describe their great apprehension between their decision to run an agritourism business and receiving their first visitors.

Extract 2

BW: With the first guests, I must tell you, there was a little worry, not particularly on my part but my husband's. In the first year I even had to cancel, pretend something that I have everything booked up or something, because my husband was saying, 'Do you want strangers? It's so scary, you never know who'll come. All sorts of things happen. They are in our house. We sleep together. Something may happen.' There was fear, especially that we would be robbed, and things, because we're in the woods, all alone, but the first people we received, they were really wonderful and well-educated. They practised medical manual therapy [*sic*]. They told us so many interesting things. And they were the first. And my husband became convinced that they were wonderful and that they did not interfere with our lives, and a little money came in, and it was also nice when they praised, admired us that we were doing up the house by ourselves and we were doing it all ourselves.

In the above extract, BW describes in some detail the anxiety she and her family felt before the arrival of the first tourists, and even admits to delaying this moment, resorting to deception and evasion. Luckily for her, the first visitors turned out to be 'wonderful' and 'well-educated'. But they did not simply 'not interfere' with the lives of their hosts, they turned out to be 'interesting' to talk to and, not least, appreciative of the hosts' efforts in doing up their house. This positive experience is not only invoked by mentioning the dispelled fears, additional income and trouble-free job, but, as evidenced by BW's acquaintance with her visitors' profession and the latters' complimentary comments towards their hosts, by presenting a picture of a close relationship between the hosts and tourists. In other words, BW's visitors have turned out to be not threatening 'others' but like-minded, benign friends with shared interests and aspirations.

It appears that being on a friendly, even intimate, footing with the visitors is an important part of running an agritourism business. We have already mentioned the identification of hosts' names in tourist catalogues and directories. The practicalities of making a telephone booking aside, hosts' names serve here a humansing function, individualising them in the same way as their farms are individual. Thus, the motivation for using names and the overall effect is quite different from what Fairclough has called *synthetic personalization*, i.e. 'a compensatory tendency to give the impression of treating each of the people "handled" *en masse* as an individual' (Fairclough, 1989: 62). With the exception of GP, who is a businessman and lives with his family in Poznań, all the interviewees declare readiness to develop close interpersonal relations with their visitors (albeit always emphasising avoidance of any imposition on those who prefer to be left alone), and seem to set great store by the relationships which do develop. In fact, for MM, contact between her family, especially her teenage children and the visitors seems to be as important a reason for starting a tourist business as the additional income (see also Extract 8 and discussion).

Extract 3
MM: When we undertook this additional activity I also considered
     that I had children of school age, who, well, we live in a small

town environment, and we had limited opportunities for development besides primary school, [and maintaining] any extracurricular interests, if any, or contact with other people. Well, I didn't know who would come here. But there are really different contacts. So I just expected such contact and development for children. This was just one of the main points beside this [financial] one. And it paid off very quickly. Friendships were made and I am very pleased about all this.

In this case, getting to know and finding out about other people is achieved not by being in the 'flow', but by experiencing it, although as MM states a moment later in the interview (not in the extract), her son is also shortly to go on a school trip to a place near Gdynia, and she is happy to think that he may be in touch there with the family who has visited them (see Extract 1). Interestingly, however, the main educational benefits to MM's family come not only from their contact with the visitors but also from their increased orientation to and awareness of their locality. As part of their brief as 'hosts', and to be able to offer visitors something in return for the time spent together, MM's children act as guides showing tourists round on cycling expeditions, and taking them to local places of interest, such as nature trails and historical monuments. MM even goes as far as to describe her tourism business not just as 'work' for the tourists but 'co-operation' between hosts and tourists.

The final instance of MM's orientation to the locality to be mentioned here is even more clearly linked to the wider, globalising processes in which she and her family partake as receivers of global flows. Through contact with other visitors, who had travelled extensively, they come to know and appreciate their own region more.

Extract 4

MM: Last year there was a gentleman who had travelled around the world for 20 years and, at this point, one could say, he's got his life sorted out and he's taking it easy. And he came here, he made us realise that we should appreciate what we've got here, because he visited places here where we hadn't been, because he was so inquisitive and he had so much time. He didn't even mind that his wife broke her arm when they were cycling and they travelled further, they explored very remote places, and he often put us to shame in that, to put it colloquially, you think the grass is greener elsewhere, and this mobilised us. Therefore, I say, it forces us to find out more about our own area, or the children to go deeper, or recently, before the last season, we had a guide course organised, by Mr. Łęcki, who is the local enthusiast. So it mobilises us, indeed forces us to put in some effort.

The above extract demonstrates how the globetrotter couple's endorsement of the touristic value of MM's area legitimises her appreciation of the local. This takes place on a number of levels: positive comparison of the area to other regions in the world, the globetrotters' unfettered interest in the area (despite the woman's broken arm), and their 'discovery' of interesting places not known to the locals (an 'eye opening' function to the local community). Moreover, this renewed interest in the locality is not purely symbolic but leads to an active undertaking – a tour guiding course organised by the local community.

MM's comments suggest that their visitors are likely to engage in the form of tourism to be conceptualised as *interaction* rather than as (or alongside) *play, seeking strangeness or authenticity, or conflict* (see Morgan & Pritchard, 1998: 7–17 for discussion of these categories). The interactive nature of agritourist holidays afforded by the small numbers of tourists staying at the farms at any one time, and the hosts' consistent efforts to actively involve their visitors in the explorations of the local, help turn the agritourist destinations into a 'chora', or interactive spaces where the tourist becomes a creative *choraster* interacting and 'growing' with other tourists and hosts, rather than a remaining relatively passive, casual, gazing *flâneur* (Wearing & Wearing, 1996).

Other interviewees tell similar stories. In response to AJ's question: 'o czym się rozmawia z turystami? 'What does one talk about with the tourists?', AD1 replies:

Extract 5

AD1: You know, about everything. About everything, I am interested, for example, in what they do and where they work, simply in a conversation I ask [them] I ask questions because I am really curious, interested. About the weather, about our work because they are also interested and they keep asking.

Here, AD1 describes mutual curiosity between herself and the tourists and identifies the 'conversation' as the main source of information about one another. But she also mentions a typical phatic topic (the weather), which suggests the possibly close but unremarkable nature of her family's relationships with the tourists (although see Coupland & Ylänne-McEwen, 2000) on different functions of weather talk in the context of travel industry and leisure).

We suggest that the relative intensity of contacts between hosts and tourists in agritourism does not follow solely from the personal involvement of the host families running their businesses (taking a booking, providing accommodation, cooking for their guests, organising outdoor activities, and so on), or from the close proximity of sharing a house with the tourists. The main factor responsible for creating the interpersonal relations is the mutual perception of hosts and guests as 'same'. Sameness here means importantly, though is not reduced to, a set of common attributes: shared ethnicity, nationality and language; it also means here the perception (at least as expressed by the hosts in our interviews) of diminishing dialectal and lifestyle differences between 'town' and 'country'. The following two extracts illustrate this point, first when AD1 responds to a question about the differences between the 'farmer' hosts and 'townsfolk' visitors, and second in response to a question about possible dialectal differences between hosts and visitors:

Extract 6

AD1: Well, there's nothing for them [visitors] to be very surprised about. This countryside is not, as I say, what people think it used to be. Once a gentleman called and well he didn't quite know how to ask this question, you know, and he says, this is the countryside, and I say, well, do not worry, sir, there's no loo behind the barn here (laughs).

　…

No, it hasn't happened. I mean, certainly our Poznań dialect here is so sing-song, and although we do speak proper Polish without it [dialect], it does exist, but it's never happened [that the differences were great]. I mean we try not to speak in this typical countryside way and we try simply [to speak properly]. I teach [my] children that way, because it's also important in my opinion, dialect is beautiful, it's a beautiful thing, but it's clear that in contacts with other people one speaks pure Polish.

Both extracts display a homogenising discourse suggesting the convergence between town and country, if not in actual behaviour then in people's aspirations: flushing toilets and attempting to speak and teach one's children 'pure' Polish seem to work effectively towards alleviating any differences imputed in the interviewer's question.

The only example of perceived 'otherness' or 'strangeness' surfacing in one of the interviews runs along the lines of professional divisions, possibly associated with a high status differential. In the following extract, while discussing vegetarian menus and visitors' culinary requirements, CD admits to having 'worried' about satisfying the preferences of a couple – two *university professors*.

Extract 7

CD: Well, she preferred vegetarian cuisine because she has some [health] issues and I was very worried. She said she couldn't [eat meat?]. She was such a nice lady that it was enough for breakfast it was enough for her to have cottage cheese and tomatoes, and this was enough. They were so pleasant. I was worried about a

Professor coming. She was such a pleasant lady. They sent us cards that they wanted to come [again]. She had some health problems, so when I made dinner I steamed fish instead of frying, but well she was such a nice lady. And they sent us [Christmas?] cards for two years, and said that they will come again. Well, she is very ill. Here, they were fine. They brought their own gear to work. This lady worked here. She sat over here, very nice.

In the above extract, CD mentions her apprehension before serving vegetarian food having probably imagined that a vegetarian diet requires levels of sophistication exceeding her cooking skills. Yet, she ends up praising the modest requirements of vegetarians ('cottage cheese', 'tomatoes', 'steamed fish') equating it with the pleasantness of the guests ('pleasant lady', 'so pleasant', 'such a pleasant lady', 'very fine', etc.), whom she probably expected to be capricious and standoffish by virtue of their occupation and relatively high social standing ('I was worried about a Professor coming'). Luckily, close contact and the manageable requirements from the visitors break the ice of initial apprehension and demonstrate to CD that even academics can be reasonable, likeable people.

CD mentions another feature of contacts between hosts and guests – exchanging greeting cards. These, being probably Christmas cards, are a form of acknowledging the existing bond, a friendly footing established during the first visit, and expression of continued interest in re-visiting the farm. This theme re-appears in other interviews.

Extract 8

AJ: And what's it like with returning visitors? Do they return as friends?

AD1: Yes, yes, we keep in touch. Christmas cards are obligatory, and if not cards then a phone call from time to time, how's your health and this and that. Of course, we [only] keep in touch with the visitors who want that.

Here AD1 states explicitly that the continued contact with former guests involves the exchange of Christmas cards and phatic phone calls. Expression of widespread friendliness and the mitigatory assurance that contact is maintained only with the guests who express interest in it demonstrate that AD1 and her family know how to balance closeness and lack of imposition; that they are adept in managing their social skills.

CB mentions shared social activities with the tourists but also emphasises that the initiative to start contact is left to the visitors. In response to a question about the main points of contact between his family and the visitors, CB states:

Extract 9

CB: Well, yes, it varies. Usually we light the bonfire [and] some
    people will come. There's also a lot of contact in the hall. They
    come to watch TV, to play [a game], to drink a beer and there's the
    greatest contact there.

What CB offers then is creating living and social spaces which enable
contact and leaving the choice of activity (shared or solitary) to the visitors. Once contact is established, the spirit of interactions seems to be
more communal rather than institutional. This is further emphasised by
little sense of difference between self and the visitors. CB and his family
no longer work the land and do not keep any animals, except a horse, a
goat and some birds for 'colour'. For the same reason, a rusting tractor is
left on the premises. However, CB does not see himself much as a
'farmer', and at some point in the interview, when his son (JB) joins in, he
claims that theirs is not so much an 'agritourism' business as 'countryside
tourism' (cf. Mühlhäusler & Peace's (2001) 'nature-based tourism' mentioned above). This is confirmed by CB in response to the question
whether tourists find the farm 'exotic':

Extract 10

CB: Well, I mean if you say exotic, then probably not, and there are
    people who sometimes come and are disappointed [that it is not
    exotic]. But they are also content one could say, because visitors
    usually have the information and they usually know what they
    are coming to.
    ...

    when children come to me for the 'green lessons' I need to take
    them to my neighbour so that they can see a real cow and a pig.
    Well, we also have a duck in the garden but this is not enough for
    them to see a [working] farm. And what I noticed about agri-
    tourism, for someone like a visitor from Warsaw it's a good thing,
    this real agritourism, but not for long. When it stinks, then it also
    stinks for me, and when one steps in shit then this is too much.

In the above extracts, CB aligns himself more with his visitors from
towns rather than with his countryside neighbours – he does not keep
farm animals like his neighbours and finds the same things repulsive as
his visitors do. Indeed, in the second half of the extract, he seems to be
positioning himself rather as an educationalist.

Several interviewees mention domestic animals as a great attraction for
tourists, mostly for children, but usually involving observation from a
distance, stroking a horse and taking a photograph with a pig, rather than
any desire to help tend the animals. The same seems to be the case with
having a go at working in the fields, gardens and orchards – according to

our informants, tourists are not keen on trying their hand at such activities. Interestingly, in both cases, this contrasts with the marketing literature, which advocates participation in country life as one of the attractions of agritourism holidays.

In sum, all our interviewees seem to identify with their (Polish) visitors to a very considerable extent. Apart from the shared national and linguistic identity, all the other potential markers of difference such as regional distance, lack of familiarity (and fear of the 'Other') and professional/ status differential are either dismissed or overcome after initial contact. Consequently, the interviewees' foreground common interests and aspirations, establishing a friendly footing with the visitors, sharing recreational/leisure areas on the farms, enjoying or aspiring to similar lifestyles and dialectal levelling. Interestingly, we can observe some divergence from the traditionally rural allegiances, especially among the farmers who have categorically re-oriented to running their farms as agritourist businesses (e.g. CB).

Foreign tourists

The seven sites discussed here receive predominantly Polish tourists, except BW, who states that her house is popular with visitors from Italy, Sweden, Holland, Belgium, France, Ukraine and Germany, all of these nationalities featuring in her visitors' book. In the remaining cases, foreign visitors are far more infrequent, and many visitors who come from abroad are either Polish ex-pats or of Polish origin.

Of course, foreign visitors are much desired by our informants as they are seen as bigger spenders than their impoverished Polish counterparts. However, even when present, some interviewees state that their interpersonal contact with foreign visitors is 'more limited'. MM, who has received one family from Germany and one from Holland, admits that they 'keep more to themselves' although she tries to involve them in some joint activities such as horse-drawn cart rides, not least to allow her children to 'polish their [German] language skills'.

Other interviewees foreground the benefits of hosting foreigners rather than communication barriers. BW, seemingly with most experience in hosting foreign visitors among our interlocutors, is convinced that apart from the financial incentive of running the tourism business with foreign tourists in mind, contacts between her family and foreign visitors are socially and culturally beneficial to both parties.

Extract 11
BW: [showing AJ the visitors' book] And you know what, they like it
    very much that they are in our families and that they are getting
    to know our country and our culture inside out, living with us.

And they benefit from this because they draw their own conclusions [about us], which are different from the [negative] publicity we get in the world [AJ: yes, the stereotype] and they often say about this that they find it charming. And they usually come with a little apprehension about what will await them that we are still worse off, and then they are pleasantly surprised. What they say is not because we insist and ask them but really because of the way they behave and act with us, we can see that they are really feeling good with us. And, as I say, the only barrier here is that not all [the people] around here, typical farmers, can communicate [in a foreign language]. For example, we are OK that we have foreigners. Here's a gentleman from Holland, Labour Minister, and this gentleman here is our Council Chairman, and they ended here, and this lady from the Dutch Parliament, they ended their trip around Poland here, and they came here for one night. I don't know whether you know German [AJ: I'm afraid not] they wrote that they very (unclear) here they were for one night, but they liked it very much [AJ: and they liked the food, too]. Yes, the food, but they all like it here. Anyway, they are shocked. It amuses me always because when we serve food they take pictures or they ask me whether Poles always eat so much (laughs), because I serve buffet style. This is probably a Dutch lady and this gentleman, I am not sure, probably of English origin, something was there, but they were here only for a short time so I don't know.

BW sees her activities on an international scale helping Poland find the *right* position in the world. Foreigners staying with Polish families learn about *authentic* Poland ('inside out') and change their stereotypes shaped by foreign propaganda ('advertising in the world'). Even though they arrive apprehensive about the lower standards of living, they leave 'charmed' and 'pleasantly surprised'. BW knows about her foreign visitors' appreciation from their spontaneous comments and observing 'the way they act'; these comments suggest to indicate close contacts between hosts and their guests, although arguably in contrast to the relationships with Polish visitors, it takes more time to get to know foreign visitors well. For example, BW is not certain of the nationalities of her visitors who stayed with her 'only for a short time'.

BW also comments on the foreign language barrier which prevents other farmers from either developing tourist business or from receiving foreign visitors. This theme is further developed in the next two extracts.

Extract 12
BW: The only problem is that some people, I don't know, those who run such [agritourism] farms can't speak [a foreign language] on

the phone because most people make their bookings or enquiries about rooms on the phone. So, [we speak] a little English, that is, our daughter does, or our friend does, if she happens to be here when we have guests, and we can [speak] German, so that we often manage in German, and this is a plus, too. We have one German, who came here for two weeks and stayed eight. He's just been here for five weeks and he's coming again. Well, there are people who keep coming back and they feel good. Also a lady from Germany, also of Polish origin, she's already [booked] this year, she was here last year for the first time and she was also pleasantly surprised because she remembers Poland and the Polish countryside was so poor, so destitute, and she liked it [here] very much and she's sent us an email that she can't wait and wants to come for two weeks. So, there are quite a few guests like that and we are glad that they are happy and that they return, phone, keep in touch, email.

Extract 13

BW: With the first foreigners there was a slight worry because of the language barrier, you know, we know very little German, so we thought, because in the old times we did not study [languages] at school, one took the odd course or had some contact, one made trips to Germany, and suddenly you need to host a Dutch man, or talk with him on the phone, or a German. And now we sit down to dinner and the conversation really [flows]. They even asked us where we learnt [German] that we [speak] well. So we managed to communicate in every area: where we work, what we do, what we like and all sorts of topics, and now there are not so many barriers. I am even glad that the children have contact with the outside world, that they get to know various foreigners and this is also an advantage and I think that it is good for the typical farmers who look for additional income, and here lies the problem that the authorities should [help] because these [agri-tourism] farms are run by people like us, who bought something, who are more open to the world and some of these ideas catch on more quickly. I could not sit idly and these ordinary, simple country families, who fear everything, they do not have much assistance, they could make one or two rooms available to tourists. And the advantage for them and for their children for the youth would be such, because country youth unfortunately has low self-esteem, maybe because parents have less money, there is not enough money for culture, to go to the theatre, for all these things that one tries to give [to the children]. There are children who know what they want but there are many children who need such help and often their parents don't know how – this should be the way for them.

BW and her family had moved into their current house in the countryside three years before from the nearby town of Nowy Tomyśl with no prior agricultural experience and no intention of cultivating the land. BW's husband still works in Nowy Tomyśl and their two daughters go to school there. Yet, throughout the interview BW chooses to talk about herself as a 'farmer' and a member of the farming community in the area. This personal and group self-identification is undermined, however, in BW's alignment with her foreign visitors and in contrast to other farmers who are unable to communicate with foreigners. Her children have contact with the 'outside world', while those from the 'typical' farming families who do not run agritourism businesses because they 'fear everything' and don't know how to start the business – do not. Thus, they not only lose out financially, but also socially and culturally in that they are unable to break out from their parochialism.

BW positions herself in the world because she lives in an environment marked by the use of foreign languages: German (she and her husband) and English (her daughter and her friend). This allows her house to be a site of the international, if not yet global, flow of people who bring income and prestige to her daily life, and broader horizons to her children. Moreover, as hosts, BW's family identify with their foreign visitors by emphasising commonalities rather than differences between them: successful communication over shared meals to the point of the foreign visitors feeling good in their home, keeping in touch and returning in later years.

In contrast to the view of the domestic tourist who may be attracted to the farms by the benefits of the unspoilt ecology and traditional, healthy food, the foreign tourist is also offered the authentic experience of life with a Polish family. This selling of Polishness is primarily economically driven and construes foreigners as 'different' and in need of being 'educated' about Polish culture, customs, food, etc. However, contacts with foreigners and foreign language use seem to be desirable not just for economic gain but also because they allow hosts to make claims to internationality, which brings them prestige and cultural advancement, away from 'traditional' farming communities. Here, the Polish national identity fostered through contact with foreigners and bilingualism can be seen as a 'new' internationality based on embracing pan-European difference rather than intra-national sameness (Jaworski & Lawson, forthcoming).

Conclusion: The Pragmatics of Agritourism Business

Patterns of interaction between hosts and tourists in Polish agritourism suggest an ongoing change in the makeup and identity of rural communities.

The declared openness to the world and people which prompts many to run agritourism businesses goes hand-in-hand with the ideologising of self and other as 'same' rather than 'different'. Agritourism is no longer the domain of farmers (e.g. GD; AD1 and AD2; JP and SP). Lapsed farmers (CD, LB and JB), townies settling in the country (BW) and business-minded city dwellers (GP) change the social fabric of the Polish countryside with their preferred aspirations and alignments coinciding more with those of their visitors rather than traditional neighbours. They are intent on preserving the authenticity of their Polish lifestyle, unique landscape and heritage, but they are also keen on shedding the exoticising image of pre-modernity associated with poor education (e.g. lack of foreign languages) or dirty and smelly farm labour (e.g. raising cattle).

Polish agritourism is marketed both internationally and locally, although the majority of guests (as evidenced in our sample) are domestic. Interestingly, our interviewees suggest that extended interaction, mutual attraction and acceptance may transcend social, national and linguistic barriers. The small-scale of the operations and the running of the business as a family enterprise encourage involvement between tourists and hosts. Therefore, agritourism fosters relationships which are less fleeting than other forms of tourism, especially package holidays (see Jaworski *et al.*, 2003b), with the hosts striving to leave an individual mark on the tourists' experience and memory, beyond the anonymous, stereotyped yet 'safe' image of the local dominant in most genres of travel writing (e.g. Galasiński & Jaworski, 2003).

As a result of these contacts with tourists, it would appear that our interviewees are redefining and reinforcing themselves in terms of a local or Polish identity. For tourists to want to visit, the hosts need to market their local-ness, or, in the case of foreign tourists, their Polish-ness. So they stress the fact that they are 'different' because they come from different parts of Poland or Europe, but, as they get to know each other, they also emphasise the shared aspects of their identity, their *sameness*. This may include, as in the case of MM, the possibility for hosts to travel to tourists' home regions in a form of role reversal. However, as in many other tourist destinations, the recipients of the global flow, i.e. the hosts, have to embrace more of the visitors' culture than vice versa, as in the discussion of the need for foreign language learning. The foreign tourists moving in the global flow merely dip their toes into Polish culture. This can lead to a redefinition of the local, whereby modern local identities are reinforced and emergent global identities are created.

Acknowledgements

We are most grateful to all our interviewees, who generously gave us time and agreed to talk to us about their work. *Dziękujemy Państwu*. We thank Annette Pritchard for her useful comments on an earlier draft of this chapter, though we take the responsibility for what remains. The research for this paper was supported by funding from the Leverhulme Trust (Grant No. F/00 407/D) to the Centre for Language and Communication Research, Cardiff University, for a larger project on Language and Global Communication (www.global.cf.ac.uk).

References

Appadurai, A. (1990) Disjuncture and difference in the global cultural economy. *Theory, Culture and Society* 7, 295–310.

Bauman, Z. (1998) *Globalization: The Human Consequences*. Cambridge: Polity.

Bourdieu, P. (1991) *Language & Symbolic Power*. Edited and Introduced by J.B. Thompson. Translated by G. Raymond and M. Adamson. Cambridge: Polity Press.

Casey, R. (2003) Defining the local: The development of an 'environment culture' in a Clare village. In M. Cronin and B. O'Connor (eds) *Irish Tourism: Image, Culture and Identity* (pp. 42–60). Clevedon: Channel View Publications.

Coupland, N. and Ylänne-McEwen, V. (2000) Talk about the weather: Small talk, leisure talk and the travel industry. In J. Coupland (ed.) *Small Talk* (pp. 163–82). Harlow: Longman/Pearson Education.

Crashaw, C. and Urry, J. (1997) Tourism and the photographic eye. In C. Rojek and J. Urry (eds) *Touring Cultures* (pp. 176–95). London: Routledge.

Fairclough, N. (1989) *Language and Power*. London: Longman.

Galasiński, D. and Jaworski, A. (2003) Representations of hosts in travel writing: *The Guardian* Travel section. *Journal of Tourism and Cultural Change* 1 (2), 131–49.

Held, D. and McGrew, A. (2000) The great globalization debate: An introduction. In D. Held and A. McGrew (eds) *The Global Transformations Reader: An Introduction to the Globalization Debate* (pp. 1–45). Cambridge: Polity Press.

Hewison, R. (1987) *The Heritage Industry: Britain in a Climate of Decline*. London: Methuen.

Hoogvelt, A. (1997) *Globalisation and the Postcolonial World: The New Political Economy of Development*. Basingstoke: Macmillan.

Jameson, F. and Miyoshi, M. (eds) (1999) *The Cultures of Globalization*. Durham and London: Duke University Press.

Jaworski, A., Thurlow, C., Lawson, S. and Ylänne-McEwen, V. (2003a) The uses and representations of local languages in tourist destinations: A view from British TV holiday programmes. *Language Awareness* 12, 5–29.

Jaworski, A., Ylänne-McEwen, V., Thurlow, C. and Lawson, S. (2003b) Social roles and negotiation of status in host–tourist interaction: A view from British television holiday programmes. *Journal of Sociolinguistics* 7, 135–63.

Jaworski, A., Coupland, N. and Galasiński, D. (eds) (2004) *Metalanguage: Social and Ideological Perspectives*. Berlin: Mouton de Gruyter.

Jaworski A. and Lawson, S. (forthcoming) Polish agritourism: Bilingualism and 'new' internationalities.

Lash, S. and Urry, J. (1994) *Economies of Signs and Space*. London: Sage.

Lawson, S. and Jaworski, A. (2006) Shopping and chatting: Reports of tourist–host interaction in The Gambia. *Multilingua* 25.

MacCannell, D. (1989) *The Tourist* (2nd edn). London: Macmillan.

Macdonald, S. (1997) A people's story: Heritage, identity and authenticity. In C. Rojek and J. Urry (eds) *Touring Cultures: Transformation of Travel and Theory* (pp. 155–75). London: Routledge.

McCabe, S. and Stokoe, E.H. (2004) Place and identity in tourists' accounts. *Annals of Tourism Research* 31, 601–622.

Meethan, K. (2001) *Tourism in Global Society: Place, Culture, Consumption.* Basingstoke: Palgrave.

Morgan, N. and Pritchard, A. (1998) *Tourism, Promotion and Power: Creating Images, Creating Identities.* Chichester: John Wiley.

Mühlhäusler, P. and Peace, A. (2001) Discourses of ecotourism: The case of Fraser Island, Queensland. *Language & Communication* 21, 359–80.

Robertson, R. (1995) Glocalization: Time–space and homogeneity–heterogeneity. In M. Featherstone, S. Lash and R. Robertson (eds) *Global Modernities* (pp. 25–44). London: Sage.

Schieffelin, B.B., Woolard, K.A. and Kroskrity, P.V. (eds) (1998) *Language Ideologies: Practice and Theory.* New York: Oxford University Press.

Silverstein, M. (1979) Language structure and linguistic ideology. In P.R. Clyne, W.F. Hanks and C.L. Hofbauer (eds) *The Elements: A Parasession on Linguistic Units and Levels* (pp. 193–247). Chicago: Chicago Linguistic Society.

Silverstein, M. (2001) The limits of awareness. In A. Duranti (ed.) *Linguistic Anthropology: A Reader* (pp. 382–402). Oxford: Blackwell Publishers. [First published in 1981.]

Smith, V.L. (1989) Introduction. In V.L. Smith (ed.) *Hosts and Guests: The Anthropology of Tourism* (2nd edn) (pp. 1–17). Philadelphia: University of Pennsylvania Press.

Thompson, J.B. (2000) The globalization of communication. In D. Held and A. McGrew (eds) *The Global Transformations Reader: An Introduction to the Globalization Debate* (pp. 202–15). Cambridge: Polity Press..

Urry, J. (2002) *The Tourist Gaze* (2nd edn). London: Sage. [First published in 1990].

Wearing, B. and Wearing, S. (1996) Refocusing the tourist experience: The 'flâneur' and the 'choraster'. *Leisure Studies* 15, 229–44.

Woolard, K.A. (1998) Introduction: Language ideology as a field of inquiry. In B.B. Schieffelin, K.A. Woolard and P.V. Kroskrity (eds) *Language Ideologies: Practice and Theory* (pp. 3–47). New York: Oxford University Press.

Wright, P. (1995) *The Village that Died for England: The Strange Story of Tyneham.* London: Jonathan Cape.

WTO (2003) www.world-tourism.org.

Appendix 1

The following are the seven promotional texts used in this study for backgrounding Polish agritourism. The language(s) of publication are indicated in parentheses.

(1) Ecotourism in the Lubuskie Region. Publisher unknown (Polish, English).

(2) The Town and Commune of Nowy Tomyśl. Published by Commune and Town of Nowy Tomyśl (Polish, English, German).

(3) Holiday on Organic Farms in Poland. nd. Published by European Centre for Agricultural and Ecological Tourism – Poland (Polish, English).

(4) Agrotourist Farms (in Nowy Tomyśl Region). n.d. Published by Nowy Tomyśl Department of Promotion and the Agritourism Association). (Polish, English, German, French).

(5) Agritourism in Poland Catalogue. n.d. Published by Indeed Poland (English).

(6) Międzychód: A Region of 100 Lakes. n.d. Published by Międzychód Council (Polish, English, German).
(7) Agriholidays – 'Willow by the Wood'. nd. Published privately (Polish, English, Italian).

Appendix 2

Polish originals of extracts translated into English in the text. The transcription conventions are as follows: = – contiguous speech; : – lengthening; underline – marked emphasis; CAPS – louder than normal voice; k- kłopoty – truncated speech; (.) – pause under 1 second; (1) – timed pause measured in seconds; (laughs) – nonverbal and other contextual information; .hhh – audible outbreath ? – rising intonation not always signifying a question.

Extract 1
MM: w: tej chwili już drugi sezon przyjedzie rodzina z Gdyni, gdzie ja (.) zupełnie byłam zdziwiona mówię co oni tutaj mają do szuka-nia właściwie z: morza nad nad no też nad wodę właściwie bo tutaj jest gro jezior .hhh i tak sobie: dziwnie tą ofertę odebrałam dlaczego tak to to się odbywa?

Extract 2
BW: pierwszych gości przyznam się panu że byla obawa nawet nie z mojej strony tylko mąż bardzo pierwszy rok nawet musiałam odmawiać gdzies tam krecić że jeszcze mam zajęte czy coś bo mąż mówi gdzie obcych ludzi tak jakoś tam strach nie wiadomo kto tam przyjedzie różne rzeczy się zdarzają są w naszym domu są razem śpimy coś się może wydarzyć gdzies tam gdzieś gdzieś tam jakiś strach tym bardziej że tu nas okradli i jakieś różne historie bo to jest gdzieś w lesie gdzieś samotnie ale pierwszych ludzi przyjęliśmy naprawdę byli ludzie wspaniali i wykształceni tam zajmowali się własnie terapią medycyny manualnej takich różnych rzeczy ciekawych tu nam też i oni własnie jako pierwsi i mąż się przekonał że że wspaniali i w ogóle nie koliduje z naszym życiem a jakiś pieniądz przyplynął i to jeszcze było przyjemne kiedy oni coś tam pochwalili podziwiali że my sami remontujemy wszystko robimy sami gdzieś tam

Extract 3
MM: podejmując się: y: tej tej dodatkowej działalności .hhh miałam na uwadze że mam takie dzieci własnie szkolne gdzie no: żyjemy w środowisku małomiasteczkowym mamy ograniczone możliwości własciwie takiego rozwoju poza szkołą podstawową jakimiś zainteresowaniami jezeli jeżeli takie są .hhh a: kontakt

właśnie z innymi ludzmi ktorymi no: n:ie wiem kto tutaj przyjedzie są naprawde różne .hhh różne kontakty .hhh właśnie
oczekuję oczekiwałam tego tego typowego kontaktu i rozwoju
właśnie dzieci to to właściwie taki był jeden z ważniejszych
punktów poza poza tym [finansowym?] i: bardzo szybko to
sprocentowało bardzo szybko zawiązay sie przyjaźnie i to jest
takie też dla mnie przyjemne

Extract 4

MM: w ubiegłym roku był pan który (.) właściwie dwadzieścia lat
podróżował po (.) świecie (.) .hhh i: i: po prostu już w tej chwili
można powiedzieć ma wszystko porobione poukładane na tyle
że że że odpoczywa .hhh i tutaj trafił i właśnie on on tak y:
uzmysłowił że że powinniśmy to doceniać co tutaj mamy
własciwie bo .hhh zwiedził takie zakątki: gdzie my żeśmy nie
byli bo taki był dociekliwy miał tyle czasu (.) .hhh że nawet nie
przeszkodziło mu to że żona rękę złamała na rowerze dalej
podróżowali dalej chodzili tam w te miejsca mie- nie do zdobycia
i właściwie nas niejednokrotnie zawstydzał że że p- po prostu
cudze chwalicie można powiedzieć tak potocznie swego nie
znacie .hhh i to nas też zmobilizowalo dlatego właśnie mówię
wymusza coś takiego żeby poznać lepiej ten swój teren czy .hhh
dzieci właśnie żeby się wgłębiły czy .hhh czy ostatnio nawet w:
przed ubiegłym sezonem mieliśmy zorganizowany kurs dla
przewodników przez y: pana Łęckiego miłośnika tutaj naszych
terenow .hhh także to też mówię mobilizuje i właściwie
wymusza w nas jakąś pracę nad nad sobą

Extract 5

AD1: wie pan co o wszystkim (.) o wszystkim mnie interesuje na
przykład co co oni robią gdzie oni pracują po prostu w roz-
mowie ja pytam zadaję pytania bo mnie to naprawdę ciekawi
interesuje (.) y: o pogodzie (.) o naszej pracy bo też też też są
ciekawi też też się tam wypytują

Extract 6

AD1: także że że no także żeby rzeczywiście no czymś byli zdziwieni
bo to już nie jest taka wieś jak jak mówię jak ludzie sobie nieraz
wyobrażają nie że kiedyś pan dzwonił (1.0) no i tak nie wiedział
bardzo jak ma zadać to pytanie no wie pani mówi no to jest wieś
ja mówię no niech się pan nie martwi wychodka za stodołą nie
ma (laughs)

AD1: nie nie zdarzyło się nie zdarzyło się to znaczy się no na pewno
ta nasza y gwara tutaj znaczy się ta poznańska jest taka śpiewna

i chociaż człowiek mówi poprawną polszczyzną bez tej bez tej to jednak y: to jest ale ni nie zdarzyło się żeby tak żeby no to znaczy się staramy się już nie nie mówimy tak typowo po wiejsku jak to się mówi staramy się po prostu i dzieci tak uczę też bo to jest ważne moim zdaniem gwara jest piękna rzecz piękna sprawa ale wiadomo że że że w kontaktach między ludźmi to (.) mówi się czysto po polsku (.)

Extract 7

CD: no i ona właśnie taką jarską kuchnię bo ona tam ma jakieś sprawy te i ja tak się bardzo bałam mówi że nie może ona była tak sympatyczna pani że (.) na przykład wystarczyło że na śniadanie to wystarczyło że miała tam biały ser i pomidory i to wystarczyło to już byli tak przyjemni ja ja to się bałam że że pan profesor przyjedzie była tak sympatyczna pani przysyłali kartki chcieli przyjechać i ona tam miała jeszcze jakieś k-kłopoty zdrowotne nie (.) także jak robiłam obiad to tam tą rybę ugotowałam nie zamiast smażyć (.) no ale była tak sympatyczna pani (.) no i przysyłali nam z: dwa lata z rzędu nie (.) kartki (.) i że jeszcze przyjadą nie (2.0) no ona tam bardzo choruje (.) tu oni oni bardzo fajnie (.) tu swoje przywieźli taki swój stojaczek do pracy ta pani pracowała o tu pod tym siedziała sobie także bardzo fajnie

Extract 8

AJ: a jak jest y: (.) z gośćmi którzy wracają czy to już czy oni wracają jako znajomi czy=

AD1: =tak TAA:K jako utrzymujemy kontakty y: kartki świąteczne to już obowiązkowo a jeżeli nie kartka to ten telefon (.) co jakiś czas a jak tam zdrowie i to i tamto także utrzymujemy kontakty z: gośćmi z tymi którzy oczywiście chcą=

Extract 9

CB: no to tak (.) tak jest różnie z reguły no to no to my zapalamy ognisko (.) ten przyjdzie tamten (.) kontakt jest tam no na sali duży tutaj przyjdzie oglądać telewizor jeden pograć coś drugi wypić piwo (.) i tam jest ten największy kontakt

Extract 10

CB: no znaczy mówiąc o egzotyce to może nie ale zdarzają się ludzie że są i zawiedzeni (.) NO o zachwyceni ale i ZAdowoleni o tak można by powiedzieć (.) no ale y: ale teraz jedynie gość ma taką informację z reguły goście już wiedza po co przyjeżdżają tu (.) […]

do mnie jak przyjadą dzieci na te tak zwane zielone szkoły (.) to ja muszę do sąsiada ich zaprowadzić żeby zobaczyli sobie krowę

świnię (.) no tam kaczka tam też u nas w ogrodzie jest ale to jest za
mało żeby akurat widziały to o gospodarstwo rolne (.) no: z tym
że (.) tak co zaobserwowałem (.) agroturystyka dla takiego gościa
z Warszawy (.) to jest fajna rzecz (.) ta prawdziwa agroturystyka (.)
ale nie na długo (.) jak za długo śmierdzi to to nawet mi śmierdzi
a jak się wdepnie raz taki w gówno to już jest też za dużo

Extract 11
BW: i wie pan co że bardzo im się to podoba że są w tych naszych w
tych naszych rodzinach i zarazem tak od podszewki nasz kraj
naszą kulturę poznają bo obcując z nami właśnie z tego wyciągają
korzyści że całkiem zmieniają zdanie o nas bo gdzieś tam ta
reklama w świecie jest inna o nas [AJ: tak tak stereotyp] i i niejednokrotnie mówią o tym, że są właściwie zaczarowani i w ogóle
przyjeżdżają z takim lekka lekkim niepokojem co tu ich będzie
czekać czy tu jeszcze u nas jest gorzej niż a: a: potem są rzeczywiście mile zaskoczeni to co mówią zresztą to sami mówią to nie
wychodzi tam że my tam nalegamy i pytamy ale rzeczywiście po
sposobie zachowania się i bycia tu z nami widzimy że rzeczywiście dobrze się czują z nami i mówię no jedyna bariera że
jeszcze nie wszyscy tutaj wszyscy tacy typowo gospodarze
potrafią się porozumieć na przykład u nas jest to dobre że mam
cudzoziemców o własnie tu jest pan z Holandii minister od pracy
a ten pan to jest u nas wojewoda i tu właśnie kończyli a ta pani z
Parlamentu Holenderskiego kończyli podróż po Polsce i właśnie
jeszcze na jedną noc zatrzymali się tutaj nie wiem czy pan po
niemiecku umie [AJ: nie niestety nie] pisali że że że bardzo
(unclear) tu jedna noc byli ale w każdym bądź razie że bardzo im
sie tu podobało [AJ i smakowało im również] tak tak tak jedzenie
ale tu im wszstkim smakuje w ogóle ich tu szokuje zawsze mnie
to śmieszy bo jak podajemy do stolu to robią zdjęcie albo mi się
pytają czy my Polacy tyle jemy (laughs) bo ja tu na przykład
serwuję sze- szwedzki stół tu chyba Holenderka ale ten pan nie
wiem czy też pochodzenia angielskiego coś tam było o tym że oni
też krótko byli także nie wiem

Extract 12
BW: jedyny problem że: rzeczywiście nieraz ludzie nie wiem co
prowadzą takie gospodarstwa nie umieją się rozmówić przez
telefon bo gro właśnie zamawia czy pyta się o kwatere przez
telefon także no tu trochę w angielskim to córka tu koleżanka
nieraz akurat trafiła na gości jak jest a my potrafimy po niemiecku
także często siv właśnie dogadujemy po niemiecku i to jest też
plusem no mamy takiego Niemca który przyjechał na dwa tygod-

nie a był osiem tygodni teraz znowu był pięc tygodni znowu przyjedzie także no są osoby ktore wracają i dobrze się czują też taka pani z Niemiec też polskiego pochodzenia już teraz na ten rok zeszłego roku była pierwszy raz też była mile zaskoczona bo pamięta Polske i polską wieś taką ubogą taką nedzną i i: bardzo sie jej podobało już teraz nam emaila przysłała że już się nie może doczekać i chce na dwa tygodnie przyjechać także także trochę gości się przewija i: i: i: cieszy to że są zadowoleni i że powracają dzwonią kontaktują się emaile

Extract 13

BW: pierwszych cudzoziemców też była jakas obawa bo bariera językowa wiadomo umiemy ten niemiecki Kali umie Kali zje tak nam sie uważało bo bo tak za tych czasów nie uczyliśmy się w szkole gdzieś tam na jakimś kursie gdzieś tam był kontakt że się jeździło do Niemiec a tu nagle trzeba przyjąć Holendra albo porozmawiać z nim przez telefon czy Niemca a tu przy kolacji siadało się i rzeczywiście ta rozmowa nawet nas się pytali gdzie się nauczyliśmy że dobrze gdzieś tam się porozu- szło się dogadać w każdej dziedzinie gdzie pracujemy czym się zajmuje- my co lubimy i na różne tematy i to w tej chwili już nie ma takich barier nawet ja się cieszę bo dzieci mają kontakt z tym światem zewnętrznym gdzieś tam poznają różnych cudzoziemców i to też jest plus i sadzę że własnie to jest też dobre dla tych typowo rolników gdzie to wiejskich rodzin gdzie szukają tego dodatkowego źródła i właśnie tu jest problem że władze właśnie powinni bo często tymi gospodarstwami się zajmują ludzie właśnie tacy jak my kupili gdzieś tam są bardziej otwarci na świat i gdzieś tam te pomysły szybciej chwytają ja bym nie umiała bezczynnie siedzieć a często ta zwykła prosta własnie takie rodziny wiejskie gdzie boją się tego wszystkiego nie mają tego wsparcia myślę mogliby takie dwa pokoje jeden udostępniać i to takie plusy i dla nich i dla tych dzieci dla tej młodzieży bo taka jest prawda że wiejska młodzież niestety jest bardziej zakom- pleksiona gdzieś tam przez to że może mniej pięniedzy rodzice mają gdzieś tam nie ma środków na kulturę na bywanie w teatrze na te wszystkie rzeczy które składa się na pomoc są dzieci które wiedzą czego chcą ale są dużo jest takich dzieci którzy które potrzebuje właśnie pomocy a często ci rodzice nie nie umieją to by był też sposób dla nich

Chapter 7
Tourist or Traveller?
Narrating Backpacker Identity

CAMILLE C. O'REILLY

Introduction

This chapter addresses the topical issue of backpacker travel, focusing on the impact of this experience on the traveller's identity and sense of self. Over the past few decades, long-term independent travel has moved from being a marginal and unusual activity to a rite of passage associated with ideals of youthful freedom, personal development and fulfilment. A growing number of people are taking the time to travel long-term, beyond the usual allotted holiday time, and more are venturing to 'difficult' destinations. Travelling for months or even years at a time, they range from young people taking a 'gap year' before further study or work to those seizing an opportunity to escape from personal problems, responsibilities or simple drudgery. Long-term international travel on a low budget has been made possible by economic and political developments brought about by globalisation, and in turn it is contributing to the cultural changes that are said to characterise the post-modern era.

The roots of this current form of long-term, long-haul tourism lie in other historic modes of travel, including early European exploration and the 'Grand Tour' of the 17th and 18th centuries. Adler (1985) suggests that 'tramping' might also be a historic antecedent. The labour-related travel of the lower classes was a sort of working man's grand tour, an institutionalised and respected pattern of travel that peaked in the 19th century and thereafter shifted from employment-related travel to something more like 'pure' tourism. Cohen (1973) writes about the phenomenon of 'drifter' travel of the 1960s and 1970s. Sometimes referred to as 'hippie' travel in places like India, it is perhaps a more direct precursor of at least some of today's backpacker travel. Of the four types of international tourist described by Cohen (1972), the drifter has least contact with the tourist industry, has no fixed itinerary or timetable, travels on a more limited budget and is more of a risk-taker. Riley (1988) provides a more recent update on the phenomenon, arguing that by the 1980s the characterisation of long-term budget travellers as hedonistic and anarchistic drifters was no longer accurate. Rather, 'the average traveller prefers to travel alone, is educated, European, middle-class, single, obsessively concerned with budgeting his/her money, and at a juncture in life' (Riley, 1988: 313). Although my own field research was carried out at least 15 years later than Riley's, her description of budget travellers might just as well have been written to characterise a significant segment of backpacker travellers on the road today (but see Davidson, this volume, for an argument against treating all 'alternative' travellers as a 'monolith').

Brown (1996) suggests that tourism is characterised by a tension between the pursuit of authenticity in the 'Other' and the search for an authentic 'Self' through experience and spectacle. In this chapter, I want to focus primarily on the pursuit of self through the experience of backpacker travel. I intend to approach the topic of identity from two related angles – the labels that travellers use to identify themselves and the activity they are undertaking, and the process of narrating their experiences. The analysis is based on extensive fieldwork with long-term independent travellers and material posted onto backpacker-oriented internet sites. The internet sites used are the discussion forums on www.bootsnall.com and 'The Thorntree' on the Lonely Planet website www.lonelyplanet.com. Discussions on these sites are organised according to subject, and topics are usually initiated by forum members. I have monitored the sites for a number of years, particularly BootsnAll.com. During a period of more intensive involvement over three months I read relevant discussions in the archives, and followed active threads as they unfolded. During this time I participated in and also initiated a number of discussions, some directly aimed at eliciting relevant material (though these were less successful than more indirect questions about current topics).

The fieldwork involved 11 months of travel on a number of backpacker circuits including eastern and southern Africa, India, Southeast Asia, Central America, Australia and New Zealand. The majority of fieldwork was carried out between June 2000 and January 2002. During this time I travelled as a backpacker, and I believe I was accepted as one of them. In addition to participant observation along backpacker circuits, I interviewed 30 backpackers while on the road. Most of these interviews were audio-recorded, taking place in a variety of locations. For example, interviews in Africa tended to take place outdoors at campsites, while those in Sydney, Australia, usually took place in a hostel, café or bar. A further 23 interviews were with travellers who had returned from backpacking more than a year before the interview. These took place in England in the first half of 2003, and were conducted over the telephone or in person. Most of these interviews were not recorded, but notes were taken on the computer while they took place. Participants were not directly asked about self-labelling in either set of interviews. The material used in this chapter was offered during the course of discussions about how the person became interested in travelling, where they had been, and why travelling was meaningful or important to them.

Interestingly, the British and some other northern Europeans (particularly Scandinavians and Irish) dominate the backpacking scene, and they remain the focus in this chapter. Southern Europeans and Americans tend not to engage in this form of travel in large numbers. While Israelis, Australians and New Zealanders do backpack in significant numbers, they do so in a different manner than Europeans in terms of routes, orientation and perhaps also attitudes and approach. Unfortunately, there is not the space to deal with these contrasts in this chapter, but for a discussion of Israeli backpackers see Uriely *et al*. (2002).

Contexts

'Wherever we happen to be at the moment, we cannot help knowing that we could be elsewhere, so there is less and less reason to stay anywhere in particular' (Bauman, 1998: 77). This could be the lament – or the call to action – of the long-term traveller, the global nomad continually in search of the next destination in pursuit of adventure, experience and authenticity. Processes of globalisation have made this pursuit both more accessible and more desirable to increasingly large numbers of people. The multi-dimensional processes of globalisation encompass economic, political and cultural spheres, which is reflected in the rise in backpacker tourism. Cheap airfares are indicative of the link between economic and conceptual aspects of the post-modern, post-Fordist condition – travel to virtually any part of the globe is affordable for a large proportion of the population of the Western world. Whether or not they ever take up the opportunity, this feeds into an imagining of other countries as potential tourist destinations and objects of desire.

The exotic 'Other' is more accessible and seemingly more knowable than ever before. As the pursuit of the authentic in the Other has characterised Western attitudes to travel, it was almost inevitable that the increasing ease of travel and the relative nearness of a myriad of exotic Others would engender something like long-term independent travel. Those who in the past might have chosen to become colonial administrators or missionaries now 'see the world' as global nomads – long-term travellers or employees of multi-national corporations – or both in succession, the former providing valuable experience for the latter. They are joined at some of the 'easier' destinations by the less adventurous, contributing to the swell in numbers of long-term travellers in recent years. These are people who might never have ventured far from home in the past when travel was more difficult and potentially dangerous, but have now taken advantage of the relative ease and affordability of long-haul travel.

The very accessibility of distant locations contributes to what some have called time–space compression (cf. Harvey, 1989). Our ability to move through space is no longer constrained by vast expanses of time: we can reach the other side of the world in less than a day by air, and instantaneously via the internet. While Urry points out that virtual travel and virtual proximity via e-mail and the internet may gradually dissolve the distinctions between online and offline, the increased contact and information thus engendered may well heighten the desire to be corporeally present in a place and hence to travel there (Urry, 2002: 268–9). Clearly there have been large-scale interactions that spanned the globe for many centuries, including the activities of explorers, pilgrims and colonial authorities, all of whom might be considered the precursors to today's tourists and backpackers. Although globalisation is not an entirely new phenomenon (cf. Robertson, 1992), it has certainly accelerated over the past century. The key differences today are the intensity and immediacy of contact, the post-colonial context and in the case of travel and tourism, the sheer numbers involved.

For backpackers, there is both an expectation and acceptance of this new context of intense and immediate global connections. Most are young enough to take it entirely for granted, and many backpackers appear to revel in the speed and intensity of jet propelled global nomadism. Contact with the comfort of home, when needed, is easily found almost anywhere in the world in the now ubiquitous internet café. Yet at the same time a key focus of backpacker travel, as with some other forms of tourism, is the search for authenticity. MacCannell suggests that 'for moderns, reality and authenticity are thought to be elsewhere: in other historical periods and other cultures, in purer, simpler life-styles' (1976: 3). Cultures that have supposedly remained 'untouched', 'traditional' and unchanged by modernity are actively sought, to the extent that some wholeheartedly believe the popular myth that the remote villagers of this or that locale have never seen a white person (Cohen, 1989). I encountered this myth on numerous occasions during the course of my research, both in my personal contacts with backpackers and in postings on traveller's websites.

Some theorists have rejected the idea of authenticity as a concept no longer relevant to the post-modern world (Baudrillard, 1983; Eco, 1987; and in relation to tourism – Rojek, 1993, 1995). As with most aspects of post-modernist theory, however, this argument can be taken too far. A post-modernist embracing of fakes and reproductions has not entirely overtaken the modernist craving for authenticity (cf. Coupland *et al.*, this volume), and certainly not in backpacker circles where the search for the authentic Other is alive and well. The paradox of the long-haul traveller who apparently feels perfectly at home in post-modern consumer society, yet seeks evidence of a way of life more 'authentic' and 'real' than their own is worth further investigation, but is unfortunately beyond the scope of this chapter (for a more detailed discussion see O'Reilly, forthcoming c).

Independent travellers seek out new and 'untouched' locations across the globe – ironically, often bringing mass tourism in their wake (Cohen, 1982; Aziz, 1999; Hampton, 1998, 1999). This raises important issues relating to connections between travel, neo-colonialism and globalisation. While many young backpackers are politically liberal and would sympathise with the anti-globalisation protests of recent years, the very act of travel is made possible by, indeed contributes to, the forces of globalisation. As Selwyn has highlighted, there are three key foundations of international tourism: it is organised on the axis of 'centre' and 'periphery', it is defined by global consumer culture, and much of tourism is concerned with a search for the 'authentic' (Selwyn, 1996: 9). Long-term independent travel raises fundamental questions about the nature of north/south relations, consumerism and mobility in the 21st century, and the increasing division of the world's population into what Bauman (1998) refers to as 'tourists' and 'vagabonds'.

Bauman's work offers insights into mobility that are particularly useful in understanding the position of backpackers in post-modern consumer society. He suggests that a key form of social stratification is now along dimensions of mobility – the freedom to choose where to be. Those 'high up' on the scale of stratification – 'tourists' by Bauman's definition – have lots of it. They can 'pick and choose their destinations according to the joys they offer' (1998: 86). 'Tourists' become wanderers because they want to. They may consider wandering to be an acceptable, even profitable, life-strategy, or they may have succumbed to the appeal of 'the true or imaginary pleasures of a sensations-gatherer's life' (1998: 92). Those low down on the scale of freedom to choose, the 'vagabonds', move because they feel they have no other bearable alternative, or because they have been thrown out from the place where they would prefer to be. Backpackers could be characterised as 'tourists' playing at being 'vagabonds', enjoying the privileges of the tourist but all the while toying with the image of the vagabond. A post-modern version of 'slumming it', this flirtation with vagabondage gives long-term independent travel a certain edginess, a tension that is compelling and for some, addictive. In his book describing the overland trail to India of the 1960s, for example, Tomory (1998) describes how some travellers can lose their access to privileged mobility, whether by accident or by voluntarily renouncing it.

A Tourist by any Other Name?

What makes a travelling individual a backpacker? From a researcher's perspective it can be difficult to clearly distinguish 'backpacker' travel from other types of tourism, mainly because of the variety of factors that need to be considered, along with individual variation in travelling habits. Inevitably, any attempt of classification will be confronted by the fuzziness of boundaries; nevertheless, it is possible to identify three broad ways of characterising backpacker travel. The first two relate to what Uriely *et al.* (2002) call 'form-related attributes' – length of time on the road (usually six months or more, sometimes extending for a period of years), and mode of travel (transport and subsistence on a very low budget, overland travel whenever possible, with levels of comfort not a primary consideration). However, probably the most important characteristic is what I call *orientation towards the task of travel* (a 'type-related attribute', in Uriely *et al.*'s terminology).

Put simply, backpackers embrace serendipity. Low levels of advance planning, no fixed timetable, an openness to change of plan or itinerary – these are the virtues preached by the faithful. The ideal traveller, at least in the eyes of most backpackers, very much resembles Cohen's (1979) drifter tourist. The extent to which backpackers conform to this ideal as they travel, however, is another matter entirely. The balance between serendipity and planning varies a great deal between backpackers, and even for the same individual during the course of a trip as the person's mood, health and desires change.

Regardless of how outsiders may perceive them, long-term globe-trotters use different labels to describe themselves, with the favourites being either backpacker or traveller. Some admit to being just another tourist, but these are few and far between. Tourist, traveller, or backpacker? The choice of label can generate a surprising amount of emotional debate. What are people trying to communicate through their choice of a particular label, or conscious rejection of another?

Any label can carry multi-faceted and sometimes contradictory meanings, and those used by long-term independent travellers are no exception. 'Tourist' is generally seen as the most pejorative from the perspective of the independent traveller. It implies following the herd, mass travel lacking in the values idealised by most backpackers. Tourists are not independent or adventurous, and do not attempt to explore 'off the beaten track'. They desire a mediated experience – they do not want to get to know a place, local people or their culture. The epithet 'tourist' is reserved for short-term, non-exotic travel or package tourism. Calling an independent traveller a tourist is likely to raise hackles and even cause serious offence. Yet a minority of backpackers are willing to admit that they really are just another type of tourist, although the positive value attached to their own mode of travel usually remains. This is illustrated by the quotes form the BootsnAll.com forum below.

The negative view of tourists and tourism is not unique to independent travellers. It has been picked up by the media and by the tourism industry itself, to the extent that a certain degree of 're-branding' has taken place at the upper end of the tourism market to avoid the negative connotations of these terms. Eco-tourism, supposedly culturally sensitive travel, charity tourism, and so on, have moved the emphasis away from travel purely for selfish reasons, attempting to imbue an aura of social responsibility to the activity. Backpackers, too, tend to see themselves as having less of a negative impact on host communities and places they visit than other types of tourists (Wilson, 1997; Hampton, 1998, 1999).

'Traveller' is the term preferred by most backpackers. If being a tourist is perceived negatively, being a traveller is positively valued. In this context the word embodies ideals of independence, mobility and freedom. It suggests that the journey itself is the focus, not just arriving at the intended destination. Using the term allows the interlocutor to tap into discourses of adventure and exploration, invoking all the assumed bravery and accomplishment of early (European) travellers. Unwittingly, of course, they are also tapping into the discourses of colonialism and imperialism, invoking the unequal global power relationships that have put Europeans in a position to have such adventures abroad. I will consider this contradiction briefly below. Finally, travelling is believed to allow the traveller to accrue cultural and symbolic capital, useful both on the road and on the return home (O'Reilly, forthcoming c). Being a tourist does not.

'Backpacker' is an alternative term commonly used by long-term independent travellers, but it is not as universally acceptable a term as 'traveller'. In high traffic areas such as Southeast Asia and particularly Australia, the term has taken on negative implications, suggesting for many a person who is mean with money, does not mix with locals, stays in grotty hostels because they are cheap, and spends an inordinate amount of time drinking, partying and taking illicit drugs. Although still commonly used and not always pejoratively, it has lost most of its street 'cred' with the advent of the 'mass backpacker' market, and in the wake of floods of gap year travellers clutching their Lonely Planet *Southeast Asia on a Shoestring* guidebooks. In spite of these difficulties, I use the term mainly as convenient shorthand for long-term, long-haul independent travellers.

Debates over whether to call oneself a traveller, tourist or backpacker are commonplace. It is surprising the amount of self-reflection that can occur when independent travellers get together. I have overheard and participated in numerous such conversations in the course of my travels, often quite heated. This is, perhaps, a measure of the importance of the experience of travel in some people's lives. An interesting example of one such debate, unusual because it has been recorded in its entirety, takes place on a traveller's website. BootsnAll.com describes itself as 'the ultimate resource for the independent traveller'. It is run by a few young men of various nationalities currently living in Oregon, USA. At time of writing one of the BootsnAll.com team had set up base in Bali, Indonesia, and another was about to do the same in Australia. The site includes places to post traveller's tales sorted by geographical location, a section for advice from fellow travellers, and discussion forums with a variety of threads that can carry on for months or even years.

One lengthy thread is on the topic of 'Travellers vs. Tourists', started in December 1999. Most postings took place over the following year, but it continues to gain contributions up to the present day. An interesting side discussion on this thread concerns labels assigned to contributions as they appear on the site. When you first sign up as a member the moniker 'tourist' appears after your first five postings, indicating your status as a new member. Once you have participated by making more than five postings, this moniker automatically alters to 'traveller'. A number of indignant postings appear in this discussion thread, protesting at having the word 'tourist' involuntarily put after their name, indicating quite clearly the extent to which people wish to avoid that label. The monikers were recently changed to Package Tourist, Contiki Bus Bunny, Armchair Traveller, and Vagabonder. The value hierarchy is still clear, and another thread is dedicated to discussing which moniker is attached to which member, and how many postings are required in order to move up the levels to the esteemed Vagabonder.

The following selection of contributions highlights the key points of the debate over labels made above, and gives a feel for common opinions on the matter. The contributions did not appear in this order. I have selected these as an interesting and reasonably representative set of comments (original spelling and style is preserved throughout).

Peter: A tourist is a person who 'visits' a country. A traveller is a person who 'gets into' a country. He/she will travel around more, get to know the customs, the people, the food and generally integrate more.

Plasticpaddy: Tourists have more money and less time. Travellers vice versa.

Frenchstick: Well basically, a traveller is a tourist who thinks they're better than a tourist cuz they're tight and live on a budget and hence have less of a cultural impact.

Bob the Dog: A traveller is leading a certain lifestyle. A tourist is just on holiday.

Lalacorpuz: It's the state of mind to start with. A traveller is instinctive, perceptive, open, a truth seeker, curious, independent minded and unafraid of changes. A tourist is only comfortable with stereotypes, narrow

	minded, a list maker, afraid of changes and not have their own mind.
Bewdy:	I have a label for you – anyone who tries to judge and pigeonhole others on such subjective grounds is a wanker!
John Glasscock:	My definition: tourist::destination traveller::journey.
Edbh:	What about backpackers? Tourist – tries to see lots of things in a short period of time. Traveller – tries to see lots of things in a long period of time. Backpacker – doesn't care what s/he sees as long as never has to go home.
Tokisi:	Travellers don't know where they're going and tourists don't know where they've been. (BootsnAll.com 2003a)

As this small selection suggests, the emphasis is clearly on the journey and getting to know local people and their culture, often accompanied by an assertion that travelling is a lifestyle or a 'state of mind'. Comparisons with mere tourists are almost always negative, used to highlight the virtues of travellers over tourists, as in the contribution by Lalacorpuz. Persistent themes appear throughout this thread highlighting the differences between tourists and travellers:

- Length of time on the road – travellers stay away from home longer, and do not face the same time constraints as tourists. This has an influence on how they travel, including what I have called the freedom to embrace serendipity.
- Budget, especially the idea that backpackers have more time than money, or that they give more of their money to the local economy – some suggest that it is not just the amount of money a traveller has, but how they choose to spend it.
- And perhaps most importantly, contributors emphasise the attitude of the traveller towards the journey, the destination and the people encountered along the way. The idea that travellers approach the task of travel differently from other tourists is important, and is often raised as the essential difference between tourists and travellers.

When backpackers do admit that there is no real difference between tourists and travellers they still tend to assert that there can be significant differences in approach to travel. What matters is not how much time you have, how much money you spend or what sort of accommodation you choose. Rather, it is openness to experience in a new place and how this affects you – it is the self that matters, and the transformative power of travel is frequently invoked. Occasionally, contributors take a more straightforward approach and suggest efforts to distinguish between travellers and tourists are nothing more than inverted snobbery, but this is very much a minority opinion.

'I Am a Traveller, Not a Tourist': Narrating Identity

People can potentially use travel to re-invent their identity on two inter-related levels – the collective and the individual. The latter has to do with a person's sense of self. The former might include, for example, class. Backpacker travel is largely (though not exclusively) a middle-class activity, and can be used to assert – or refute – a particular class position. While on the road travellers often indulge in a degree of 'slumming it', flirting with the experience of poverty and rejecting middle-class values however temporarily, while having that all-important safety net should they need it. In essence they are tourists in Bauman's sense of the word, and not vagabonds. The cultural and symbolic capital that travel affords can be used to enhance position and status when the period of travel is over, but for most backpackers it is not likely to significantly alter their class position.

On the return home, a period of extended travel can be presented as a badge of social status to peer groups and employers. My own research and that of others (see, e.g. Riley, 1988) suggests that many travellers do use their experience to improve employment prospects, an area that encompasses aspects of both collective and individual identity. Handled in a particular way, taking a year out to travel can communicate qualities that many employers find desirable – particularly in relation to what Urry (1995: 167) calls 'aesthetic cosmopolitanism'. Urry's model of aesthetic cosmopolitanism includes: the idea that one has the *right* to travel anywhere and to consume all environments; a *curiosity* about all places, peoples and cultures; an *openness* to other people's culture and a willingness/ability to appreciate some elements of language/culture of place one is visiting; willingness to take *risks* by moving outside of tourist bubble; an ability to *locate* one's own society and its culture in terms of a wide-ranging historical and geographical knowledge; a certain *semiotic* skill – the ability to interpret tourist signs and know when they are partly ironic. These skills and qualities are transferable, and are particularly suited to the current expectations of flexible employment conditions.

The development of a sense of self relating to desirable characteristics that confirm one's image to oneself and others, including descriptive adjectives like 'educated', 'fulfilled' or 'adventurous,' is perhaps even more central to the narration of identity than establishing a place within a collective identity such as a particular class or ethnicity. In fact, for

MacCannell (1976, 1992), tourism is about the alienated modern individual attempting to discover a sense of self. For many, there is an acute self-consciousness about place in the world, not so much to do with collective identity but rather with one's identity as a 'social individual' (Desforges, 2000).

Leaving aside the question of collective identity, in the rest of this section I will focus on sense of self and individual identity. In an article on identity and travel biography, Desforges (2000) suggests two key moments in which travel is important to identity: (1) when the decision is taken to travel; and (2) upon homecoming, when narrating travel experiences as part of the process of presenting a new self-identity. To this I would add a crucial intermediary moment – (3) during the journey itself.

For people making the decision to travel long term, the first key moment is largely a process of justification to oneself, an employer, and perhaps to sceptical or worried friends and family. How do you explain that you plan to postpone further study, give up that perfectly good job, sacrifice that flat with the great location, and leave friends and family behind? Some simply say that they have 'always wanted' to travel and see the world, and leave it at that. For many, though, a reference to personal development is enough to gain acceptance from significant others. For gap year travellers it is often about 'education'; for older travellers, it may be about a change in direction; for others who are experiencing some form of life crisis, it may be about 'finding myself'. It is significant that almost every person I have interviewed during the course of my research felt the need to 'set up' the trip in a context of personal development, whether this was a primary or more peripheral reason for taking the trip.

Case Study One: Before the big trip

How to explain the decision to travel has been the topic of a number of discussion threads on BootsnAll.com. One 23-year-old writes that his girlfriend's mother is having difficulties coming to terms with their decision to spend two years travelling around the world, and asks for advice on what to say to her parents during a 'chat' about their plans (BootsnAll.com, 2003b). In another thread, an 18-year-old looks for ideas on how to broach the topic with his parents, now that he has made the decision to travel (BootsnAll.com, 2003c). The message and responses to 'Court', a recent graduate from university, are in many ways typical. Court writes:

> How do I convince them that I'm going to be okay? … My father has been less-than-supportive. I finance all my own travel so it's not like I need his approval/money but I'd like to at least convince him I'm not 'messing things up' by not getting a job right away. I've gone for the 'it

makes me more worldly' approach but he, like some other people, sees it as a 'not knowing what you're doing with your life' weakness. He also likes to remind me that it's not a thing for 'young females' to do … It doesn't help that I'm turning down a job in a tough market … to travel. (BootsnAll.com, 2003d)

Advice offered in the responses focuses on personal fulfilment and how travel might positively impact on one's future employment prospects. One response encourages Court to 'make mention of skills you've picked up as a result of your travels, which might enhance your marketability. You might also use this approach with your father, emphasising the concrete benefits you expect from your travels'; another comment states: 'you might well be surprised at the changes in yourself as the result of extended travel' (BootsnAll.com, 2003d). Yet another writer advises Court to put together a 'qualifications package' for her father to review, including:

information on the countries I'd be going to; financial breakdowns of how I'd budget and how I'd saved; correspondence between me and some friends abroad; my general itinerary including means of transport, safety, etc.; also some information on my potential future plans and how travel will be a benefit to me and others whom I come in contact with; and finally, a short (and purposely moving) essay on how important travel was to me. (BootsnAll.com, 2003d)

While it may be unusual for backpackers to feel the need to make such a formal presentation to their parents, it is clear that most feel the need to justify their decision to their significant others, and the majority tend to do so in these terms.

The intermediary key moment, which I would suggest is the most crucial, takes place during the journey itself. For those who spend months or years on the road it may in fact be more like a series of moments. It is during the course of the journey that the traveller works through the process of re-inventing the self – having new experiences, meeting new people, and incorporating these into a revised identity. This is accomplished largely through narrating the story to oneself and others. The narration can take many forms, from a private internal dialogue or keeping a diary to public discourse including letters, e-mails and discussions with fellow travellers (O'Reilly, forthcoming a).

Many travellers make regular entries in travel diaries while on the road, even if they do not keep a diary when at home. These private discourses are an opportunity to work through the significance of experiences without fear of outside judgement. Letters and individual e-mails are another way of narrating the travel experience, still personal but not completely private. The relatively new genre of the 'group e-mail' is a hybrid combining aspects of personal letter and more public travelogue. Because e-mail still retains an air of privacy,[1] group e-mails can give surprisingly intimate accounts. Yet they are written with a collective audience in mind and with the knowledge that they might be read by strangers. With the advent of internet cafés in all but the remotest parts of the world it has become common practice to write a single newsy e-mail recounting the latest adventures, which is then sent to everyone on a list that might include friends, family and former colleagues. Group e-mails allow the traveller to narrate experience and re-invent themselves while the journey is still taking place, preparing friends and family for a potentially transformation upon the traveller's return.

Oral as well as written narratives are important while on the road. Travellers' tales are regularly exchanged with fellow backpackers, often in a form that would be familiar to recreational fishermen, employing a degree of exaggeration and occasionally pure fiction in an effort to outdo each other. Comparing illnesses, describing remote locations devoid of other tourists and explaining the outrageous difficulties involved in journeying from A to B are the mainstays of backpackers' stories (see Elsrud, 2001 for a discussion of backpacker adventure narration).

Competitive storytelling is an opportunity to build up credibility in the insular world of the long-term traveller, but it is also a chance to develop and test out narratives of self, identity and personal history that will be used in different contexts on the return home. The relationships made during travel are very often fleeting affairs, lasting a day or a month, but rarely continuing after the return home. In fact the general assumption is that relationships made on the road will be short-lived. These 'single serving friendships' are important for testing out new identities, because there are no long-term ramifications unless both parties actively pursue the relationship beyond the end of the trip. Thus the nature of the relationships made on the road can facilitate the re-creation of self.

Case Study Two: On the road

Alan (pseudonym), an Australian backpacker who had been on the road for about 18 months, agreed to add me to his group e-mail list for the final months of his journey through South America and Europe in 2001. His e-mails came in a similar format each time: a title indicating where he was and a general theme; the main body written in the style of a letter; and a final section called 'Culture for the Uncultured' where he lists points both serious and amusing about the places and people he had encountered in a particular country. Addressed to 50 friends and family, Alan's e-mails move between thoughts and observations about the places he visits and self-reflection. The following excerpts are typical:

[Writing about Brazil] …They have a passion for living, music and the arts. Incredibly hospitable and genuinely want you to have a good time in their country. They love parties and any sort of gathering with people and energy. They will talk to people with no barriers and are incredibly open. When you meet someone on the street you give the girls a kiss on each cheek and the men a typical handshake with the other hand patting the shoulder or arm. Very touchy people which is another gesture highlighting their warmth and openness. I like their style…. The openness of the people has been very good for my spirit. I have never been the most open person myself and Brazilian encouragement has helped me grow. Shy people don't seem to exist here. They all seem to know you have to 'give it a go' to learn, and there is always a lot of encouragement to dance, to kiss a girl passionately in the street, or to go and watch the sunrise after partying all night.

Later in the same message he says:

A little on the real purpose of my trip, self development. The fact that I'm by myself helps a lot. I have no connection to home and nobody knows me. I've realised this allows a subtle form of greater freedom where your 'normal' behaviour does not exist. I'm ultimately by myself and plans can be changed at will if the situation calls. People and places are different allowing me to experience other ways of life encouraging [me] to question my own beliefs and values. Having to talk to other people and meet new people all the time is surprisingly easy. I've learnt a lot about individuals, cultures, attitudes, interests, differences and, of course, the similarities among all of us.

This selection is rather more contemplative than some of his other missives that focus on humorous anecdotes, but it is not out of keeping with the mood of his group e-mails as a whole. Alan is a keen observer and an articulate writer, perhaps more so than your 'average' backpacker. However, he is not unusual in his views about the transformative experience of (particularly solo) travel, nor in the way that he uses narratives about his travels to develop and express a sense of self.

On the return home, the challenge is to translate cultural and symbolic capital gained while travelling into a transferable form in a sedentary context. What contributed to the accumulation of cultural capital on the road will not necessarily go down well when no longer in the company of fellow travellers. Travellers do not balk at discussing the state of their bowels or the relative merits of using antibiotics to cure a bout of diarrhoea, but this is hardly considered appropriate dinner party conversation at home. Boasting that you did not bother to take malaria prophylactics may make you sound cool to other travellers, but it comes across as reckless and foolish to family and potential employers. And long-winded descriptions of a 12-hour bus journey that ended up taking 24 is just plain boring to the uninitiated (and admittedly to many veteran travellers as well).

People use the experience of travel in different ways depending on a number of factors, including the extent to which they wished the journey to result in self-discovery or a re-invention of self. For those who started out travelling in the recreational or diversionary mode (Cohen, 1979),[2] it may come as a surprise to find that they have changed while away. Those who set out hoping to achieve some form of self-realisation or find a new, more fulfilling sense of self can have the opposite problem, feeling that they face the same difficulties as before they left. For the professional backpacker in the experimental mode, the return home can be profoundly alienating, leading to dreams of further journeys in the near future (see O'Reilly, forthcoming b, for a detailed typology of backpackers).

Regardless of the traveller's circumstances on the return home, however, the transfer of capital takes place largely through narration – telling the story in the right way to the right people, and of course coming to terms with it yourself. Some travellers describe difficulties with their CVs after a long stint of travelling, not sure how to present the experience in a way that will be attractive – or at least not off-putting – to employers. Others find that friends and family rapidly tire of their stories and photos, making it difficult for the returned traveller to try out new narratives and assert their new sense of identity. A very common complaint is the sensation that while everything has changed for you, nothing much has changed at home while you were away. It is not always possible to plug back into an old role after the trip – but it can be difficult to avoid the pressure to do so.

Case Study Three: Reflecting on the experience

The impact of the travel experience, whether it is ultimately perceived as very significant or relatively minor, is unique for every individual. Nevertheless, common to all former travellers is the need to make sense of the experience through narration and to translate its value into different contexts at home. In the following three quotes, people who first backpacked between one and 10 years ago reflect on the experience in relation to career path, personal identity and sense of self in the world (all names have been changed):

Fran, a freelance journalist:
Travelling gave me an awful lot of confidence. My father said I was a different person afterwards, a lot more confident, more up front with people. I wouldn't have dreamt of haggling before, but I came back and I now haggle at John Lewis [department store] even – if there was a

slight mark on a dress or something, I would get a reduction! Being a go-getter has helped in my career as a free-lance journalist. I might not have survived in the job if hadn't got the confidence from the travel. I probably wouldn't have stayed in it, because it would have been too hard. There's a lot of competition in food and wine writing, so it's very difficult to succeed.

John, formerly an investment banker:
[Telling his favourite travel anecdote.] When I was in Tanzania, I'd ended up going on a week long safari and then had a day or two left [in Arusha before going home]. There was this guy called Rasta who persuaded me to go on a walking safari to a nearby village. It was a beautiful sunny day. I can remember this Maasai guy joining us in full kit but with Wellington boots. Tromping over the ridge with these guys, it occurs to me that it's a dangerous thing to do with my camera and money, no one knows I'm here, and they've got a big knife. I had the equivalent for them of a year's wages or more on me. We ended up at a cannabis plantation, staying in mud huts – it turns out that Rasta was on a ganja gathering trip and just took me along. Most people go on this sort of trip in a tour bus, but it was much nicer to go with a few locals and meet their friends along the way. When we got back to Arusha I was supposed to be going off to the airport. But they'd locked my hotel for the weekend and my bags were in there. The Rasta guy got all the urchins of the city to fan out and track down the owner to get my bags. He then got me on this crowded local mini-bus to the airport with all my purchases of statues on my lap. A fight broke out between two women on the way, and this guy next to me telling me how Westernised he is. Then he stands up and has a piss out the window, standing over people. He then clambers over people to sit back down and have the conversation again. It turns out the bus stopped 12 km from the airport turnoff in the dark – and my companion told me I'd be bound to get mugged on the way if I walked. So he speaks to a Maasai guy in the corner who is getting off at same spot, a 40 to 50 year old guy who didn't look very tough was supposed to protect me. We got out and this Maasai guy had one hand on his knife and other hand on his loaf of Sunblest bread he was carrying. It felt strange being protected by an old and withered guy, with me being over 6 feet tall. Eventually I got a lift, but they refused to take my [Maasai] friend because he had a knife. When I finally got to the airport I saw all these guys in their safari outfits who came up on a coach, talking to their tour guides. I felt like I'd had an authentic African experience, while these guys spent four times as much and had a pretend, plastic experience and were smug about it.

Mark, a travel guide writer:
[Talking about why travelling is important to him.] The reasons have changed completely, radically. I'm not even sure if could have said why it was important 10 years ago, beyond 'seeing the world' or 'seeing how other people live'. It was much more an expression of me, being about me, for me – with me at the centre. I just happened to be somewhere exotic or somewhere I was familiar with from holidays. Now if I travel it is often for work, which is different anyway ... Travel has given me a perspective, a larger backdrop against which I can draw myself. Not getting too metaphorical, but being able to identify myself in relation to the world by being as lucky to see as much as I have. It's that sense of perspective that I was dying for at university, but then I didn't even know what it was that I didn't have. I was so bored and pissed off and aimless in school and university – so unattractively negative ... When what I really wanted was to get the perspective I wanted from leaving.... The sense of freedom [I have now] to make decisions – to do big things like [quitting my current permanent job], getting married and moving flat all in the space of a month. It's down to learning these things.

Narrating travel experiences in these three key moments is part of what Giddens (1991) identifies as the reflexive project of modernity, the ongoing development of self-identity. The transformation of experience gained while travelling into social and cultural capital at home takes place through narratives that demonstrate the possession of important personal qualities, such as those Urry collectively labels aesthetic cosmopolitanism. As such, backpacker travel should be understood as much more than a simple holiday or an escape from the 'real' world – for those who choose to undertake long-term travel, it is fundamental to a sense of self and social position.

Conclusion: Backpacker Identity, Narratives, Symbolic Capital

I suggested above that backpackers tend to prefer the term 'traveller' because of its associations with freedom and exploration. There is a contradiction, however, between this seemingly innocent discourse of adventure and self-discovery and the reality of unequal global power relationships in which it takes place. The study of tourists, including backpackers, is generally approached in one of two ways – the critical or the phenomenological. The former might be exemplified by Boorstin (1964), Fussell (1980) or the more recent work of Kaur and Hutnyk (1999), who argue that 'the traveller is not an innocent, nor just curious' and ask 'how different are we to troops on the march' (p. 3)? The latter, in terms of backpackers, might be exemplified by Riley's (1988) or Cohen's (1972, 1973, 1979, 1982, 1989) attempts to both explicate and understand.

Are backpackers unwitting post-colonial agents of cultural imperialism, or adventurous global wanderers taking advantage of the opportunity to experience the human condition in all its richness? Can we accept at face value the self-representations of these travellers who see themselves on the adventure of a lifetime and/or on a quest for experience and self-discovery? Some might say that their claims for increased cultural understanding and enrichment ring hollow beside damning critiques of Orientalism and cultural imperialism, witting or unwitting. Yet we cannot dismiss out of hand the experiences of our informants as mere delusions or contrivances that mask the reality of tourists as 'troops on the march'. It is possible to gain an understanding of the backpacker phenomenon on both levels, that of the lived experience of the tourists as well as of travel in the wider context of a globalised, post-modern consumer society. A serious consideration of the latter is outside the scope of this chapter, but I have made an attempt to contribute to the growing body of knowledge making up the former.

The extent to which long-term independent travel is bound up with people's sense of self and identity is indicated by the intensity of feeling generated by the labels 'tourist', 'traveller' and 'backpacker'. Being a tourist is common – it is not transformative, and lacks the qualities valued by backpackers. Journeying through space and time is a key element of the transformative experience, as are the endurance of discomfort and illness. Though not actively sought, neither are they avoided – for many, they are an integral part of the experience. Tales of ill health, risky situations and danger are the badges of achievement proudly worn by the veteran traveller, as important as the list of countries visited and the length of time clocked up on the road. The ability to transform cultural and symbolic capital gained while travelling into a form that will be of use at home relies in large part on an ability to narrate experiences in an appropriate way. In this sense, travellers' tales are much more than mere stories – they are the process through which travellers re-invent themselves, communicate their new identities and enhance their social positions.

Notes

1. This air of privacy seems to persist in spite of recent cases where private messages were made embarrassingly public by the exponential forwarding capacity of e-mail. In one highly publicised case a sexually explicit message sent by a woman to her lover was forwarded repeatedly until it reached an estimated million readers around the world. Nevertheless, e-mail retains the feel of a private exchange more akin to a telephone conversation than the more formal genre of the letter.

2. Cohen's (1979) 'recreational mode' refers to a type of tourist experience geared towards 'taking a break' from the pressures and busyness of ordinary life, associated with entertaining but fundamentally shallow experiences. The 'diversionary mode' is similar to the recreational mode, but it is associated with those who experience life at home as alienating. While recreational type tourists seek relaxation, diversionary types seek escape. In the 'experiential mode', the tourist seeks to observe the authentic lives of others without joining in, while those in the 'experimental mode' wish to experience the authentic life of others as a way of seeking an alternative to their own culture. Many backpackers look for an experiential or experimental type of experience.

References

Adler, J. (1985) Youth on the road: Reflections on the history of tramping. *Annals of Tourism Research* 12, 335–54.

Aziz, H. (1999) Whose culture is it anyway? *In Focus* (Tourism Concern). Spring, 14–15.

Baudrillard, J. (1983) *Simulations*. New York: Semiotext.

Bauman, Z. (1998) *Globalization: The Human Consequences*. Cambridge: Polity Press.

Boorstin, D.J. (1964) *The Image: A Guide to Pseudo-Events in America*. New York: Harper & Row.

BootsnAll.com (2003a) Online document: http://boards.bootsnall.com/2/OpenTopic?a=tpc&s=712096715&f=455098755&m=555098755

BootsnAll.com (2003b) Online document: http://boards.bootsnall.com/2/OpenTopic?a=tpc&s=712096715&f=209091657&m=6883012296

BootsnAll.com (2003c) Online document: http://boards.bootsnall.com/2/OpenTopic?a=tpc&s=712096715&f=179090755&m=2063048196

BootsnAll.com (2003d) Online document: http://boards.bootsnall.com/2/OpenTopic?a=tpc&s=712096715&f=179090755&m=2013034127

Brown, D. (1996) Genuine fakes. In T. Selwyn (ed.) *The Tourist Image: Myths and Myth Making in Tourism* (pp. 33–47). New York: John Wiley.

Cohen, E. (1972) Towards a sociology of international tourism. *Social Research* 39, 164–89.

Cohen, E. (1973) Nomads from affluence: Notes on the phenomenon of drifter–tourism. *International Journal of Comparative Sociology* 14, 89–102.

Cohen, E. (1979) A phenomenology of tourist experiences. *Sociology* 13, 179–201.

Cohen, E. (1982) Marginal paradises: Bungalow tourism on the islands of southern Thailand. *Annals of Tourism Research* 9, 189–228.

Cohen, E. (1989) 'Primitive & remote': Hill tribe trekking in Thailand. *Annals of Tourism Research* 16, 30–61.

Desforges, L. (2000) Travelling the world: Identity and travel biography. *Annals of Tourism Research* 27, 926–45.

Eco, U. (1987) *Faith in Fakes*. London: Secker & Warburg.

Elsrud, T. (2001) Risk creation in travelling: Backpacker adventure narration. *Annals of Tourism Research* 28, 597–617.

Fussell, P. (1980) *Abroad: British Literary Traveling Between the Wars*. Oxford: Oxford University Press.

Giddens, A. (1991) *Modernity and Self-Identity: Self and Society in the Late Modern Age*. Cambridge: Polity Press.

Hampton, M. (1998) Backpacker tourism and economic development. *Annals of Tourism Research* 25, 639–60.

Hampton, M. (1999) Same same, but different. *In Focus* (Tourism Concern). Spring, 6–7.

Harvey, D. (1989) *The Condition of Postmodernity*. Oxford: Basil Blackwell.

Kaur, R. and Hutnyk, J. (1999) *Travel Worlds: Journeys in Contemporary Cultural Politics*. London: Zed Books.

MacCannell, D. (1976) *The Tourist: A New Theory of the Leisure Class*. New York: Schocken.

MacCannell, D. (1992) *Empty Meeting Grounds: The Tourist Papers*. New York: Routledge.

O'Reilly, C. (forthcoming a) Performing backpacker travel.

O'Reilly, C. (forthcoming b) From drifter to gap year: Mainstreaming backpacker travel. submitted to *Annals of Tourism Research*.

O'Reilly, C. (forthcoming c) 'Traveller' good, 'tourist' bad: Backpacker travel in (post-)modern consumer society.

Riley, P. (1988) Road culture of international long-term budget travellers. *Annals of Tourism Research* 15, 313–28.

Robertson, R. (1992) *Globalization*. London: Sage.

Rojek, C. (1993) *Ways of Escape*. London: Routledge.

Rojek, C. (1995) *Decentring Leisure: Rethinking Leisure Theory*. London: Sage.

Selwyn, T. (1996) *The Tourist Image: Myths and Myth-Making in Tourism*. New York: John Wiley.

Tomory, D. (1998) *A Season in Heaven: True Tales from the Road to Kathmandu*. London: Lonely Planet Publications.

Uriely, N., Yonay, Y. and Simchai, D. (2002) Backpacking experiences: A type and form analysis. *Annals of Tourism Research* 29, 520–38.

Urry, J. (1995) *Consuming Places*. London: Routledge.

Urry, J. (2002) Mobility and proximity. *Sociology* 36, 255–74.

Wilson, D. (1997) Paradoxes of tourism in Goa. *Annals of Tourism Research* 24, 52–75.

Part 4

Performance and Authenticity

Chapter 8

Tourism Performance as Metaphor: Enacting Backpacker Travel in the Fiji Islands

STEPHEN DOORNE and IRENA ATELJEVIC

> *All the world is not, of course, a stage, but the crucial ways*
> *in which it isn't are not easy to specify*
> (Goffman, 1959: 72)

Introduction

Central to the emergence of 'new' theorisations of tourism is the embrace of the 'de-differentiation of the economy and culture' (Crang & Malbon, 1996; Amin & Thrift, 2000; Sayer, 2000). These new trajectories of tourism have contributed to the situation of tourism and leisure as a critical realm for understanding the broader issues of culture and society in a global era (e.g. Urry, 2002 [1990]; Squire, 1994; Lanfant, 1995; Crain, 1996; Rojek & Urry, 1997; Morgan & Pritchard, 1998; Ringer, 1998; Aitchinson, 1999). This chapter seeks to enhance these 'new' projects in the context of identity formation and to simultaneously elaborate on new arenas through which these processes are being articulated. Morgan & Pritchard's (1998) analysis of tourism imagery within wider social and cultural forces to some extent paves the way for this discussion by illustrating how meanings, produced and consumed by tourism image(in)ing, are grounded within circuits of a wider cultural discourse. With reference to Stuart Hall's (1997) holistic analysis of culture and by using a wide range of case studies, they show how destinations and their people have been portrayed, packaged, presented, read and mediated within cultural circuits of power, knowledge and social practice.

In this context, we respond to the call that 'tourism studies must investigate the sensual, embodied and performative dimensions of change in tourism cultures' (Franklin & Crang, 2001: 14). The study of the representation of culture through performance has an established lineage in tourism studies both in terms of critical examinations of 'staged authenticity' (Turner & Ash, 1975; MacCannell, 1999 [1976]; Greenwood, 1978; Smith, 1978; Adams, 1984; Britton & Clarke, 1987; Crick, 1989), as well as reflexive exploration of the social dynamics through which cultural production takes place (Boissevain, 1996; Kirshenblatt-Gimblett, 1988). Most recently, however, the emergence of theoretical perspectives that conceptualise tourism as performance moves beyond the passive gaze of the visual towards the embodiment of the acts of production and consumption.

In *Tourists at the Taj*, Edensor (1998) introduced an extensive account of the tourist performance metaphor, examining the diverse enactments that centre upon the Taj Mahal stage. He reviews a few notable explorations of tourism as a set of performances referring to Adler's (1989) pioneering work on travel as 'performed art' and Crang's (1997) examination of tourist workers as 'cast members'. Similarly, Perkins and Thorns (2001) explore representations of adventure tourism in New Zealand, challenging Urry's (2002 [1990]) notion of the tourist gaze of sightseeing, and unravelling these activities as a 'performance' associated with an active body, heightened sensory experience, risk and vulnerability.

In his later work, Edensor extends the argument to contend that 'tourism is a process which involves the ongoing (re)construction of praxis ... [whereby] the whole of social life can be considered as performative' (Edensor, 2000: 322) . Similarly, Franklin and Crang (2001: 17–18) claim that: 'the cultural competencies and required skills that make up tourist cultures themselves suggest a "Goffmanesque" where all of the world is indeed a stage'. More recently, Coleman and Crang's (2002) edited volume represents an extensive collection of seeing tourism as embodied and performed engagement with places, and demonstrates the mutual entanglement of practices, images, conventions and creativity.

It was Goffman (1959) who pioneered the approach to interpersonal communication based on the dramaturgic or performance analogy, where individuals and groups engage in individual and collective performances when and where they meet. Goffman observed that these meetings take place as if on a stage ('frontstage' and 'backstage'), where the performer and performing groups are each others' audiences. Backstage is a place where performers collect themselves before their frontstage encounters and where they retire after them. The stage contains a range of resources that are utilised in the performance, including props, scenery, service staff and so on, but the performance is controlled principally through what Goffman identifies as 'impression management' (Goffman, 1959: 203ff.), the act of controlling of the signs and cues one 'gives' (consciously, directly) and 'gives off' (unconsciously, indirectly) to the audience. Ultimately, the performer has little control of the impressions he/she gives off, and this difficulty may produce an asymmetry between the 'giving' and the 'giving off' of impressions.

In this chapter, we draw on Goffman's conceptualisations of the presentation of self as a performance with a specific focus on the behaviour of backpackers in Fiji. The use of the performance metaphor provides a theoretical lens through which socio-cultural practices of 'consuming' tourism can be captured, observed and examined in terms of language, actions and socio-strategic behaviour (Dann, 2002).

Our discussion focuses on three elements which form the basis for this 'production' of travel experiences. Firstly, we examine the dramaturgical context of performance to illustrate in general terms the nature of backpacker performance. Secondly, we observe the physical setting and aspects of the stage in the case of Fiji Islands. Thirdly, we discuss casting of characters and the social positioning of self amongst other actors and the wider social environment. Following this, we examine various roles learned and performed in the process of tourism 'consumption', including the roles played when part of an audience. Finally, we look more broadly at 'production' as a composite of roles scripted, prescribed or improvised, depending on contextual factors, where underlying social discourses literally take place.

We argue that the concept of performance provides an important critical framework around which practices and processes running through tourism can be observed, particularly the processes of identity construction, cultures of consumption and communication. We begin with a discussion of this broader context of consumer culture, whereby backpacker travel represents one of the forms through which one can formulate identity and generate cultural capital.

The Culture of Consumption, Identity and Backpacker Travel

The contemporary global economy has become characterised by an intensity and sophistication of the semioticisation of consumption where production is increasingly aestheticised, attaching visual representations to material objects (Britton, 1991; Rojek, 1995, Lurry, 1996; Ateljevic, 2000). Luckacs (1971), for example, provides the notion of an endless commodity logic through a synthesis of Marx–Weber, a conceptualisation which was subsequently extended by the Frankfurt School of critical theorists: Marcuse (1964), Lefebvre (1971) and Adorno and Horkheimer (1971). The Frankfurt School maintains that the logic and rationality of commodity production has been transferred into the leisure sphere, producing greater opportunities for controlled and manipulated consumption of the masses. Essential to this development has been the formation of what these critical theorists call *the culture industry*, which has become a filter for leisure time pursuits, cultivating all activities which are able to alleviate the mundaneness of everyday life. The phrase 'culture of consumption' emerged to acknowledge the importance of culture in ensuring consumption, where leisure and tourism become significant features of contemporary capitalist society (Featherstone, 1987a, 1991; Rojek, 1995; Sharpley, 1996).

Following Bourdieu (1984) and Urry (2002 [1990]), Britton (1991) places tourism in the context of the contemporary cultural economy, within which groups and individuals increasingly construct their identities through their consumption preferences and lifestyle choices which signal taste and one's position in society. As the 'culture of consumption' evolves in terms of 'you are what you buy' and 'where you go away' (Featherstone, 1987b), a burgeoning contemporary literature is addressing the relationship of material culture, consumption and identity (e.g. Glennie & Thrift, 1993; Crewe & Lowe, 1995; Jackson & Holbrook, 1995; Pearce, 1997; Miller, 1995, 1998; Miller *et al.*, 1998; Jackson, 1999).

Over the last decade, backpacker travel has appeared as representative of a travel lifestyle, an expression of consumer identity, as well as a coherent cultural form and industrial complex (Ateljevic & Doorne, 2001). In this sense, the analysis of backpacker tourism forms an integral part of broader theoretical discussions of tourism as a contemporary cultural and social practice. Desforges (1998), for example, explores the notion of consumer identity through the practice of 'collecting places', as a way in which travellers relate to the 'Other'. With respect to perceived 'authenticity' he identifies its markers as the absence of travel industry and other tourists. Drawing on Bourdieu (1984), he discusses travel as a form of cultural capital, which serves as a sign of distinction and enables the traveller to gain access to elevated social classes and their privileges. Munt (1994: 108) similarly discusses the relationship of class and the 'new petite burgeoisie' who are 'best conceived as ego-tourists who search for a style of travel which is both reflective of an alternative lifestyle and which is capable of maintaining and enhancing their cultural capital' (see also Mowforth & Munt, 1998).

Desforges (2000) explores these issues further referring to Giddens' (1991) notion of self-identity and a 'fateful moment' of life in which travel is drawn upon to re-imagine the self. Elsrud (2001) also uses Giddens' idea that identity is left to individuals to conceive through the means they are offered by society. In this context Elsrud argues that Western travellers undertake 'risky' travel because they come from a society that demands from them the ability to cope successfully with risk. By differentiating their identities relative to 'primitive otherness' travellers construct their identities through the practice of telling stories about risks associated with the physical self (e.g. illnesses, dangerous foods, malaria). Ateljevic and Doorne (2001, 2003) observe a dynamic heterogeneity amongst backpacker travellers whose internal transformation of self is normally accompanied by its projected expression through the construction of a visual identity, grounded in habitus, or the behavioural dispositions that evolve around class, gender, age and ethnicity (Bourdieu, 1984). In this respect, backpacker travel represents a contemporary cultural condition reflecting the 'tourist sign economy and the images of escape, freedom and relaxation which it produces' (Rojek & Urry, 1997: 19). The following section provides the background context in which these concepts are further explored in the case of backpacker travel in the Fiji Islands.

Backpacker Travel in Fiji

The Fiji Islands are firmly branded in the global tourism industry as a 'tropical paradise' destination saturated with the iconic imagery stereotypical of island holiday environments, notably blue skies, palm trees, clear turquoise blue sea, 'idyllic' islands surrounded by coral reefs, muscular warriors and submissive maidens. As Hall and Page (1996: 1) observe, Fiji lives in the minds of prospective tourists as the 'quintessential tourism image of sun, sea, surf and sand'.

Since the 1960s, Fiji's tourism development has been largely dominated by transnational capital investment in hotels and resorts targeting mostly families, couples and honeymooners. As such Fiji is regarded by many as a 'classic' example of tourism dependency, leakage and 'enclave tourism' (e.g. Britton, 1978; Plange, 1996; Stanley, 1996). In more recent years, however, with the well-known events of political unrest and changing tourism market structures, the emergence of the backpacker market is being considered as a mechanism for overcoming the inherent problems produced by the traditional structures of the Fiji tourism industry. Backpacker travel is normally associated with an extended length of stay, diverse patterns of behaviour and expenditure distribution (spatial and sectoral). Consequently, there is considerable interest in cultivating backpacker markets in order to stimulate local, small-scale industry development (Fiji IVS, 2002). The backpacker market has in recent years become a crucial component of the government's tourism policy largely due to its perceived contribution to Fiji's 'triple bottom line' development goals integrating economy, employment and the conservation of culture and tradition (Fiji Taskforce, 2001).

Fiji has been a budget destination in recent years, largely due to 'resorts' such as Beachcomber Island and transit accommodation in the gateway Nadi, and is now firmly established on the global backpacker trail (Fiji Taskforce, 2001). However, the backpacker sector has experienced significant growth recently in line with general trends occurring within worldwide tourism industry in which an estimated 20% of all international travellers are young people, predominantly travelling as 'backpackers' (Tourism New Zealand, 2003).

For backpackers, Fiji is frequently included as a stopover destination on around-the-world-tickets and is, consistent with other markets, perceived as a '4S holiday' providing relief from the 'hard work' of Asian travel and the busy schedules and adventure consumption of New Zealand and Australia (Ateljevic & Doorne, 2001). The most recent Fiji

International Visitors Survey (2002) displays the characteristics of the backpacker being predominantly young and white (74% being under 29 years of age and 11% being aged 30 to 39), originating from the United Kingdom (57%), North America (17%) and from the rest of Europe (16%). The composition of the backpacker market in Fiji arguably reflects what Desforges (1998) and Munt (1994: 109) describe as Western middle-class youth seeking 'alternative travel' as a means to accumulate on 'cultural capital' (see also O'Reilly, this volume).

Method

The theoretical shift in tourism studies mentioned above has been accompanied by significant progress in the methodological sophistication of research, particularly with respect to the role of the researcher and the multiplicity of research methods. It follows that this more complex research approach necessarily reveals a more complex world. The reflexivity of the researcher is a critical dimension of the research process that involves the evolution of research from its conceptual foundation through trust-building to the interpretation and analysis of 'data' (Harding & Hintikka, 1983; Evans, 1988; Smith, 1988; Denzin, 1997).

For this research we use a phenomenological approach combining ethnographic fieldwork and semi-structured interviews with 27 backpackers in various locations in the Fiji Islands. The research methods also included participant observation and informal conversations, which involved tracing everyday interactions and making visible issues surrounding the performance of backpacker identities. Given this research design, we were sometimes actors of our own roles, supporting actors in the performances of others, and at other times as part of the audience. Our roles saw us 'frontstage', 'backstage' and part of the social backdrop, but always an integral part of the myriad of performances taking place around us.

The interview data were analysed to 'obtain comprehensive descriptions that provide the basis for a reflective structural analysis that portrays the essences of the experience' (Moustakas, 1994: 13) and to validate our observations and sense of what was taking place. As Giorgi (1985) argues, the phenomenological approach lifts the analysis beyond mere description by reflective analysis and interpretation of the research participant's story. As has been mentioned, our analysis is guided by Goffman's conceptual framework in which the presentation of self is conceptualised in terms of performance, dramaturgical practices and strategies. Our discussion draws on our reading of the research environment supported by the narratives of respondents where necessary to remain sensitive to the perspective of the subject and retain the integrity of our interpretation. The reader will notice that discussions of self and the casting of others is driven mostly by our interpretation of observations partly due to the unwillingness of respondents to openly discuss their behaviour or that of others. Discussion of discourses on the other hand is supported more directly by narratives.

Before engaging fully with the analysis it is important to clarify our key analytic terms borrowed from Goffman's (1959) work discussed above. *Performance* may be described as all the activity of a given participant on a given occasion which serves to influence in any way any of the participants. When individuals are in the continuous presence of each other, we can refer to this as interaction or an encounter. When continuous with a regular grouping of people, we refer to this as social relations or relationships. *Role* is the enactment of rights and duties attached to a given status; a social role will 'involve one or more parts and each of these parts may be presented by a performer on a series of occasions to the same kinds of audience or to an audience of the same persons' (Goffman, 1959: 16). We use the term *performance team* or *team* to refer to any set of individuals who cooperate in staging a single routine. For dramaturgical effect we also use the terms 'supporting' actors, 'bit part', or 'extras' as appropriate to tease out the subtleties of team based performances.

Setting involves furniture, décor, physical layout and other background items which provide the scenery and stage props for the spate of human action played out before it. Geographically speaking, setting tends to remain in one place so that those who intend to play a particular performance cannot do so until they have brought themselves to it, and must terminate that particular performance when they leave it. In certain circumstances we see the stage setting moving with the performers (bus, boat, etc.). *Stage* is essentially a bounded region, bounded that is by limits to perception. Boundaries can be physical, cultural, social or temporal.

Finally, a note on the transcription conventions. All the extracts are rendered in conventional orthographic style. We use '…' where either the narrative is interrupted or the respondent simply lets a thought or idea 'hang' before picking up another idea or adding to the previous one. Additional interpretive information is included in parentheses (like this). The identities of all our informants have been anonymised.

The dramaturgical context of performance

The act of backpacker travel forms just one part of the larger 'life' production of self. The particular roles enacted in Fiji form an integral part of the construction of the 'global traveller' element of accumulated cultural capital. This role will be a composite of various characters played by the individual according to the destination and dominant consumption themes. As noted earlier, Fiji is conceived largely as a rest and relaxation destination demanding particular performances of self, relationships with other travellers and relationship with 'locals'. If an individual has travelled to similarly themed destinations previously, this may involve a re-enactment of behaviours, actions and strategies learned elsewhere, with perhaps some modification to the local environment and audiences. If the individual has been pursuing other types of backpacker travel, the arrival in Fiji will require them to learn new characters and may demand some re-interpretation of the role to accommodate them. The assumption that different stages demand different performances is observable at the country/destination level, as well as at the level of particular premises. Some resorts emphasise 'party' behaviour, others are places to 'chill out' and relax, yet others to engage in particular activities (village visits, snorkelling, bush walks).

Integration with other travellers is essential to the enactment of backpacker travel; their role in the Fiji context is frequently to affirm the acceptance of the individual as a member of what would be projected to audiences back home as a *secret society*. It should be noted that other actors also form various conceptions of audience. On one level the individual performs for themselves in their larger 'production of life'. The travel experience provides opportunity to experiment with new roles which can be built upon over time. The other members of the cast represent an important audience in this activity as they become the reference against which successful performances or modifications are critically reviewed.

The social structure of an individual's 'life at home', i.e. where they usually reside (family, friends, work colleagues) has a wider, more significant audience for whose benefit characters and roles are rehearsed (cf. O'Reilly, this volume). This particular audience is accorded strategic consideration because this is the environment the traveller will return to. The overwhelming desire of most travellers is to return in some way different from when they left. Whilst many appreciate that the setting they will re-enter will probably have changed little when they return they must count on their enhanced cultural capital, and provide the necessary evidence, as a foundation for engineering strategic maneuvers in their social, family life or careers or places of work. Given that these concerns are common to other members of the cast, themselves each enacting their own strategic performances, these collaborative performances are normally played out with cultivated exclusivity. Relationships with locals or hosts (staff, villagers) in Fiji form a human backdrop; the cultivation of superficial friendships has the capacity to further enhance the individual's performance as the 'global traveller'. For the most part, relationships with locals revolving around functional service activities, that is, the stage crew who facilitate the performance.

In order to meet the above expectations, certain elements of the experience need to be set in place, beginning with the physical *setting* and associated signifying style elements upon the stage which precondition the subsequent enactment of a desired role – the global traveller taking time out on a tropical island. One of the most important physical elements of the tropical island experience is the now iconic construct featuring the white sand beach offset against a backdrop of the Pacific Ocean horizon and palm trees.

The Backdrop and Setting the Stage

Much of the conditioning of demand for such settings can be attributed to a standardised imagery of Pacific destinations which is notably consistent across the spectrum of tourist markets. Indeed these elements were regarded as so essential to the overall performance that they were not negotiable in decision-making behaviour. The stages providing this backdrop come pre-constructed as the myriad of small-scale 'resorts' catering to this market, particularly in the Mamanuca and more recently Yasawa island groups. Once 'in place' the travellers then proceeded to identify particular stages upon which they will enact the art of being a backpacker. The representation of landscape is carefully captured in photographs and stories, and to authenticate the performance by signalling that the actors are/were 'really there'.

> I like to take photos of what I would like to look at again and really remind me of Fiji and what it was really like and like the remoteness of the island we stayed on, I've tried to get a good few photos demonstrating the remoteness and how many people were there, that sort of thing ... the idea of paradise.

The backpacker industry is inherently socialised, moulded and modified to fit into the understanding and expectations of the market in which it is presented ('the idea of paradise'). Control of the setting is an advantage during interaction. This control allows a *team* of performers to introduce strategic devices for determining the information an audience is able to acquire. Thus settings which are controlled by others and which are governed by different rules are less conducive to successful performance. The décor and props are what can be considered as the fixed sign equipment. Each stage displays a familiar ordering of props (bar, tables, drinks, menus, music systems, etc.), yet as noted earlier, resorts on the islands are increasingly differentiated relative to one another. Subtle cues of imagery, layout and word of mouth suggest corresponding performances whilst conforming to a uniform backpacker genre. A dance floor (sand) and large music system in the bar area will signal a party theme, whereas craft work, postcards and photographs will suggest more introspective behaviour and intimate socialisation.

Stages have *front* and *back* regions. The backstage is the place where an individual can relax and disengage from their performance and must be regionally bounded to meet that need – normally out of sight. The toilets or the individual's own room provide places away from the audience gaze where the performer can behave out-of-character, knowingly contradict their current performance, or indeed to engage in private performances which may never be aired to an audience other than themselves. Commonly, backstage time is dedicated to preparations for front stage activities such as checking costume, hair, jewellery, or adjusting swimsuits so tan lines are accentuated and so on. The backstage can also be a place where collusion or collaboration takes place between team members producing its own backstage performance.

It is nowadays common for backpacker accommodation establishments to have rooms available in addition to the traditional dormitory. The dormitory has obviously limited backstage utility. The feeling of needing to constantly perform a particular role due to the relentless presence of others also contributes to the need for some travellers to move regularly and frequently.

We can also consider the travel period itself as an extended backstage experience away from the familiar audiences of the home environment. As such an individual may feel obliged to behave out-of-character with that in their home environment in the same way that a backstage environment may prompt uncharacteristic actions.

A further backstage is of course the backstage where the staff working at the resort can behave out of character. These are clearly separated regions with physical, cultural and social boundaries. We observed travellers who stumbled into the staff coffee/smoking room confronted by the awareness that they were intruding in a 'foreign' stage, their lack of knowledge about suitable characters and roles to play normally leading them to extract themselves apologetically or with humour (playing the 'dumb whitey') from the situation.

The regions beyond the bounded area of the resort can be seen as a residual 'outside', and anyone from that region is an 'outsider'. The dynamics of social relations in resort environments means that on occasions individuals may feel liberated by being outside, for example, in neighbouring village surrounds, in a bush environment, or away down the beach, and at other times stifled by the unfamiliarity and lack of control outside environments present.

When a performance is given it is normally given in a highly bounded region. In the West performances are normally indoor performances; in the tropics therefore there is also the added novelty of being able to take what would normally be an indoor performance outside or to environments where physical barriers of confinement in a building are removed. A beach in front of a bar at midday can in one context be an idyll for the sun worshipper but in another location a place to drink and 'party', reminiscent of popular soft drink commercials.

The resort environment is for a temporary period the 'home turf' and should necessarily include a certain set of props in order to function effectively. The director therefore plays a key role in facilitating the opportunity for individuals to play the part of the backpacker in various ways, and in some cases to inject themselves into the setting to 'window dress' in an almost ceremonial manner. The role of the director is principally to provide a stage supported by service staff whereon social relations of performance can 'take place'.

The Casting of Characters (Self and Teams)

In backpacker resorts, the social life forms the core of the play, its scenes commonly composed of partying, lying on the beach, meals, and occasional day trip activities (snorkelling, village visits, bush walks). The identity of characters is negotiated around a number of sensual and embodied aspects, such as bodily deportment and dress, dance, sexual practices, practices around consumption of alcohol and sometimes other drugs, and practices around displays of physical intimacy in public spaces. The individuals craft their performances in discursive spaces through the props and costumes of particular clothing, notably bikinis, surf wear, and wrap-around 'sulus' (sarong). The characters are often highly sexualised displaying suntanned bodies with tattoos and piercing, and seek to enhance their attractiveness by actively cultivating collaborative relationships with those who project similar performances of self.

Experience will lead an individual to assume that individuals of a particular kind can be found in a given social setting. Assessment of others will rely on either what they say about themselves and/or on documetary evidence provided that they are who they say they are. These 'sign vehicles' are a means of conveying this information in such a way that screening of potential cast or *team* members can proceed without having to socially engage everyone in conversation.

From the audience perspective (the audience being other members of the cast) the congruence of the two form the basis of validation. The symbols are used to convey information that others are known to attach to these symbols. An audience member will evaluate the asymmetry of the performance in terms of the ungovernable (what is said) aspects of expressive behaviour to check upon the validity of what is conveyed by the governable. A male bragging about adventurous or drunken 'mateship' with local Fijian men would be evaluated against the behaviour of the individual in the presence of local men at the current resort and the respect they accord him. The extent to which the story matches expressive behaviour may be taken as an indication of the believability of other stories. As such an individual may feel obliged to re-enact the same performances over time or indeed to turn a desired identity into reality through performance.

Travellers will often travel with a companion or friend either for the entire duration of their trip or just a part of it as new friendships are made on the way. These relationships take the form of cooperation, a kind of collusion or understanding between individuals who are ostensibly involved in presenting their own performances. Naturally, travelling with friends from home may have the effect of constraining an individual's attempts to try new performances depending on the level of freedom accorded by the other. Friendships formed with others 'on the road' provide the opportunity to perform the same character in different stages and through different roles for each character in a kind of reciprocal dependence. Women's friendships appear very different to friendships between men. Where the latter communicate as individuals through interest in projects, activities and ideas, women's relationships tend to be bounded by complicity and exchanges of confidences, information and experiences. The choice of stage partners will depend on the level of trust they are able to share. Those who constitute an unpredictable performance risk are to be avoided.

New arrivals are on one level immediately accepted into the fold as honorary members only later to have to find their way to allegiances and relationships with appropriate groupings. The set of dispositions expressed through body language and communication define the level of skills and accumulated cultural capital. The life experience of backpackers' performance becomes indicative of one's status in the backpacker casting community, to go from more 'seasoned' centre stage or lead role performers to less experienced (usually younger) supporting actors.

We should also be aware of the 'personal front' an individual assembles which includes sex, age and ethnicity characteristics, size and looks, posture, speech patterns, facial expressions, bodily gestures and clothes. Some of these characteristics are relatively fixed (*appearance*), others relatively mobile or transitory (*manner*) and can vary from one moment to the next throughout a performance. There is an expected consistency between appearance and manner and there is an expected coherence between setting, appearance and manner. Subtle expressions of interpretation of these standards form the basis of differentiation between various groupings of the backpacker market. Individuals assume these existing roles so they will be readily distinguishable from other groups. Collusion within groups may, depending on the circumstance and the individuals, tactfully conceal exclusiveness from other non-members or snobbishly advertise it to others.

Staff and village locals who spend time in and around the resorts play important roles as supporting cast. Staff play a technical role rather than a scripted one. It is not within the scope of this study to delve into the complexities of cross-cultural perspectives other than to note that we should also be aware of the front and backstage performances of staff and locals in encounters and the day-to-day activities of the resort. The barman, whilst friendly, will maintain an image of disinterest in the affairs of the traveller. In the service environment, it is apparent that backpacker tourists frequently perceive they have a 'moral right' to receive certain treatment of particular quality standard related to their position of 'guests'.

'Outsiders' provide opportunities for discourses about 'Third World' cultures, lifestyle and values to be validated. There are commonly few deviations from the accepted script in which one-dimensional locals live happy, simple, and contented lives free of the trappings of Western urban society. These scripts also rarely confront the asymmetrical power relations through which poverty and underdevelopment are necessary facilitators of the travel experience.

> They are always so happy because they have nothing … no computer and stuff like that. If everything goes here slow and in Sweden everything goes fast and you have everything there. So I think yeah … really good they are happy and they dance. I admire them because they live such simple lives and they are happy any way you know.

Outsiders are also cast to authenticate the role of the worldly wise traveller through the positioning of themes and scenes relative to other places and associations, sometimes as a statement about Western order, predictability and conservatism. Here, the respondent discusses the circumstances around capturing an image and in doing so reveals the role that image plays in the construction of his identity.

> There was a shot I took in Sigatoka of these guys and they looked about as dodgy as you could get … they were mini-van drivers, but they looked like Colombian drug vans. One of them had like big aviators and they all sort of were like quite shifty around each other and I got this photo of this guy with his legs back against the wall, sort of looking quite … and I took it on a zoom lens … it was a bit sneaky, out of the window. He was an interesting character. I wouldn't have liked him probably catching me taking that photograph I think.

With the casting of actors comes a corresponding framing of an audience for whom scripts will be drafted, rehearsed and performed according to the perception of their values and expectations and their anticipated reaction to the images and stories presented.

Playing and Learning Roles

Individuals will have to act so that they intentionally or unintentionally express themselves, and others will in turn have to be impressed by them in some way. The performance serves not only short-term interests but may also have longer-term strategic significance. When an individual appears in the presence of others there will usually be some reason for them to mobilise activity so it will convey an impression to others that supports this strategic interest.

> [I send postcards of] a beautiful white beach because that's what it must be like and you kind of sometimes send that just because you really kind of ... maybe you want to believe it yourself but maybe just you want everyone to believe you're in paradise. It's never the place, it's always the people you're with that makes it amazing.

The physical removal of the individual from home surroundings to new environments and social context provides an ideal petri-dish for the incubation of new characters, the concealment of past behaviours, the revelation or reinterpretation of pasts, and the rediscovery of aspects of their character suppressed by routinised daily life. The time frame also provides sufficient time for these characters to be nurtured and developed so that they may resist suffocation by the 'same old, same old' routines and strong enough to carry them forward to new life roles. There is a natural asymmetry in this communication which can take the form of an 'information game'.

Self-belief is a critical part to the formation of character. We should not see performance as putting on a show solely for the benefit of other people but the act of self-belief in the impression of reality an individual attempts to engender amongst whom they find themselves. The *mask* presented by the character is the role they strive to live up to, the truer self who they would like to be. The mask becomes second nature and is an integral part of personality.

Through individual performances each setting has its own inertia of roles. The perpetual arrival and departure of travellers through a resort means that new arrivals will take cues from those who are already there as to the appropriate behaviours associated with particular stages; they in turn will be the reference point for these cues for new arrivals following them. In this way each resort maintains difference from other establishments and maintains an identity which persists over time despite much coming and going. The coherence of setting with manner and appearance also serves to resist radical realignment by those who would attempt inappropriate performances.

A further role often played is that of the 'learned beggar' (see Cohen, 1973), where displays of wealth are played down in order to foster the impression that standards regarding birth, culture, or moral earnestness are the ones that prevail. Recently the emergence of 'Flashpackers' amongst the backpacker population represent an interesting contradiction to the traditional backpacker ethos with displays of conspicuous consumption and materiality, perhaps driven by the need to signal social status of their home environment without which individuals feel socially naked. It is not uncommon to see, for example, young women 'dressing for dinner', wearing makeup, jewellery, high heels and expensive evening gowns, drinking cocktails before dinner. The performance is one which has been played before, here the novelty is its very incongruence with the local environment. The backstage preparations, with hairdryers and mirrors, is a graphic illustration of team performance. More remarkable is the attire of the young men who accompany them and the absence of deviation from the uniform surfwear.

Sexuality and gender relations also produce multiple bisections of the social realm. The other requirements of decorum outside of the requirements of handling of others in a conversation may have moral requirements. Rules regarding the non-interference and non-molestation of others, and sexual propriety provide opportunities for the exploration of socio-cultural boundaries. Male travellers seek sexual encounters with other travellers and thus have relatively culturally unchallenging experiences, whereas female travellers are also sanctioned to seek sexual encounters with local males. The local males themselves are not subject to the cultural constraints regarding sex with foreigners that local women are.

Sexual relations between group members do not necessarily interfere with the prevailing social dynamics. In a group of five or six for example, basic alignments between one conjugal pair and another, or between sexes, can be easily set aside as participants readily shift and re-shift team alliances from audience to team member unrehearsed but guided by prompts in the conversation.

The Roles of Audience

In 'everyday' life (Goffman, 1959) the role of audience is highly reflexive as the part an individual plays is adapted to the parts played by others present effectively compressing the role into two. An audience may assume that the performance presented to them is all that there is to the individual who acts out the performance. 'Audience segregation' occurs when the performer takes care not to repeat the same performance to two audiences, especially if those audiences are known to one another. On the other hand the performer is careful to make points of detail consistent; for example, length of time in 'high status' places in case they are cross-validated by different audiences.

The role of the audience is to give a proper amount of attention and to exercise tact in holding back a willingness to project their own performances and in providing appropriate cues and feedback to the performer. There is a core element of trust and loyalty to the play being staged to the extent that audiences must fill these roles in order that the production may take place. Errors of judgement or lapses of consistency by a novice performer, for example, will often be ignored or overlooked in the interests that 'the show must go on'. Travellers' tales, the normal display of cultural capital, are usually led by a dominant actor yet a fair and even opportunity for others to perform is a core value. It is considered inappropriate to hog the limelight at the expense of others and overall a sense of 'decorum' tends to prevail even when travellers' tales appear overtly competitive in nature.

More experienced travellers have not just travelled more widely or for longer but have a broader vocabulary and lexicon of sign cues. In conversation, an experienced traveller will be able to ascertain the experience of others through their response to particular details which would normally prompt certain responses.

> The first island we went to … we were just walking on the beach and saw some locals sitting in their house or whatever and walked up and said hi and they invited us for kava of course, sat around and talked to them for a long time … just talked to them and they showed us around a little bit.

The ability to affect familiarity or playing down of high value sign cues is a mark of high cultural capital, but one which is lost on the unfamiliar. The performer exercises expressive control in being able to adapt a performance to the perceived appropriate level for the audience in question, leading in part to the tendency of clique formation and the segmentation of the backpacker population generally. This behaviour often forms the basis of small talk when encounters are first initiated. They provide an efficient means by which individuals sort themselves socially.

Goffman argues that everyday performances in Anglo-American society often must pass a strict test of aptness, fitness, propriety and decorum and that individuals are often more preoccupied by the standards of their own activity to notice the standards which are unthinkingly applied. Many of our respondents identified a core motivation to travel as being the need to escape the 'suffocating' constraints of social performance in favour of a social environment where the rules of the game are more flexible and open to adaptation.

> I had a day when I had a new mirror delivered to the office and I turned around and I kind of caught a glimpse of myself sitting back on the phone to clients and it was my father sitting in the chair, I'd put on weight … big red braces and I just thought, geez I'm 25, this is nuts! I looked like my father. I had a bit of a panic attack and started thinking about getting away.

Backpacker travel generally has the core characteristic of seeking other cultural environments expressly for the dual purposes of freeing oneself from the overly familiar rules of performance and replacing them with rules from other cultures, or more commonly, enjoying the opportunity to act obliviously to local customs. The previously mentioned differentiation between one resort and another suggests that individuals effectively shop around sampling different ways of performing and trying on different roles towards a strategic objective. In the case below the need to satisfy expectations of the audience is emphasised as is the implicit relationship between identity and image.

> I don't know if it always happens but that's part of the reason … get a sun tan. Getting a sun tan is certainly … well I don't know about other countries, but for English girls, getting a sun tan and going home is really quite a big thing I think. When people come away to sort of change their image … nobody wants to go home and look the same as they did before.

The act of performance is naturally subject to human foibles and errors of judgement. The impression of reality fostered by performance can be fragile and shattered by relatively minor mishaps. One of the drivers of the regular mobility displayed by the backpacker population can be attributed to the removal of self from performances which have gone wrong or which have been less than successful in achieving the desired impression. Scenes of embarrassment or discomfort or indeed boredom can be quickly and easily replaced with a fresh start at the next place, all the time learning from past experience.

> … as [anonymous] was saying, to reinvent yourself completely.

Some individuals use this transient environment to give deliberately false performances and masquerade as someone they would prefer other people to think they are. These performances are sometimes influenced by the performances of others by borrowing stories, lines and mannerisms normally towards the attainment of an idealised identity. The successful maintenance of affected characters requires a constant social distance through which the audience is held in a state of mystification in regard to the performer. Whilst this action may be used by those seeking to masquerade, the state of audience mystification is also key to the performance of the new self on the return home. The various roles and characters a traveller assumes are in part rehearsal for the return home, a kind of psychodrama or *anticipatory socialisation* where time is taken to learn the performance. Too much detail may threaten to shatter carefully constructed impressions. Editing of photographs before display, for example, will reduce chances of the audience gaining anything other than the desired impression. The on-the-spot editing capability of digital cameras was noticeably favoured by many for their ability to facilitate these strategic representations.

'The Tourism Production': Discourses of Backpacker Performance

The cultural context of backpacking in Fiji reveals a number of ways in which the 'other' is conceived and perceived and the reflective nature of long-term budget travel. The apparent ease of backpacking in the island groups may to some extent encourage more mainstream tourist roles amongst backpackers and an apparent lack of interest in the cultural context beyond superficial encounters with 'locals'.

> … we haven't done that for Fiji [researched appropriate behaviours and local customs] and I find that quite interesting that we hadn't because when … I did Wellington learning about the manners of the country and what's polite and what's not polite, but for some reason we just plonk ourselves on the beach and do nothing.

Many backpackers note that travelling in Fiji is relatively introverted socially as compared to other destinations, social relations being largely confined to the 'resort bubble'. This amplified cultural context itself accentuates the cultural characteristics of 'outside' environments yet casts them firmly as backdrops to the main production.

> [at the resort] … they were still living in a village … which was nice because we got to see what Fiji … you know … it shouldn't be like home otherwise you wouldn't choose to go travelling there.

Other extras are cast in the 'eye candy' role by resort managers and are similarly interpreted in ways which conform to an accepted script, here reminiscent of the 'noble savage':

> And then that evening they … it was their island dance show and they all came out all covered in oil and skirts … and then they were doing all this very macho dancing and proper like sort of baton with fire on the end and actually spinning it around faster and faster and then lying down and spinning it … at which point all the girls were just sat there going oh my God … oh my God … they're very gorgeous … and they were just absolutely beautiful … white smiles … lovely big eyes … very … lovely … and really … just really friendly … you know you can tell someone's just really warm and genuine.

Children are frequently included as extras in photographs in part because the social connotations of playing with children are notably absent, but also because they form a counterpoint for a raft of perceived ills pervading Westernised lifestyles. Similarly, the cross-cultural context frequently reminds the actors of the social constraints on the roles they would normally perform in their home environments.

You know like a mother's letting their children going ... just go off into the water and play with people, when they barely can't swim and trusting them to be ... in England, if a man picked up a child or ... like some of the boys have here picked up the children and thrown them around ... in England you would have to really watch you know ... people would be watching you wondering whether ... you know.

As noted earlier backpackers are by no means a homogeneous group but are highly segmented most notably around the issue of travel experience. Young travellers are perceived to be inexperienced, commonly favouring 'packaged' backpacker products which feature party culture and group activities. This socio-cultural segmentation of backpackers is naturally associated with a differentiation of the corresponding tourist complex.

So you find differences between ... because that's what we found in New Zealand for example, that more and more people would travel on these backpacker networks are younger than the people over 25 to late 20s, early 30s, identifying other options like buying their own car ... and all these kind of things.

Conforming to established patterns, roles and behaviours is fundamental to articulating the identity of individuals in time and space. Just as important, however, are the experiences which deviate from the accepted script and demand new interpretations of each character and their role. The ability to ad lib and improvise as part of the overall performance remains a core feature of the backpacker role despite the increasingly mainstream structure of the industry worldwide. Improvisation achieves its highest cultural capital when the unexpected is able to be assimilated as 'normal' or 'passé'.

The director–actor relationship is by no means perfect and is often subject to misrepresentation if the director creates scenes which deviate from the script such as when the tourist–traveller discourse is challenged:

I think as well I was quite surprised because we are backpackers and when we stayed in Nadi, they put your serviette on your lap and all that sort of thing ...

The importance of improvisation as a defining characteristic of backpacker travel is underlined when inconsistencies to that role are encountered, in this case mores and customs which constrain the backpacker's traditional 'grazing' approach to consuming cultures and indigenous lifestyles:

I didn't realise you wouldn't be able to just go to a village and walk around and sit and talk to people ... that you actually have to be invited or taken in ... when you feel you're invited somewhere it's nice but it also makes you less relaxed, you feel like you're on a tour group ... it's nice to be able to just wander around but you feel like you have to ask to go to these places.

Drug culture is a traditional part of backpacker culture particularly in developing country destinations, and Fiji is no exception, particularly with respect to marijuana use. The role of drug culture varies between resorts, some being alcohol focused while others implicitly tolerating marijuana use amongst both hosts and guests. As distinct from some South East Asian destinations 'designer' and 'hard' drugs are relatively uncommon in Fiji. Not only does the drug attitude of particular resorts produce a corresponding shift in the role and script each character will assume while there, encounters with drug culture illustrate the extent to which backpacking is often associated with rethinking one's own life script and reinterpreting discourses of power and control:

> I think that's part of travelling ... you realise that some of the things that you've lived your life by have maybe ... I mean I've always been incredibly anti-drugs and all this kind of stuff ... and I suddenly thought God I've based all this decision on something I know nothing about and how on earth can you do that ... I think rather than just becoming a puppet of my parents ... they don't like drugs, I don't like drugs, but I don't know whether they base their things on just ... the all drugs are bad type thing or whether they actually tried drugs.

Encounters on the edge of comfort zones appear to stimulate departures from the accepted script to the realm of improvisation, normally accompanied by introspection of previously unchallenged values and the discourses pervading them. As well as the boundaries constructed by legal systems, cross-cultural relationships reveal a similar set of boundaries demanding new interpretations of meaning. As noted earlier, the characters projected are often highly sexualised revealing the relative absence of social constraints on sexual relations, and for women, opportunities to engage in cross-cultural (sexual) encounters.

> Martin ... my Fijian friend said that it's been rated in a magazine, the third best place to get sex in the world ... on Beachcomber Island ... was the third best place to go out and get sex. I think people drank a lot and there was a lot ... you know quite often we went into the dorm and there were people having sex just in the dorm ... yeah ... all over the beach at night there were people ... you'd wake up ...

It is not unusual for young women to pursue their self-imposed goal of having sex with a different partner on every island visited be they other backpackers or local men whereas male travellers predominantly seek sex with young women travellers. For women, the sexual act itself is less of a topic for discussion than the way in which the cultural divide is challenged by pushing the cross-cultural boundaries of courtship:

> ... it is hard to know with Fijians, where you stand. If somebody ... if a guy said to you, look do you want to go and walk along the beach? Automatically you'd think, well no I don't want to do that because you know if I walk along the beach with him then you know ... am I leading him on ... that sort of thing. But at the same time you feel like you don't know their culture and if you turn them down, it could be ... they could be purely innocent and it could be really rude.

Issues of how to manage encounters are common in conversations amongst women. Individually some cross-cultural encounters revealed the extent to which sexual relations in their own 'Western' culture are highly prescribed and cynical of overt romanticism and naivete.

> I just thought that he'd be really sort of clingy and horrible and he wasn't at all ...we went and sat on the beach and he can play the guitar and sing ... which I love and very few English guys can sing ... so he was playing guitar and we were both singing together, which at home you just wouldn't do because it would just be too cheesy and horrible, but there it was really nice.

Tourism, Performance and Interpretation: Beyond the Metaphor

Central to the concepts discussed here is their perpetual nature, that the way people behave is the basis of social relations. We should not assume that calculated performances are necessarily false, contrived or designed to mislead; rather we should see them in the context of how people wish to lead their lives in the settings which surround them, and as a means through which they might aspire to a better future. In most day-to-day encounters performances are routine, unselfconscious and habitual. What is interesting about the backpacker case is that the performances represent specific strategies to gain leverage with which they are able to manœuvre themselves to different positions in these relations.

In most societies and cultures there is a major or general system of stratification and in most societies there is an idealisation of the higher strata and some aspiration on the part of those in low places to move to higher ones. Upward mobility involves the presentation of proper performances. Proper performances necessitate the proper sign equipment and familiarity with the management of it; from here the signs can be used to embellish and illumine daily performances with a desirable social style. The performance of individuals tends to incorporate and exemplify the officially accredited values of society as a whole and more specifically of backpacking as a sub-cultural form. In this sense performance is an expressive rejuvenation and reaffirmation of the moral values of the culture and wider society.

We should remain aware of the extent to which certain roles and performances will vary from destination to destination, particularly at the national level. Fiji is a desirable destination because it provides opportunities for certain types of behaviour and will undoubtedly be highly influenced by its dominance of travellers from the United Kingdom. Other backpacker destinations have very different characteristics to their tourism orientation. It would be interesting to explore performances in other places where the cultural, social and/or environmental context is different from that described here to find out the nature of general and specific performances. Many of the performances we have focused on here are in fixed, relatively controlled settings. A further avenue of research therefore would be the exploration of tourist performances in comparatively unregulated, mobile, transitory environments, where encounters are less predictable and where there is more cultural interchange than is characteristic of backpacker travel in Fiji. Further and much broader opportunities for research also emerge when we consider the perspective of hosts and those involved in facilitating the art of tourism.

Goffman's analysis reminds us that the performance of the tourist, in this case the backpacker, is itself an act of production of tourism: that tourism is ultimately about the personal journey of the individual facilitated by the complex machinery and relationships of industry, government and community.

> A correctly staged and performed scene leads the audience to impute a self to a performed character, but this imputation – this self – is a *product* of a scene that comes off, and is not a *cause* of it. (Goffman, 1959: 252)

What began as an interesting excursion on a relatively untravelled theoretical path has emerged as an immensely powerful interpretive perspective with seemingly endless scope to mine the metaphor for further symbolism. So neat the fit, the temptation to advance the performance metaphor as a defining theorisation of tourism is for the moment carefully avoided. Notably absent in the literature is a body of research which critically examines performance in the context of entrepreneurship. Given recent theorisations arguing the circularity and inseparability of production and consumption, the crystallisation of the 'tourists as performers' concept has the potential to contribute significantly to a seamless and holistic interpretation of the tourism phenomenon.

The voices of our respondents frequently appropriate the terminology of performance practice, yet explicit recognition of tourism as performance remains, at least from the industry perspective, relatively taboo ('tabu'). At the theatre, we are obliged to suspend reality and see the actors only for the characters they play rather than as actors playing those roles. Similarly, tourism demands the complicity of tourists, that they engage in at least partial denial of their tourist identities and enter its mythical realm of real, authentic and unmediated experience. In this context the analytical liberty of applying the language and terminology of the theatre should not be regarded as a progressive layering of meaning but the reinterpretation of an existing reality. In this sense, performance ceases to resemble a metaphor, a mode of representation, but rather a way in which people live and create their lives.

At the methodological level, Goffman's dialectic between the impression a performer 'gives' and the impression they 'give off' remains a constant challenge to performance focused research. The previously noted 'information game' implicitly incorporates a personal and 'back region' to a performance which will always elude the researcher, and so it should. The interpretive dimension throws up its share of challenges for the researcher between the human interpersonal level in which friendships and relationships are formed and the more abstract consideration of tourism impacts in developing countries where backpacker behaviour set against profound disparities of wealth can appear, at best, distasteful.

Whilst popular conceptualisations of tourism involve the movement of the body in time and space in order to experience 'something different', we argue that the success of this activity is largely dependent on the ability of individuals to perform a series of relatively prescribed yet adaptable roles. In the case of Fiji, these roles are constructed and performed relative to an individual's global travel behaviour. Furthermore, the traveller performances we observed are just a small part in the broader performances of social life and consumption practice. We are constantly reminded of the extent to which consumer classes are 'at one' with the nuances of meaning and symbolic interpretation which are central to performing cultures.

References

Adams, K.M. (1984) Come to Tana Toraja, 'Land of the Heavenly Kings': Travel agents as brokers in ethnicity. *Annals of Tourism Research* 11, 469–85.

Adler, J. (1989) Travel as performed art. *American Journal of Sociology* 94, 366–91.

Adorno, T.W. and Horkheimer, M. (1971) *Dialectic of Enlightment*. New York: Herder & Herder.

Aitchinson, C. (1999) New cultural geographies: The spatiality of leisure, gender and sexuality. *Leisure Studies* 18, 19–39.

Amin, A. and Thrift, N. (2000) What kind of economic theory for what kind of economic geography? *Antipode* 32, 4–9.

Ateljevic, I. (2000) Circuits of tourism: Stepping beyond a production-consumption dichotomy. *Tourism Geographies* 2 (4), 369–88.

Ateljevic, I. and Doorne, S. (2001) 'Nowhere left to run': A study of value boundaries and segmentation within the Backpacker Market of New Zealand. In J.A. Mazanec, G.I. Crouch, J.R. Brent Ritchie and A.G. Woodside (eds) *Consumer Psychology of Tourism, Hospitality and Leisure* (pp. 169–87). London: CAB International.

Ateljevic, I. and Doorne, S. (2003) Culture, economy and tourism commodities: Social relations of production and consumption. *Tourist Studies* 3, 123–41.

Ateljevic, I. and Doorne, S. (2004) Theoretical encounters: A review of backpacker literature. In G. Richards and J. Wilson (eds) *The Global Nomad: Backpacker Travel in Theory and Practice* (pp. 50–76). Clevedon: Channel View Publications.

Boissevain, J. (1996) Ritual, tourism and cultural commoditization in Malta: Culture by the pound? In T. Selwyn (ed.) *The Tourist Image: Myths and Myth Making in Tourism* (pp. 27–43). Chichester: John Wiley.

Bourdieu, P. (1984) *Distinction: A Social Critique of the Judgement of Taste.* London: Routledge & Kegan Paul.

Britton, S. (1978) *Tourism in a Peripheral Capitalist Economy: The Case of Fiji.* Wellington: Micrographics Bureau, Government Printing Office

Britton, S. (1991) Tourism, capital and place: Towards a critical geography of tourism. *Environment and Planning D: Society and Space* 9, 451–78.

Britton, S. and Clarke, W. (eds) (1987) *Ambiguous Alternative: Tourism in Small Developing Countries.* Suva: University of South Pacific.

Cohen E. (1973) Nomads from affluence: Notes on the phenomenon of drifter–tourism. *International Journal of Comparative Sociology* 14, 89–103.

Coleman, M. and Crang, M. (eds) (2002) *Tourism: Between Place and Performance.* Oxford: Berghahn.

Crain, M. (1996) Negotiating identities in Quito's cultural borderlands: Native women's performance for the Ecuadorian tourist market. In D. Howes (ed.) *Cross-Cultural Consumption: Global Markets, Local Realities* (pp. 125–37). London: Routledge.

Crang, P. (1997) Performing the tourist product. In C. Rojek and J. Urry (eds) *Touring Cultures: Transformations of Travel and Theory* (pp. 37–54). London: Routledge.

Crang, P. and Malbon, B. (1996) Consuming geographies: A review essay. *Transactions of the Institute of British Geographers* 21, 704–11.

Crewe, L. and Lowe, M. (1995) Gap on the map? Towards a geography of consumption and identity. *Environment and Planning A* 27, 1877–98.

Crick, M. (1989) Representations of international tourism in the social sciences: Sun, sex, sights, savings, and servility. *Annual Review of Anthropology* 18, 307–44.

Dann G.M.S. (2002) The tourist as a metaphor of the social world. In G.M.S. Dann (ed.) *The Tourist as a Metaphor of the Social World* (pp. 1–17).Wallingford: CAB International.

Denzin, N. (1997) *Interpretative Ethnography: Ethnographic Practises for the 21st Century.* Thousand Oaks, CA: Sage.

Desforges, L. (1998) Checking out the planet: Global representations/local identities and youth travel. In T. Skelton and G. Valentine (eds) *Cool Places: Geographies of Youth Culture* (pp. 175–92). New York: Routledge.

Desforges, L. (2000) Travelling the world: Identity and travel biography. *Annals of Tourism Research* 27, 926–45.

Edensor, T. (1998) *Tourists at the Taj: Performance and Meaning at a Symbolic Site.* London: Routledge.

Edensor, T. (2000) Staging tourism: Tourists as performers. *Annals of Tourism Research* 27, 322–44.

Elsrud, T. (2001) Risk creation in travelling: Backpacker adventure narration. *Annals of Tourism Research* 28, 597–617.

Evans, M. (1988) Participant observation: The researcher as research tool. In J. Eyles and D. Smith (eds) *Qualitative Methods in Human Geography* (pp. 197–218). Cambridge: Polity Press.

Eyles, J. (1988) Interpreting the geographical world. In J. Eyles and D.M. Smith (eds) *Qualitative Methods in Human Geography* (pp. 197–218). Cambridge: Polity Press.

Featherstone, M. (1987a) Lifestyle and consumer culture. *Theory, Culture and Society* 4, 55–70.

Featherstone, M. (1987b) Leisure, symbolic power and the life course. In J. Horne, D. Jary and A. Tomlinson (eds) *Sport, Leisure and Social Relations* (pp. 113–38). London: Routledge.

Featherstone, M. (1991) *Consumer Culture and Postmodernism*. London: Sage.

Fiji International Visitors Survey (2002) Ministry of Tourism and Stollznow Research.

Fiji Taskforce (2001) *Enquiry into the Backpacker Segment of Fiji's Tourism Industry*. Bangkok: PATA.

Franklin, A. and Crang, M. (2001) The trouble with tourism and travel theory? *Tourist Studies* 1, 5–22.

Giddens, A. (1991) *Modernity and Self-identity: Self and Society in the Late Modern Age*. Cambridge: Polity Press.

Giorgi, A. (ed.) (1985) *Phenomenology and Psychological Research*. Pittsburgh: Duquesne University Press.

Glennie, P.D. and Thrift, N.J. (1993) Modern consumption: Theorising commodities and consumers. *Environment and Planning D: Society and Space* 11, 603.

Goffman, E. (1959) *The Presentation of Self in Everyday Life*. New York: Doubleday Anchor.

Greenwood, D.J. (1978) Culture by the pound: An anthropological perspective on tourism as cultural commoditization. In V. Smith (ed.) *Hosts and Guests: The Anthropology of Tourism* (pp. 129–38). Philadelphia: University of Pennsylvania Press.

Harding, S. and Hintikka, M. (eds) (1983) *Discovering Reality: Feminist Perspectives on Epistemology, Metaphysics, Methodology and Philosophy of Science*. Dordrecht: Riedel.

Hall, S. (ed.) (1997) *Representation: Cultural Representations and Signifying Practises*. London: Sage and Open University.

Hall, C.M. and Page, S.J. (1996) Introduction: The context of tourism development in the South Pacific. In C.M. Hall and S.J. Page (eds) *Tourism in the Pacific: Issues and Cases* (pp. 1-15). London: International Thomson Business Press.

Jackson, P. (1999) Commodity cultures: The traffic in things. *Transactions of the Institute of British Geographers* 24, 95–108.

Jackson, P. and Holbrook, B. (1995) Multiple meanings; Shopping and the cultural politics of identity. *Environment and Planning A* 27, 1913–30.

Kirschenblatt-Gimblett, B. (1998) *Destination Culture: Tourism, Museums, and Heritage*. Berkeley, CA: University of California Press.

Lanfant, M.F. (1995) Introduction. In M.F. Lanfant, J.B. Allcock and E.M. Bruner (eds) *International Tourism: Identity and Change* (pp. 1–23). London: Sage.

Lefevbre, H. (1971) *Everyday Life in the Modern Life*. Harmondsworth: Allen Lane.

Luckacs, G. (1971) *History and Class Consciousness*. London: New Left Books.

Lurry, C. (1996) *Consumer Culture*. Cambridge: Polity Press.

MacCannell, D. (1999) *The Tourist: A New Theory of the New Leisure Class* (2nd edn). Berkeley, CA: University of California Press. [First published in 1976].

Marcuse, H. (1964) *One Dimensional Man*. London: Routledge.

Miller, D. (ed.) (1995) *Acknowledging Consumption*. London: Routledge.

Miller, D. (ed.) (1998) *Material Cultures: Why Some Things Matter*. London: University College.

Miller, D., Jackson, P., Thrift, N., Holbrook, B. and Rowlands, M. (1998) *Shopping, Place and Identity*. London: Leicester University Press.

Morgan, N. and Pritchard, A. (1998) *Tourism Promotion and Power: Creating Images, Creating Identities*. Chichester: John Wiley.

Moustakas, C. (1994) *Phenomenological Research Methods*. Thousand Oaks, CA: Sage.

Mowforth, M. and Munt, I. (1998) *Tourism and Sustainability: New Tourism in the Third World*. London: Routledge.

Munt, I. (1994) The 'Other' postmodern tourism: Culture, travel and the new middle classes. *Theory, Culture and Society* 11, 101–23.

Pearce, S. (ed.) (1997) *Experiencing Material Culture in the Western World*. London: Leicester University Press.

Perkins, H.C. and Thorns D.C. (2001) Gazing or performing? Reflections on Urry's tourist gaze in the context of contemporary experience in the Antipodes. *International Sociology* 16, 185–204.

Plange, N. (1996) Fiji. In C.M. Hall and S.J. Page (eds) *Tourism in the Pacific: Issues and Cases* (pp. 205–18). London: International Thomson Business Plan.

Ringer, G. (1998) *Destinations: Cultural Landscapes of Tourism*. London: Routledge.

Rojek, C. (1995) *Decentring Leisure*. London: Sage.

Rojek, C. and Urry, J. (eds) (1997) *Touring Cultures: Transformations of Travel and Theory*. London: Routledge.

Sayer, A. (2000) Critical and uncritical cultural turn. In I. Cook, D. Crouch, S. Naylor and J.R. Ryan (eds) *Cultural Turns/Geographical Turns* (pp. 166–82). Harlow: Prentice Hall.

Sharpley, R. (1996) Tourism and consumer culture in postmodern society. In M. Robinson, N. Evans and P. Callaghan (eds) *Tourism and Culture Towards the 21st Century Cultural Change* (pp. 220–56). Sunderland: The Centre for Travel and Tourism.

Smith, V. (ed.) (1978) *Hosts and Guests: The Anthropology of Tourism*. Oxford: Blackwell.

Smith, S. (1988) Constructing local knowledge: The analysis of self in everyday life. In J. Eyles and D. Smith (eds) *Qualitative Methods in Human Geography* (pp. 17–38). Cambridge: Polity Press.

Squire, S.J. (1994) Accounting for cultural meanings: The interface between geography and tourism studies re-examined. *Progress in Human Geography* 18, 1–16.

Stanley, D. (1996) *South Pacific Handbook*. California: Moon Publications.

Tourism New Zealand (2003) *The Backpacker Market in New Zealand*. Wellington: Tourism New Zealand.

Turner, L. and Ash, J. (1975) *The Golden Hordes: International Tourism and the Pleasure Periphery*. London: Constable.

Urry, J. (2002) *The Tourist Gaze* (2nd edn). London: Sage. [First published in 1990].

Chapter 9

Wales Underground: Discursive Frames and Authenticities in Welsh Mining Heritage Tourism Events

NIKOLAS COUPLAND, PETER GARRETT and HYWEL BISHOP

Introduction

'Authenticity' and 'heritage tourism' are locked in a treacly critical antagonism. If heritage tourism is a symptom of 'the disease of nostalgia', then critics will want to debunk it for its inauthenticity – its myopic and rose-tinted versionising of preferred histories, packaged for consumption. But self-aware critics will be wary of signing up to the principle of authenticity that underpins this stance. Authenticity tends to be thought of as a moribund casualty of late-modernity. If critics see it this way, they can locate another myopia – a naive, pre-critical faith in structured certainties. Trapped in this double bind, tourism research's engagement with the concept of authenticity seems at this point to have stalled, although the problem may have as much to do with the ethos of criticism as with the theoretical nexus itself. Our argument will be that issues of authenticity *do* define much of what is distinctive in the design, implementation and experiencing of at least some forms of heritage tourism, but that it is self-defeating to frame the debate through totalising and critically precious questions like: Is heritage tourism inauthentic?

We take a more sociolinguistic approach and ask how the discourse practices of heritage tourism events can themselves deploy or invoke notions of authenticity. How are authenticity and inauthenticity worked into the talk and texts of such events? What resources do the events make available to participants for reading the values we associate with authentic experience? To address these questions we analyse textual data from three sites, which are all 'visitor attractions' linked to mining industries in Wales. The texts in question are a diverse set from the three sites. They include promotional literature (leaflets and web pages) and display texts positioned within sites themselves, such as poster displays explaining the history of mines and local communities. But we also examine fragments of spoken interaction – texts that form part of visitors' engagement with heritage displays, and in this case specifically tour guides' talk. All three types of text generate meanings and values associated with authenticity, but authenticity in different frames (Goffman, 1974, 1981), different structures of meaning and value. We hope to show how different, internally coherent systems of authentic experience inform these texts. Moving away from what we believe are excessively unitary discussions of 'heritage inauthenticity', we suggest that specific heritage tourism events in specific discursive frames actually offer their visitors rather rich resources for authentic experience.

The first of the three sites we deal with is Big Pit: National Mining Museum of Wales / Y Pwll Mawr: Amgueddfa Lofaol Genedlaethol Cymru (http://www.nmgw.ac.uk/bigpit), located in Blaenafon, Torfaen, in south-east Wales. Big Pit is a constituent institution of the National Museums and Galleries of Wales and is therefore currently a free (sponsored) attraction, as well as being part of a UNESCO sponsored World Heritage Site. The second is Rhondda Heritage Park (http://www.rhonddaheritagepark.com/), which has been historically and critically interpreted by Bella Dicks (Dicks, 2000). Rhondda Heritage Park is located on the site of the Lewis Merthyr Colliery in Trehafod, Rhondda Cynon Taff, in the south Wales Valleys. Dicks describes in detail the complex history of sponsorship that created and currently sustains the site, which is owned and funded by Rhondda Cynon Taff County Borough Council. The third site is the privately owned Llechwedd Slate Caverns (http://www.wales-underground.org.uk/llechwedd/; see also http://www.llechwedd.co.uk/) in Blaenau Ffestiniog, Gwynedd, north Wales. The second and third are both paid-entry sites; neither is promoted bilingually via the web.

All three sites share some general characteristics. Each one is a rearticulation of Welsh mining communities, their work practices and lifestyles. The Rhondda Valleys – there are two, although they are often referred to in the singular – are a powerful icon of Welsh, British and global industrialisation (Williams, 1985; Davies, 1993; Smith, 1999), as is the south Wales Coalfield generally, whose eastern limit is defined by Big Pit. The slate mining industry of north-west Wales started earlier, was on a far smaller scale and was less obviously ravaged by rapid and ruthless deindustrialisation during the second half of the 20th century (Lindsay, 1974). Nevertheless, the three visitor sites take their main themes from a shared narrative and material repertoire. This includes big-scale natural phenomena, harsh and short lives, child labour underground, risks and tragedies, strong and resilient communities, political activism, dirt, dark and depth, vernacular culture, and a detailed inventory of material objects and technical terms associated with mining – 'drams', 'roadways', 'Davey lamps', 'black damp', 'mandrels', and so on. Each site gives visitors access to 'the mining experience in Wales' by means of various exhibitions and tours, but with different affordances and emphases in each case. The three sites feature on a longer list of mining-themed tourist sites and exhibitions in Wales whose title – *Wales Underground* (see http://www.wales-underground.org.uk/) – we have borrowed for this chapter.

Before we turn to the data we take a short tour around the literature on heritage tourism, where two review chapters – by John Urry and John Frow – seem particularly helpful. Although they treat much the same research material, the differences between them indicate the different assumptions one can bring to tourism research and to a discussion of authenticity.

Urry's Worries and Frow's Frown

John Urry begins his review of approaches to tourism with Daniel Boorstin's view of tourism as a series of 'pseudo-events' (Boorstin, 1964; Urry, 2002: 7), which is where tourism research seems to have opened its complex relationship with the concept of authenticity. In a chapter on heritage and history, Urry considers Robert Hewison's (1987) acerbic line on heritage and the decline of Britain. Hewison's view of heritage as 'bogus history', as reactionary and as part of 'what is wrong with Britain', is recycled in many historical reviews of tourism theory. He is a familiar critical target for reviewers, presumably because he is seen as over-determining authenticity and equating it with 'real history'. His argument is along the lines of: 'if history matters, we should do it properly', begging all the obvious epistemological questions about what 'proper history' might be and how it might be achieved.

Urry then takes in Dean MacCannell's influential argument (1999 ([1976]), contradicting Hewison. In this alternative view, tourists are engaged in an authenticity quest, seeking out the authentic values and experiences that modern life denies them. MacCannell's argument appears to rescue tourism from the global charge of 'being inauthentic'. It even dignifies tourism practices, asserting the agentive capacity of tourists and their powers of cultural discrimination. This early opposition between Hewison and MacCannell in fact makes it clear that tourism has a highly vested interest in authenticity, using the concept to discredit or to validate the cultural practice of tourism itself. This involves making rather reckless assumptions about authenticity and about how it can be accessed.

For example, MacCannell's view positions heritage tourism partly as a response to the belief that 'real lives' are lived 'backstage' rather than 'on stage' or 'on the front stage' so that they are not typically amenable to tourist inspection. The 'frontstage' versus 'backstage' contrast seems to invoke Erving Goffman's dramaturgical sociology of social interaction, although his theorising of social life as drama is far more nuanced than this (cf. Goffman, 1997: 95ff., see also Doorne & Ateljevic, this volume). Sociolinguists will read MacCannell as offering a version of William Labov's much debated and often criticised 'observer's paradox', being the claim that we are unable to directly observe the sorts of untainted and 'natural' language data that we need to observe (Labov, 1972). Urry writes that, in response to the problem of accessing 'backstage' cultural practice, 'the people being observed and local tourist entrepreneurs gradually come to construct backstages in a contrived and artificial manner' (2002: 9), by which he means heritage tourism displays.

These closely related distinctions between 'frontstage' and 'backstage' and 'real' and 'contrived' are based on several questionable assumptions. The view that the reality of 'real life' is amenable to inspection, if only we can access its covert places and practices, is a thoroughly idealised and romanticised view of social life in its 'natural' state. It has surfaced repeatedly in sociolinguistics, for example, where concepts such as 'natural speech' and 'the vernacular' (people's base-line ways of speaking) have been commonplace (see Labov, 1972 and the critique in Coupland, 2001a, 2001b). It seems unlikely that we can convincingly devise criteria for recognising or even theorising the unsullied socio-cultural realities that (some) tourists (arguably) seek. Correspondingly, it seems unnecessary to dislocate 'culture' from 'cultural performance' (see below), and second-order recontextualisations of cultural practices may in fact merit particular attention. The overriding point is that authenticity needs to be addressed contextually, and that we have to move the debate on from categorical claims about whether first-order or second-order manifestations of culture are inherently favoured or disfavoured sites for authenticity. We would certainly want to keep the social 'contrivance' of authenticity in focus, following the premise that, however we define authenticity, it must be a quality of experience that is constituted discursively.

To some extent voicing our own reservations, and although authenticity is fundamentally implicated in the mainstream theoretical discussions that his chapter reviews, Urry himself shows rather little enthusiasm for authenticity as a simple explanatory concept in tourism research. He makes the important observation that cultural remaking happens in non-tourism contexts as well (2002: 9, see also Rojek & Urry, 1997). This echoes anthropological linguists' stance on cultural performance as repeated entextualisation (e.g. Bauman & Briggs, 1990). This is the view that culture is a set of constantly re-enacted discursive forms, with each performance orienting both to its precursors and to its new local context. This is an emancipating idea for tourism research, because it invites us to inspect the texts of tourism encounters with an open perspective on what their cultural representations achieve, in particular contexts. It invites us to construe representation as a complex, contextualised and contextualising process, rather than as the display or reproduction of pre-formed cultural content.

On the whole, Urry's chapter is more concerned with documenting shifts in tourism practices, in the UK but also globally, and with the distinctive qualities of different genres and instances of tourism attractions. He sees a general growth in the heritage sector of tourism, particularly in the UK and in areas where there has been rapid de-industrialisation, 'particularly because of the apparently heroic quality of the work, as in coalmine or steel works' (Urry, 2002: 97). The implication is that heritage tourism is a growing cultural practice which needs its own historical and political accounts, and this is surely right. Urry reminds us that heritage tourism services diverse local needs, such as pressure from local groups seeking to hold on aspects of 'their' history (where issues of ownership are interestingly complex), efforts to maintain skills associated with particular trades, community regeneration projects, as well as local commercial initiatives (Urry, 2002: 101). Dicks' account of Rhondda Heritage Park is similarly strong on these functional considerations, as is Sharon Macdonald in her (1997) analysis of a heritage centre on the Isle of Skye in the Scottish Hebrides.

Perhaps the most important facet of Urry's perspective for our own research is his argument that heritage displays are amenable to different patterns of interpretation in different contexts (2002: 102). This view, implicitly in his discussion but crucially for us, breaks the assumption that qualities of authenticity or inauthenticity are inherent in heritage displays themselves. So, people visiting 'their own' heritage sites, as local people or as people from a linked diaspora (Cohen, 1997), might be expected to bring ambitions and sensitivities to such events which differ from those of other groups of tourists. Urry's over-arching theme of 'the tourist gaze' specifically foregrounds diverse ways of looking and diverse constructions of value in tourist experiences, which is precisely our analytic concern with the *Wales Underground* instances in this chapter.

As a more abstract theorist of culture and postmodernity, John Frow (1997) can afford to be much less grounded in social functionality. Starting points for his essay on 'Tourism and the semiotics of nostalgia' are Plato, Baudrillard and Deleuze and their treatments of the simulacrum – the copy. Frow then introduces what he calls the 'three more or less standard moves' in discourse on tourism (Frow, 1997: 69). The first two of these are the Boorstin stance, as we discussed it above, which Frow says is the 'least interesting' of the moves, and the MacCannell stance on tourism as authenticity quest, with the associated problem of so-called 'frontstages' and 'backstages'. Frow suggests that MacCanell

> elaborates something like Baudrillard's theory of a historical regime of simulation in which the difference between original and copy falls away, and indeed where the very existence of an 'original' is a function of the copy. (Frow, 1997: 70)

This entertaining relativist paradox is unrevealing when we try to apply it to tourist experiences, especially if judging the status of 'an original' is a matter for tourists themselves rather than for all-seeing cultural critics. It may or may not be true that visitors to Rhondda Heritage Park become sensitised to an 'original Rhondda culture' through their gazing at reconstituted mineshafts and artefacts. But whatever sense of cultural authenticity they imbibe, it is not because 'the original' is evinced only through the existence of 'the copy'. Authenticity's trick is to persuade us that 'the original' pre-exists and evaluatively outweighs 'the copy', and the challenge is to see how this is achieved. Whatever, Frow agrees with Cohen's analysis that authenticity is an eminently modern value which is defined in the self-conscious and commodified present. Moderns seek out 'traditional cultures' which are unaware of their own relativity (Cohen, 1988; cf. Greenwood, 1989).

Frow's third move is represented by Jonathan Culler's formulation of the paradox of authenticity:

> The paradox, the dilemma of authenticity, is that to be experienced as authentic it must be marked as authentic, but when it is marked as authentic it is mediated, a sign of itself and hence not authentic in the sense of unspoiled. (Culler, 1981: 137, quoted in Frow, 1997: 73)

This is the idea captured in the well-worn tale of a tourist photographer eyeing a prefigured tourist 'view' and saying 'Wow, that's so postcard' (see Urry, this volume). Taking this perspective, Frow suggests that heritage tourism is locked into a 'spiral of simulations' (1997: 74). Tourist invasions of ever-more-remote sites progressively de-authenticate them, further confounding the authenticity quest. Paradoxicality dominates the interpretation. The tourist is excluded from experiencing social reality. Frow cites Anthony Giddens' (1990) thoughts about the disembedding of social relations from local spaces into 'stretched time-space matrices'; tourist spaces become 'non-places ... characteristic of [late-] modernity' (Frow, 1997: 75). Tradition is not only recontextualised in heritage tourism but 'invented', as in Eric Hobsbawm and Terence Ranger's (1992) influential treatment, to the effect that 'even the most "authentic" traditions are ... effects of a stylized simulation' (Frow, 1997: 77).

Frow's interesting discussion is densely loaded with perspectives and it is sometimes difficult to distinguish his own critical positions from those of authors he cites. It is difficult to be sure that he intends to uniformly or definitively relativise out the value of authenticity for tourism research, but he certainly does a good bit of this. On the 'functional' side, he cites Patrick Wright (1985), at length and with a degree of approval, on the remembrance function of some sorts of heritage – 'affirming continuity with the dead' (Frow, 1997: 78). But he constructs himself as a critic revelling in paradox and infinite deferral, not least when we remember that Frow suggests that his three 'moves' – three theoretical phases of tourism research – become 'less uninteresting' as they become less specific and more nihilistic. It is in his most personal paragraphs that he is also most damning of heritage:

> [I]t remains crucial to guard a deep suspicion of the auratic [aura-bearing] object, whatever the uses to which it may seem to lend itself. Nostalgia for a lost authenticity is a paralysing structure of historical reflection. (Frow, 1997: 79)

It seems that Boorstin lives, after all! And then, here is Frow on tourism in general:

> Exalting the *non-*'modern—the natural, the non-Western, the traditional, the exotic, the primitive, the different—it [tourism] brings whatever corresponds to these imaginary terms within the sphere of their categorical opposite, a 'modernity' constructed in this relation, and destructive of the very otherness it celebrates. (Frow, 1997: 101)

This condemnatory flourish, with which the essay ends, is surely itself a Culler-esque metasign. Frow refuses to be 'paralysed', which would not be an authentic stance for a self-respecting cultural critic, and he eventually signs up to an easy anti-tourism.

Authenticity in the Discourse of Wales Underground Events

Aligning rather more, then, with John Urry's concerns about over-simplifying and under-contextualising authenticity than with John Frow's ultimate condemnation of the tourist enterprise, we turn to our data. As we suggested earlier, we are interested to assess the various dimensions of talk and text where authenticity is in different ways invoked in the language of *Wales Underground* events. 'Event' is a key notion in our approach, in the sociolinguistic sense of 'speech event' introduced by Dell Hymes (1974). One reason for not running too quickly to generalisations about authenticity in heritage tourism is that each of the 'visits' or 'experiences' or 'facilities' we are focusing on is constructed and experienced as an event through several distinct communicative episodes. These episodes imply and predispose different ways of potentially orienting to a piece of Welsh mining heritage, through what Hymes calls 'norms of interaction' and 'norms of interpretation' associated with culturally specified event types. 'A visit' to any one of the three sites in our data might typically elicit different orientations, even by any one individual visitor, held either in sequence or concurrently. This is in addition to different styles of enactment constructed within or across events staged by sites' designers. In this way we are trying to develop a 'multifunctional' or 'multiple goals' perspective on heritage authenticities, drawing generally on literatures in discourse analysis where the multifunctionality of language in use is axiomatic (Halliday, 1978).

As participants in a complex, partly prefigurable, episodic event, many visitors will first engage with a site by viewing some form of promotional publicity for the facility, perhaps a website, a television commercial, a leaflet or a booklet. These texts are carefully prepared to attract visitors of different sorts who predictably have different priorities for their visits. Then, all three of our sites have self-publicising and self-introducing texts and scripts which socialise visitors into the experience they are about to have. These include 'orientation' notices and posters, some of which carry dense historical linguistic and visual texts. But we could also include other text types which we do not have space to consider here – road signs identifying 'heritage sites' (these are distinctive brown signs in the current UK convention), information printed on tickets, or introductory spoken scripts by ticket-office staff describing tours and facilities. Tours themselves have a complex sociolinguistic structure, featuring small talk and banter by tour guides, which contrasts with their more scripted narratives and explanations, and question/answer sessions. As Dicks describes for Rhondda Heritage Park (where these are a dominant feature), some sites have elaborate audio-visual tableaux, with voiced characters describing their 'personal' experiences of working underground in particular roles at particular periods. Across this wide range of genres, text types, sub-events and ways of participating communicatively, issues of authenticity and inauthenticity play out in complex ways. In following sections we illustrate discourses around authenticity by looking at specific instances of the three text types we mentioned earlier: (a) promotional texts, (b) orienting posters, and (c) tour guides' banter.

There is some overlap with the 'communication approach' Dicks (2000: 70ff.) develops for her research on Rhondda Heritage Park (which provides an invaluable context for our own work in many ways) and the constructivist approaches to tourism research (e.g. Cohen, 1988; Bruner, 1994; Olsen, 2002; Shepherd, 2002). But, despite for example Dicks' comments about text construction and her use of interview transcripts, social construction in these treatments is not generally analysed in relation to semantic structures of language texts per se. Our own method has been to assemble whatever situated texts are available to us, through our own visits to the three sites, and to trawl them for their explicit or implicit constructions of authenticity in different value frames. We collected advertising leaflets, guidebooks, education packs and printed pages from relevant websites. We made field notes to record details of audio-visual performances, guides' commentaries, both scripted and extemporised, and details of our own personal exchanges with tour guides. The result is a diffuse corpus of linguistic and textual material which goes some way to representing the communicative experiences associated with the three *Wales Underground* sites.

Like Bruner (1994), our method of engaging with authenticity is to start by unpacking its key semantic dimensions. In earlier research, Coupland (2003) has suggested five qualitative traits which, in concert, are taken to define the authenticity of objects and experiences. Authentic phenomena have (1) *ontological solidity* (existing in essence, as core rather than peripheral phenomena), (2) *historicity* (they have survived and 'have history on their side'), (3) *systemic coherence* (they are properly constituted in significant contexts), (4) *consensus* (they are authorised and accepted as such within a particular constituency), and (5) *value* (they are revered and endorsed as 'mattering', they are anchoring points). Our commentaries pick out these qualities as they are worked into particular texts. The five traits or criteria have a general heuristic value for the analysis; we do not present them as a fully cogent or exhaustive 'theory' of authenticity. But they do help us to identify the range of semantic resources available for the discursive construction of authenticity.

Promotional texts

Texts 1 and 2 are reformatted from different hard-copy promotional leaflets advertising Big Pit. The first is a section on Big Pit from the general Wales Underground leaflet. The second is an extract from *The Big Pit Story*, a 30-page illustrated booklet for sale at the site which combines historical facts, colour photographs, quotes from miners (*Mining Memories*) and a section on *What the Children Say*, a 'testimonial' section.

Text 1: The Wales Underground Leaflet's Entry on Big Pit

The real underground experience! Big Pit is the UK's leading mining museum. It is a real colliery, which gives visitors the opportunity to take an authentic underground tour and walk the same passages walked by miners, who for 200 years extracted the precious mineral that powered the industrial revolution.

Going underground. Kitted out in helmet, cap-lamp and battery pack, you descend 300 feet (90 metres) to an underground world of coal faces and levels, airdoors and stable. With just the light of your cap-lamp to light the inky darkness and an ex-miner as your guide, you get a real sense of life at the coal face.

Underground tours run daily between 10am and 3.30pm. Voted Tour of the Year and Welsh Family Attraction of the Year by the Good Britain Guide (2002).

Blaenafon – World Heritage Site. Blaenafon had a pivotal role in the beginnings of the Industrial Revolution. A revolution that transformed the landscape, culture and society of not just the South Wales valleys, but of the whole world. The wider impact of Blaenafon's unique industrial heritage was recognised with the award of World Heritage Status.

Planning your visit. Underground tours take approximately one hour. Please wear warm clothing and sensible footwear. Free coach and car parking.

Access. Big Pit welcomes accompanied wheelchair users, please phone and book your underground tour in advance. An Access Guide is available on our website. Children must be at least one metre tall to go underground.

Big Pit is currently in the last phases of re-development. However, it is open to the public. With support from the Heritage Lottery Fund, the Wales Tourist Board, the European Union and several private trusts and funds, we are spending nearly £7 million on the site, restoring the surface buildings and ensuring a more enjoyable experience for visitors in the future.

Visitors can still enjoy a tasty meal or snack from the 'Flavours of Wales' menu in the original miners' canteen and buy quality souvenirs of your visit from the gift shop.

Text 2: The Big Pit Story (page 2)
'Big Pit Blaenafon, which in its heyday employed 1300 men and produced more than 25,000 tons of coal a year, is now a very special museum. Nothing is contrived or invented here – Big Pit is the real thing. It looks much as it did on that February day in 1980 when the last miners clocked off. There is the same clutter of buildings around the pit shaft, and the wheels of the winding gear still revolve every day.

The difference today is that most of those who now make the descent to the pit bottom are not miners, but people who have never ventured underground before... With former miners acting as guides, visitors learn something of what it was like living in one of the toughest working environments of all.

Visitors to Big Pit find that many of their preconceived ideas of coalmining are false. For some, their very first sight of the place is itself a surprise. They imagine that a colliery, especially one in South Wales, must inevitably be on the floor of a valley, hemmed in by towering hills and rows of terraced houses. But Big Pit stands high on the bracken-clad moors of north Torfaen, swept by invigorating winds and commanding extensive views.

Lexis on the theme of authenticity appears at the surface of both these texts. 'Real', 'authentic' and 'original' appear as adjectives in Text 1; Big

Pit is described as 'the real thing' in Text 2, which also directly denies the qualities of 'contrived' and 'invented'. The quality of 'real' is attributed to the colliery itself in the phrase 'a real colliery' – where the word 'colliery' is itself a more authentic variant than 'mine' or 'coalmine' according to vernacular usage within the industry in south Wales. But lexical claims to authenticity – using adjectives 'real' and 'authentic' – are not generally sufficient to conjure authentic experience; witness 'the real thing' that is reputedly Coca-Cola. Culler's paradox might apply here, if we believed that direct claims to authenticity mark their targets to be necessarily *in*authentic by virtue of the act of claiming itself. But this seems to be far too stringent an interpretive rule, and it is more reasonable to argue that a textual claim that Big Pit 'is a real colliery' neither achieves nor precludes a sense of its authenticity for visitors. Rather, we have to look at the texts' less overt semantic operations and how they might frame authenticity for visitors. If we do this, we see that the five qualities of authenticity are quite widely thematised.

The projected authenticity of Big Pit as a colliery in Texts 1 and 2 is based in large part in its material historicity and continuity as a structure and space. Temporal expressions therefore have an authenticating function in the discourse, e.g. 'for 200 years' (time-depth) and 'still revolve' (practice maintained across time). Hard material objects ('helmet, cap-lamp and battery pack', 'clutter of buildings', 'pit shaft', 'wheels', 'winding gear', etc.) have a timeless quality, and the awkward term auratic might therefore be appropriate for them. Nouns like these are distributed in the texts referring to solid ontologicals with the specific value of historicity. Their authenticating quality of coherence is based on their 'proper fit' within the iconography of mining.

So if Big Pit is indeed convincingly characterised as 'the real thing' in these texts, it is because the texts marshal the core semantic attributes of authenticity which then go on to be fulfilled in other facets of the visit event. It is not that there is no disjunction between 'the real, original Big Pit' and 'what is available now in the heritage tourist version of Big Pit', and authenticity in that direct sense is not at issue. In fact the texts represent this disjunction clearly in phrases like 'looks much as it did' (entailing 'similar but different') and 'the same passages walked by miners' (entailing shifted human participation in the same spaces). But the texts conjure sufficient elements of material ontological sameness and continuity to warrant a plausible claim to being 'real' in the local context of a heritage reconstruction. Many heritage tourism sites have this appeal of offering opportunities to engage with places and objects that were formally exclusive domains of manual work. The experience of 'being there' (what we conventionally refer to as 'first-hand' experience) and seeing or touching ('direct' or 'unmediated' experience) the physical paraphernalia of the domain is one affordance for achieving a sense of authenticity. In summary, we can identify *material historical authenticity* as one coherent discursive frame operative in the data. Texts draw attention to this affordance and are themselves a resource for visitors to define their visit as authentic.

At the same time, Texts 1 and 2 amply represent the consumption frame within which a materially authentic Big Pit is amenable to be visited. Nouns like 'experience', 'museum', and 'tour' lexicalise tourist activities directly, and Text 1 refers to Big Pit's standing in the tourism institutions' internal awards system ('Voted Tour of the Year'). Contextual demands on visitors ('wear warm clothing', 'must be at least one metre tall', etc.) and the site's provision for them outside as well as inside the tour ('buy quality souvenirs', 'free coach and car parking') are also mentioned. The commercial service basis of the encounter is therefore clearly marked in the texts, even in connection with non-pay sites like Big Pit. In our view these elements of meaning constitute a second general frame – a frame of *legitimate tourist consumption* – through which visitors are *also* invited to contextualise their participation in *Wales Underground* events. Whatever historical and cultural authenticities they may seek out and experience during visits, the events and their texts offer them ways to function, and function authentically, as consuming tourists.

Texts 1 and 2 interestingly juxtapose semantic features from the two value frames mentioned so far, and they seem entirely capable of sustaining the two systems in parallel. In terms of the grossest 'authenticity' versus 'tourism' duality that we met in the review section, we would be forced to see an incompatibility between them. In fact there are some interesting phrases in those texts where the syntax implies a compatibility between concepts that are, in conventional semantic terms, anomalous. 'The real underground experience' is one of these phrases; 'take an authentic underground tour' and 'a real sense of life at the coal face' are others. In prescriptive mode we might ask: Can a tour in itself be authentic?, etc. But the issue is of course not one of 'non-standard syntax'. These phrases creatively blend values from two ideological frames, expressing the potential for second-order authenticities in heritage displays. They concede certain primary authenticities – there is no move in the texts to describe the experience of mining practice achieved by Big Pit visitors as anything other than 'a *sense* of life at the coal face'. Tourists are well aware that their own participation in 'the mining experience' is, in one frame, a simulated participation. In Goffman's (1981) terms they are fully ratified as participants in some roles (audience members, onlookers, car drivers, etc.) and only selectively ratified in others (they wear helmets, battery packs and lamps in Big Pit, but they do not drill, shovel and sweat). In their 'sensible footwear' with 'free parking' they could hardly be more aware of their role specificities. As legitimately consuming tourists they can only aspire to 'learn something of what it was like'. But in another frame they are positioned to experience the material historical authentic-ities of *Wales Underground*.

Individual attractions differ in the degree to which they foreground these two and other value frames. Llechwedd Slate Caverns in fact offer many of the same physical and material resources as Big Pit – the impos-ing depth and darkness of the mine workings, mining implements, drams, roadways, etc. – and broadly the same historical continuities. But publicity material for Llechwedd, as in *Wales Underground*'s entry in its hard-copy leaflet, tends to prioritise the tourist consumption frame (see Text 3).

Text 3: Wales Underground on Llechwedd Slate Caverns
Ride Britain's steepest passenger railway into the spectacular Deep Mine while the ghost of a Victorian slate miner guides you through ten dramatic son et lumiere sequences, and past the underground lake used for two Hollywood films. Ride the Miners' tramway through enormous man-made caverns, and demonstration of ancient mining skills. Explore the surface museum, or the Victorian Village where pub and shops use re-minted Victorian coins obtainable from the Old Bank.

The text is grammatically structured as a series of imperatives ('Ride...', 'Ride...', 'Explore...'), which function as invitations or chal-lenges. This is a genre-marking convention for texts promoting active tourism 'experiences'. Verbs 'ride' and 'explore' combine meanings of activity and agency which position visitors as controlling and choice-exercising consumers. (Contrast the declarative verb forms in 'visitors take a tour' or 'visitors learn' in the Big Pit texts, above.) Superlative expressions ('Britain's steepest...') and the piling up of pre-modifiers in noun-phrases ('the spectacular Deep Mine', 'enormous man-made caverns', etc.) are markers of a product advertising genre. Their effect is to pack out the nominal entities with a semantic density that predicts an intensity of experience – here, during a visit. All three texts above draw on these stylistic resources, but they cluster more densely in the Llechwedd promotion.

In the consumption frame, hyperbole is normative. Expressing size and grandeur in the material historical authenticity frame is therefore discur-sively difficult, which might explain Text 1's use of only numerical values for depth. Adjectives like 'spectacular', 'dramatic' and 'enormous' in Text 3 imply consumption values – the sensory impact of an environment on visitors – just as the material resource of 'the underground lake' in Text 3 is validated by saying it has been 'used' in 'two Hollywood films', rather than by describing it as a natural phenomenon. 'Ancient mining skills' seems to establish more discontinuity than continuity between the original circumstances and the present day, just as 'ghost of a Victorian slate miner' exoticises the visit into the realm of the fantastic rather than the culturally remembered.

Orienting posters

A third value frame for *Wales Underground* events is associated with what Bella Dicks calls 'memorialist discourse', which she defines as 'reminiscences composed of the personal, the detailed and the idiosyncratic', and which she opposes to 'a spectacle-oriented theatre model' (Dicks, 2000: 188; see also 148ff.). By 'theatre model' she means the staging of audio-visual displays, which were designed for Rhondda Heritage Park by professional companies. Dicks provides a rich historical account of efforts made in the conceiving and designing of Rhondda Heritage Park to build a dignified, accurate and 'locally relevant' display, although she also shows how financial and technological considerations led to the exhibits being professionalised, which in practice undermined the memorialist objective. Nevertheless, some of the key texts that *Wales Underground* events make available are strong constructions of the distinctive qualities of mining people and communities, 'how things were', and particularly 'how hard it was'.

Issues of authenticity are clearly at the heart of 'memorialist discourse', including a heritage display's ambition to present an enduring record of the true values of defunct mining communities. There is a clear pedagogic purpose behind these displays and their texts, explaining former cultural forms and practices, instructing visitors about them, and reminding those within the culture about their value. The pedagogy is in turn driven by a moral assumption – that documenting, knowing and remembering 'matters'. Historicity is therefore once again a dominant dimension of authenticity in this third value frame, but history in the definition, redefinition and validation of community – the frame of *community authentication*.

Figures 9.1 and 9.2 are photographed details of two of a series of posters displayed in a museum-like space at Rhondda Heritage Park which is used as a waiting area for visitors, before they take the standard tour. Figure 9.3 is a photograph of one detail of the museum area, showing artefacts from a Welsh kitchen from around 1890; Figure 9.4 is a photograph of the main foyer area, beyond the service desk, from which tours begin. These images show how the 'orientation' phase of a Rhondda Heritage Park visit builds historical community context for the tour to follow. Visitors move through a visual/artefactual collage of historical scene-setting detail, and it is in this context that they may read texts like those in Figures 9.1 and 9.2 from the poster display. Such texts explicitly dignify the Rhondda communities for whom mining was a primary rationale.

Figure 9.1 'The price of coal' – poster, Rhondda Heritage Park

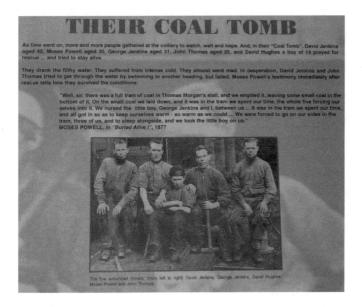

Figure 9.2 'Their coal tomb' – poster, Rhondda Heritage Park

Figure 9.3 'Welsh kitchen' – detail of the museum area, Rhondda Heritage Park

Figure 9.4 Foyer – entrance to the museum, Rhondda Heritage Park

The community authentication frame is built around themes such as poverty, risk, death, struggle, camaraderie, technical competence, ritual and order. Narratives of risk, death and struggle fill out the texts of Figures 9.1 and 9.2, 'The Price of Coal' and 'Their Coal Tomb', both of which document disasters in the south Wales Coalfield. The texts are not purely windows on the facts of disastrous accidents. They offer a moral agenda for visitors to carry with them throughout their visits – and no doubt beyond this – as an interpretive frame. Notice 'of course' in the second paragraph of Figure 9.1. 'Of course' conventionally marks the proposition to which it is attached as an obvious or taken-for-granted one. The text therefore constructs an opposition between the taken-for-grantedness of regular deaths in collieries and the singularity of the 'heroic and historic events recorded here' (in the first paragraph). The second paragraph repeats the contrast more forcibly with the suggestion that 'Tynewydd's loss of just four men and one boy may seem little more than an irrelevant historical detail'. The text is opening up issues of scale and of value: how much are 'just' these five lives worth? How should we properly react?

The question is politicised, partly through the text's implication that these deaths might be seen, *by someone*, as 'an irrelevant historical detail'. In contrast, the text (whose authorship is anonymous and therefore perhaps claims to be consensual – 'saying what we all think') proposes that these are 'shocking statistics' (right panel, paragraph 4). The grammar of the texts positions mineworkers as people affected not only by natural disaster ('trapped', 'drowned', 'killed') but by the decisions of others, being 'called upon to struggle through hell'. Note Moses Powell's powerless 'sir', similarly, in the text directly above the image in Figure 9.2. The main image in Figure 9.1 adds the idea of the victims' powerlessness, after death, to maintain dignified graves (or 'tidy' graves, as it would be in Valleys vernacular English). The reconstituted shop-front in Figure 9.4 echoes the tidy simplicity of a Valleys street, just as the kitchen fire and mantelpiece in Figure 9.3 connote a simple functionality. These two displays fill out some of the material particularities of hard-lived Valleys lives, and challenge us to deny their continuing 'relevance'. The poster display's function is to begin to redress a lack of control and autonomy, which reaches out beyond the lifespan of the dead. The text mentions the 'steady dripping away of life, which found no place in newspapers or record' (Figure 9.1, right panel, paragraph 4). These texts and the reconstructed environments *are* a belated record. The texts borrow from the genre of obituary. Even though the five 'entombed' miners in Figure 9.2 survived, they are now dead and their ordeal needs to be recorded.

This is where the theorising of heritage bites. The critical view that 'heritage tourism de-authenticates' flies directly in the face of efforts – of the sort documented historically by Dicks and in the historicising texts and displays we have just considered – to dignify individuals and communities. And dignification requires authentication as a prior process: before we can 'pay our respects' we must inspect 'the realities of life as it was underground'. No doubt a case could be made that the particular images and stories displayed as orientation at Rhondda Heritage Park are historically selective and that they privilege a 'victim's view' of *Wales Underground*. But that doesn't seem to be the main issue in, for example, John Frow's third-phase theorising of authenticity. His case was that, in our tourist quests, authenticities recede before us as signs of themselves. There is no doubt that the Rhondda mining community is idealised in the sorts of representation we are considering, but how does it 'recede', rather than being made more vital or more accessible? Our best answers would lie in detailed ethnographies of different visitors' engagement with these representations and narratives, which go beyond our analytic scope here. But we assume that at least some visitors will entertain the community authentication frame in ways that are emancipating for them. It will allow them to establish or to revisit personal or family coherence with the mining communities that defined the Rhondda Valleys as a distinctive (and for many, a prototypically 'Welsh') cultural formation.

Tour guides' banter

The fully institutionalised texts we have considered so far are only some of the discursive resources available for working through issues of authenticity during visits. The final domain we consider here is the talk of tour guides, and again this falls into different genres. Our repeated visits to *Wales Underground* sites make it clear that, even across different tour guides within the same tour, the content of guides' commentaries is to an extent standardised. Largely the same historical facts (e.g. details of the ownership of mines), quantitative details (e.g. heights and depths, tonnages of coal and slate produced), and demonstrations (e.g. how a Davey lamp works, how a drilling tool was used, total darkness underground) find their way into most guides' comments. Commentaries are only partly monologic, however, and the convention for guides at each of the three sites we visited is to encourage question/answer sequences and, outside of this, a general air of informality and spontaneity. Particularly during the two colliery tours, both of which are guided by ex-miners, guides maintain a stream of 'banter' with visitors and occasionally with other guides. In this section we reproduce fragments of guides' talk which we again take to bear on authenticity.

Tour guides at mining heritage sites who are ex-miners occupy complex slots in the discursive ecology of visits. As guides they have an institutionalised documenting role; they are required to present the experience in the way it is designed to be presented. To this extent they are mouthpieces for content and perspectives authored elsewhere. But as ex-miners, they are also a key part of the 'living historical content' of the display, recreating aspects of their original lives at work underground. Then again, they are reflexive interpreters of that content, authorised to vivify it and elaborate on it as independent authors in their own regard. Not surprisingly therefore, they are able to accommodate and articulate the different value frames operative in an event. Our ethnographic notes captured some of the ephemera of guides' banter, most of it at Big Pit. Descending the shaft at Big Pit, one guide says to an older female visitor:

Text 4
Do you want to come home with me? Do you want to have a Welsh cwtch?

Another, who has asked visitors where they are from and whether they are Welsh, says:

Text 5
I haven't got a good voice (.) I'm not Tom Jones (.) but I wish I had the money

The same guide, when he has just told us his age, says:

Text 6
I'm sixty years old and it's me who do have the headaches now

At pit bottom, when the visiting group is entering the cage to ascend the shaft, a guide says:

Text 7
Going up in the shaft we turn the lights off so you can see the natural daylight (.) and so that if the cable breaks you can't see where you're falling

Another says:

Text 8
Mind your (h)eads on the pipes (.) or mind your heads I should say (.) when you think about it logically it's the cheapest way to be buried

These fragments are a mix of teases and minor improprieties which might seem to stand outside of the predictable genre of tour guides' talk. Dark humour about accidents and death and mock-sexual overtures (a *cwtch* is a 'cuddle') to visitors may not seem to be solicitous guiding. But the guides are doing self-stereotyping. This is true of their vernacular speech styles: compound verbs like 'do have' are a Valleys English dialect feature; the 'correcting' of aitchless '(h)eads' to 'heads' in Text 9 shows metalinguistic sensitivity to dialect. Some of their quips play off the serious and pervasive pedagogy (see Texts 1 and 2, above) about mines as risky environments in which many people died. As elements of heritage content, the guides are performing the discursive 'key' or 'tone' of life underground, the camaraderie and resilience that is mythologised as a quality of community in the more directly pedagogic, scripted texts. To quote from *The Big Pit Story* booklet (see Text 2, above), 'With former miners acting as guides, visitors learn something of what it was like living in one of the toughest working environments of all'. As Text 1 claimed: 'you get a real sense of life at the coal face'.

The banter is of course performed knowingly. We even have one piece of textual evidence of how it can be pre-scripted. Text 10 is an exchange between two tour guides (with the name 'Dai' fictionalised) that we noted at Rhondda Heritage Park, at the start of a tour:

Text 9
Guide 1: hello Dai (.) that was a hell of a draft when you came through
          that door b'there look?
Guide 2: no it's the beer mun

In fact there was no apparent 'draft' through the opened door (on a particularly hot day) and the pat timing of the exchange clearly indicated that this was not 'fresh talk'. It was a set-piece joke ('draft' as flatulence), setting the guide's relational style at the beginning of the tour. Banter might even be a performance requirement of the role, and we noticed a few other apparently formulaic exchanges between guides of this sort. But are formulas and scripting of this sort 'damaging simulation'?

The frame of legitimate tourist consumption validates the local 'entertainment' function of an event. Guides' mild sexual teasing, dark humour about mining accidents and punning sit easily within this frame, but, at least for some visitors, it may also bear significance within the frame of community authentication. We saw how threat to life and a mining community's resilience to threat are recurrent themes in that frame. Expressions like 'you can't see where you're falling' in Text 7 and 'the cheapest way to be buried' in Text 8 have an inescapable historical salience at the level of the Rhondda mining community, even when voiced humorously in the local circumstances of a visit. They bridge intertextually to the themes of the orienting posters that we considered earlier. Valleys dialect, doing banter and indeed the guides themselves are metasigns – manifestations of community, and of Rhondda community 'then' as well as 'now'. In different interpretive frames the individuals we are referring to as 'tour-guides' feature simultaneously as contemporary entertainers and as socio-historical icons.

There were moments in our visits when guides did self-positioning rather explicitly. On one occasion a tour guide at Big Pit suggested to a group of visitors:

Text 10
Don't take us serious. Try to recreate a bit of atmosphere (.) that's what it's all about

The comment seemed to be an implicit apology for a teasing exchange. But 'what it's all about' was amenable to different interpretations. The frame of tourist consumption positioned 'us' and 'you' in Text 10 as 'tour guides' and 'visitors', respectively. But in the visitor role we felt entitled to 'take him serious' in a wider socio-historical context that the event had sensitised us to repeatedly. Two centuries of repressive industrial relations, of oppressive manual work underground, and of building and destroying Rhondda communities, loomed behind an ephemeral 'bit of atmosphere'.

Conclusion: Performance, Authenicity and Discourse

The frame analysis approach we have been following is, as we said in the introduction, axiomatic in sociolinguistic approaches to discourse. Like notions of front/backstage, fresh talk and participation frameworks it is originally attributable to Erving Goffman, who had no hesitation about modelling all aspects of routine social interaction through the concepts of performance and dramaturgy (see Doorne & Ateljevic, this volume). As Goffman says, 'all the world is not, of course, a stage, but the crucial ways in which it is not are not easy to specify' (1997: 106).

But we do not need to read Goffman as debunking authenticity, *tout court*, in favour of pervasive performance. Analysing discourses of authenticity forces us to be circumspect about authenticity and performance alike. Social actors *do* seek out and value authenticity, often behind complicating layers of communicative strategies, norms and representations. Constructivism has banished simplistic assumptions about 'natural behaviour' and ideology-free social categories; that critical battle is won. Authenticity is clearly only approachable as a felt or an attributed or negotiated quality of social experience. It is certainly not a pre-discursive phenomenon offering itself for inspection, even if its main device is to imply that this is precisely the case. But rather than banishing authenticity and revelling in a supposed infinite regress of signification, we have gone after 'the discursive construction of authenticity'. We have found it to be a reasonably manageable empirical task, even though our readings of texts are inevitably open to reassessment by others. The concept of framing lets us see that, even in the politically contested and sometimes vilified context of 'heritage tourism' (which we are ultimately unhappy to treat as a unitary thing, but which most definitely entails cultural performance), there are multiple discursive routes into authenticity.

We have commented on three broadly differentiated frames, each of which, we hope to have shown, allows access to its own version of authentic experience. The materiality and timeless forms of grand-scale underground sites are one relevant construction. The very different but systemically coherent values of day-out tourism – more geared to commercial, practical and recreational concerns than to ontological and historical ones – are a second. Authenticating narratives and performances of retreating communities access a third frame, offering some people the means to renegotiate their own moral values and their historical senses of self. There are almost certainly other frames and more complex inter-relations among frames to be teased out in the data.

Our main conclusion is that critical commentaries of 'the necessary simulacra of heritage tourism' are hugely reductive. The argument that the globalising new economy is stripping away what we might have understood to be 'real community' (cf. Raymond Williams, 2003) is of course convincing. It would be hard to find clearer instances of the decimation of working-class industrial communities than the mining valleys of Wales. Monica Heller, for example, puts this case convincingly, and her summary phrase 'the commodification of authenticity' (Heller, 2003) does capture the inversions of community structures and identities that have followed the trashing of old-style production-based economies – in francophone Canada just as in Wales. We have not set out to dignify heritage or apologise for tourism. Our starting point has simply been that heritage, as John Urry argues, is an increasingly dominant cultural manifestation and one that we need to understand better. Heritage *does*, as Kirshenblatt-Gimblett (1995) shows, introduce new complexities of cultural representation, and necessarily complicates the processes by which we construct and experience authenticity.

But we have argued that authenticity, as a discursive construction of cultural ontology, historicity, coherence, consensus and value, is *not* simply outlawed or made redundant in heritage domains, and we have introduced some data that we believe make this point for us. In fact the discursive formats of heritage tourism events, at least in the instances we have examined, create distinctive opportunities for the construction of authenticity – or more accurately authentic*ities* in the plural, and much of the theoretical havoc caused by the term 'authenticity' stems from accepting its universalising singularity. Disconcerting though this may be, authenticities are always relative. As we have mentioned, the value component of authenticity always reflects a particular social consensus and the coherence of a particular system. Our focus on the diversity of discursive frames that mining heritage constructs for its participants is one way of operationalising this principle. Heritage performances prove *not* to be a resolute obstacle to authentic experience. We should not be surprised at this, given wide-ranging accounts in other research fields (Coupland, 2001b – comments on sociolinguistic aspects) of how cultural value and a meaningful sense of the real is increasingly located in performances – personal or institutional. The acceleration of this tendency is a hallmark of late-modernity.

Acknowledgements

This research is supported by a grant to Cardiff University's Centre for Language and Communication Research by the Leverhulme Trust, under the general title of *Language and Global Communication*, 2001–2006 (grant F/00 407/D; see http://www.global.cf.ac.uk/), which we gratefully acknowledge. The grant supports different empirical strands, including *Welsh Language and Welsh Identity under Globalisation*, to which this chapter contributes. We are grateful to Adam Jaworski and Annette Pritchard for their very valuable comments on an earlier draft.

References

Bauman, R. and Briggs, C. (1990) Poetics and performance as critical perspectives on language and social life. *Annual Review of Anthropology* 19, 59–88.
Boorstin, D. (1964) *The Image: A Guide to Pseudo-Events in America*. New York: Harper & Row.
Bruner, E. (1994) Abraham Lincoln as authentic reproduction: A critique of post-modernism. *American Anthropologist* 96, 397–415.
Cohen, E. (1988) Authenticity and commoditization in tourism. *Annals of Tourism Research* 15, 371–86.
Cohen, R. (1997) *Global Diasporas*. London: University College London Press.
Coupland, N. (2001a) Language, situation and the relational self: Theorising dialect style in sociolinguistics. In P. Eckert and J. Rickford (eds) *Style and Sociolinguistic Variation* (pp. 185–210). Cambridge: Cambridge University Press.
Coupland, N. (2001b) Dialect stylisation in radio talk. *Language in Society* 30, 345–75.
Coupland, N. (2003) Sociolinguistic authenticities. *Journal of Sociolinguistics* 7, 417–31.
Culler, J. (1981) Semiotics of tourism. *American Journal of Semiotics* 1, 127–40.
Davies, J. (1993) *A History of Wales*. Harmondsworth: Penguin.
Dicks, B. (2000) *Heritage, Place and Community*. Cardiff: University of Wales Press.
Frow, J. (1997) *Time and Commodity Culture: Essays in Cultural Theory and Postmodernism*. New York: Oxford University Press.
Giddens, A. (1990) *The Consequences of Modernity*. Stanford, CA: Stanford University Press.
Goffman, E. (1974) *Frame Analysis: An Essay on the Organization of Experience*. New York: Harper & Row.

Goffman, E. (1981) *Forms of Talk*. Philadelphia: University of Pennsylvania Press.

Goffman, E. (1997) *The Goffman Reader*. Edited by C. Lemert and A. Branaman. Malden, MA: Blackwell Publishers.

Greenwood, D.J. (1989) Culture by the pound: An anthropological perspective on tourism as cultural commoditization. In V.L. Smith (ed.) *Hosts and Guests* (pp. 180–95). Philadelphia: University of Pennsylvania Press.

Halliday, M.A.K. (1978) *Language as Social Semiotic: The Social Interpretation of Language and Meaning*. London: Edward Arnold.

Heller, M. (2003) Globalization, the new economy and the commodification of language and identity. *Journal of Sociolinguistics* 7, 473–98.

Hewison, R. (1987) *The Heritage Industry: Britain in a Climate of Decline*. London: Methuen.

Hobsbawm, E.J. and Ranger, T. (eds) (1992) *The Invention of Tradition*. Cambridge: Cambridge University Press.

Hymes, D. (1974) *Foundations in Sociolinguistics: An Ethnographic Approach*. Philadelphia: University of Pennsylvania Press.

Kirshenblatt-Gimblett, B. (1995) Theorizing heritage. *Ethnomusicology: Journal of the Society for Ethnomusicology* 39, 370 –85.

Labov, W. (1972) *Sociolinguistic Patterns*. Philadelphia: University of Pennsylvania Press.

Lindsay, J. (1974) *History of the North Wales Slate Industry*. Newton Abbot: David & Charles.

MacCannell, D. (1999) *The Tourist* (2nd edn). London: Macmillan. [First published in 1976.]

Macdonald, S. (1997) A people's story: Heritage, identity and authenticity. In C. Rojek and J. Urry (eds) *Touring Cultures* (pp. 155–75). London: Routledge.

Olsen, K. (2002) Authenticity as a concept in tourism research: The social organization of the experience of authenticity. *Tourist Studies* 2, 159–82.

Rojek, C. and Urry, J. (1997) Transformations of travel and theory. In C. Rojek and J. Urry (eds) *Touring Cultures: Transformations of Travel and Theory* (pp. 1–19). London: Routledge.

Shepherd, R. (2002) Commodification, culture and tourism. *Tourist Studies* 2, 183–201.

Smith, D. (1999) *Wales: A Question for History*. Bridgend: Seren.

Urry, J. (2002) *The Tourist Gaze* (2nd edn). London: Sage. [First published in 1990].

Williams, G.A. (1985) *When Was Wales?* London: Black Raven Books.

Williams, R. (2003) *Who Speaks for Wales? Nation, Culture, Identity*. Edited by D. Williams. Cardiff: University of Wales Press.

Wright, P. (1985) *On Living in an Old Country: The National Past in Contemporary Britain*. London: Verso.

Chapter 10

'Just Perfect!' The Pragmatics of Evaluation in Holiday Postcards

CHRIS KENNEDY

Introduction

Postcards are a major tourist market product if one judges by their ubiquity in shops and other outlets in holiday locations. The custom of sending postcards remains an important social practice as a means of communicating, while on holiday, with friends and relations who have remained at home. Linguistic aspects of holiday postcards are under-researched with most researchers more concerned with the visual images presented (e.g. Lofgren, 1986; Edwards, 1996; Geary & Webb, 1998; Whitaker, 2000; Pritchard & Morgan, 2003). In this chapter, I discuss the social meanings attached to postcards as cultural artefacts (Edwards, 1996) and, using data from a corpus of holiday postcards, investigate in particular the significance of evaluation in the genre, its interpretation by readers/recipients, and its various linguistic realisations. I shall be referring only to present-day 'holiday' postcards.

Collecting and Analysing the Corpus

The corpus which provides the data for this article consists of 100 holiday postcards written in 1995 by male and female 18–20 year old undergraduates from an English university to their male and female friends of the same age during a summer vacation period. The writers were tourists and were writing home to their friends.

'Opportunity' data collection was used in that two female undergraduate students asked their fellow students to give them any holiday postcards they had recently received during the summer vacation from friends. More than 100 were collected and a random selection was used to create the required number. Although this is a relatively small corpus, it can be regarded as a reliable and valid sample of the discourse community represented, that is young British undergraduates. No doubt some postcards were withheld by students because of the delicate nature of the content but I do not believe this has appreciably skewed the data since such postcards are likely to be relatively rare given the nature of the postcard as a public document. The holiday postcard genre (see below for a definition of 'genre') is highly predictable in linguistic terms and a collection of 100 from a relatively small set of writers means that we can make reasonably reliable and valid claims from the linguistic evidence provided by the data. No attempts are made however to generalise outside the genre and outside the discourse community represented.

Once the 100 postcards had been collected, the message on each one of the postcards was typed into a database as an individual Word file and then converted to *ascii* format for computer analysis. The message was typed exactly as it appeared on the postcard with no corrections or amendments made, and examples and extracts from the corpus are quoted in this article as they were written in the original data. The only exception is that, for the purposes of this chapter, any personal names given on the postcards were changed to preserve anonymity. Spelling 'errors' and other writer idiosyncrasies have been retained.

The corpus was then analysed using the Oxford Wordsmith Tools and the Longman Mini-Concordancer. Both programmes are accessible and easy to use. The Longman program is no longer available, but Wordsmith Tools can be ordered and downloaded from the OUP website. The programmes are able to process at speed large amounts of linguistic data to provide frequencies and to sort the data in various ways. Investigators wishing to discover how a particular linguistic item is used within the database can key in the item and the program will produce all the instances of the item together with its surrounding linguistic context. We shall see outputs of the programs as we proceed through this chapter.

Postcards as part of a literacy event

Tourists engage in a number of practices and take part in various social events while on holiday, both linguistic and non-linguistic, and one of the most important from a social point of view is the sending of holiday postcards. The literacy event (Street, 1995) that we have characterised as 'sending postcards' involves much more than the physical act of sending. The event can be broken down into a series of acts, most, but not all, necessary and obligatory, on the part of the writers/senders (and later readers/recipients). Underlying the event is the overall specific intention to communicate with those at a distance. The acts that make up the event include seeking an outlet selling postcards, selecting a postcard (at this point the recipient is explicitly considered for the first time and influences the choice of postcard especially its visual element), purchasing the card, composing the message, (when the recipient becomes a part of the communication) and posting.

The transmission of postcard from sender to recipient then takes place. On receipt the recipient 'reads' the card (both the visual and linguistic messages), perhaps discusses it with interested third parties, and may do a variety of things with it. It may be disposed of, perhaps after an acceptable time has elapsed. It is significant that postcards and by extension their senders are shown a degree of respect and assigned a social value since on receipt postcards are generally not immediately thrown away as for example circulars and other 'junkmail' might be. The postcard may be preserved for a while, perhaps attached, showing the picture rather than the text, to a kitchen noticeboard or refrigerator in a domestic context, or to a filing cabinet in a work context. More unusually, it may be added to an informal or formal postcard collection. Where subsequently the recipient and the sender linguistically interact with each other, whether face-to-face or remotely (for example, via letter, telephone, or email), there is usually a social obligation on the part of the recipient, often in the context of a follow-up conversation about the sender's holiday, to mention with an expression of thanks receipt of the postcard. If the recipient does not mention receipt, the sender will often enquire of the recipient whether the postcard arrived. If potential recipients or those who perceive themselves as such have not in fact been sent a postcard, they may well mention this fact, and express various degrees of offence, either directly to the sender or to a third party.

These reactions indicate the degree of social pressure associated with the sending of postcards and the sociocultural importance of postcards and their transmission in at least a British holidaying culture. The literacy event which we know today as the sending and receiving of holiday postcards is embedded in the culture in question. Other cultures may not have such a literacy event. In order for it to take place, certain preconditions which lead to the development of a present-day 'holiday postcard industry' must be met, including the existence of a developed economy with no restrictions on travel, people with available time and spending power for holidays, and a market for holidays which involve travel away from the immediate locality. I am of course referring here solely to the holiday postcard genre. Phillips (2000: 12–13) makes the point that in the early 20th century postcards were used for a variety of functions other than reporting on holiday experiences, much as the telephone and the email is used today (cf. Pritchard & Morgan, this volume).

Postcards as artefacts

The physical object of the postcard affects the literacy associated with it since it limits the quantity and type of language used. The postcard is normally a rectangular shape with standard measurements roughly 15x10 cms (though this will vary and larger sizes and 'fancy' shapes are available at greater cost). Generally one side of the postcard is devoted to an often idealised image relevant to the tourist location. I do not unfortunately have space here to discuss image relevance (i.e. who selects the postcard images and why), but whether the image is of a rural scene or a factory, which participants are portrayed and what they are doing is dictated by the ideology of the culture and is motivated by the identity and image the country or region concerned wishes to make public. Specific reference can be made to the image in the message though this is comparatively rare in the data that forms the basis for this article.

The reverse, non-image, side of the postcard is divided into two halves – the left-hand side for the sender's message; the right-hand for the recipient's address and postage element. The small space available limits considerably the feasible length of the message which has to be short, in turn affecting the content and the way it is expressed. Senders are aware of this limitation. One writer in the present corpus declares 'So much to say so little room'.

What might appear from the above a mundane characterisation of postcards does in fact illustrate at least four important aspects of what I shall call the 'genre' of holiday postcards. First, the postcard is a multimodal artefact (Kress & van Leeuwen, 2001) with visual as well as linguistic messages which have social meanings attached to them. Secondly, the postcard as the primary product of a literacy event is at the centre of an involved and complicated chain of linguistic and non-linguistic actions and there is a high degree of intertextuality linking the parts of the chain together. Thirdly, there is considerable social interaction both linguistic and non-linguistic between writer/sender and reader/recipient. Fourthly, the postcard despite being a small and seemingly trivial literacy artefact is in fact valued especially by recipients out of all proportion to its physical size.

Postcards as genre

Where a set of texts share the same communicative purpose and social ends they tend to share the same ideational, interpersonal and textual meanings (using Halliday's now familiar terms – Halliday, 1978) and exhibit as a result a common set of linguistic characteristics. The common name give to such a similar set of texts is 'genre' (e.g. Swales, 1990; Bhatia, 1993) and I shall be considering holiday postcards as a genre in the sense defined.

The purpose of postcards as acts of communication is to express feelings of solidarity between sender and recipient. The sender's wish to show that those not accompanying them on holiday and separated from them in space and time have not been forgotten. Similarly those not on holiday (the recipients) like to feel that they have been remembered by senders. Indeed as we have seen above, offence can be caused if a holiday postcard is not sent.

It is the act of sending that is important and we might conclude that the content (part of Halliday's ideational aspect of language) is not of concern to either sender or recipient in that it is not preserved, analysed or acted upon (although it is reacted to). Content is not regarded as serious, and is ephemeral, and in many ways the holiday postcard text is a form of phatic communion expressing social solidarity so that content becomes irrelevant.

However, to conclude this would be overstating the case. The major purpose of the genre in question is undoubtedly interpersonal (express-ing solidarity) but that purpose can only be achieved by senders if they select appropriate content (ideational meaning) and have the relevant linguistic resources to create a coherent message (Halliday's textual meaning). What is said, how it is said, and how it is put together in discourse is important in any successful act of communication.

One only has to look at attempts to manipulate holiday postcards in literature (e.g. Lodge, 1991) or their use in advertising, or deliberately to flout the conventions of the genre to see how important these linguistic inter-connections are. An example is given below. The postcard was delivered to my address and followed the normal layout of the postcard. Physically the artefact had the appearance of a postcard, except that the message was not hand-written, but was reproduced in typed italics (as an imitation of handwriting) with the line breaks as shown below.

> *Having a wonderful time.*
> *My wife, two kids and myself took the*
> *return ferry from Dover, hotel*
> *accommodation with breakfast for one*
> *night and 14 days AA Five Star Vehicle*
> *cover for an unbelievable price. It's so*
> *cheap we've booked the same again in*
> *June for just £188!*
> *You should try it!*
>
> *AA Overniter package deals available at*
> *AA shops.*
> *For further details call into your nearest*
> *AA shop*
> (address of local shop follows)

It is clear that we have here two genres – that of the holiday postcard and that of the advertisement. The copywriters have selected some features which they associate with the holiday postcard, notably the first sentence, the positive evaluation of the holiday experience ('unbelievable price'; 'so cheap'), and use of exclamation marks. (In fact, such evaluative features are shared with the genre of advertising). However, the text quickly flouts the conventions of the holiday postcard genre and moves into the advertisement genre. Relationships are known and there is a high degree of shared knowledge between senders and recipients of holiday postcards, so the writer of a holiday postcard would only need to use the form *we* rather than specify his wife and two children as participants. An unnecessary (for the holiday postcard) amount of detailed information follows with specific details and prices of the holiday package. The copy-writers need to provide this information to communicate the value of the package, while the writers of holiday postcards typically deal in more general non-specific information to create impressions rather than to communicate facts. Writers of holiday postcards, at least in the corpus presented in this chapter, do not typically talk about packages. If they did, a possible re-write of the advertisement to conform to the holiday postcard genre might read something like:

We got a great package,

omitting all the detail the copywriters regard as essential for their purposes.

The example above illustrates the major social purpose of the holiday postcard. The genre is *relational* (i.e. its purpose is to foster positive relationships) rather than *transactional* where the communicative purpose is to achieve defined ends and objectives. This accounts for the rapid switch in the language used in the example above from relational to transactional when the selling function of the message becomes salient.

Much research (e.g. Coupland, 2000; Koester, 2002; Holmes & Stubbe, 2003) shows how important the relational is, how it interacts in many situations with the transactional, and, indeed how, without it, much transactional work could not be achieved. In the case of the holiday postcard genre the relational element is likely to have a relevance to transactional ends in the longer term, since preserving a friendship may smooth subsequent transactional demands. Its immediate effect, however, at least in the cultural group being investigated (British university students) is predominantly relational and the postcards in the present corpus, therefore, belong at the relational end of the relational-transactional cline.

Two further contextual elements are significant. First, the text is hand-written often under time constraints with little pre-planning; no drafting is possible and space is restricted (as we have seen normally the left-hand blank half of the postcard). Secondly, the holiday postcard is a public document since it is not sealed (as a letter normally is) and can therefore can be read by those responsible for its transmission to its destination, and by those who share the recipient's address. It is interesting to note that there now exist on the market 'postcards' with an envelope attached. It would be interesting to find out why people buy these hybrid forms in preference to traditional postcards and whether the linguistic content of the private 'letter' postcard is in fact different from that of the public 'open' postcard.

Phillips (2000: 14), talking of postcards in general, lists some interesting strategies adopted by those wishing to disguise their message in some way, including using codes and writing the message upside down in relation to the address. An extreme example of the consequences of there being a potential public reader of postcards is found in the Lonely Planet guidebook advice to be positive and praising when sending postcards from North Korea so that they may be delivered more quickly. The implication is that postcards in the present political system in that country are read by the authorities and that speed of delivery correlates with degree of positive comment.

Additional Features of the Holiday Postcards Corpus

The following is one example from the data.

Dear Pat, Having a great time here in Florida. The weather's sunny and hot. We spent all day Sunday at Watermarine! We all got sunburnt, but none more than Alex. Went to Universal Studios yesterday and encountered their first powercut ever! Typical! Never mind we're off to Disneyworld now. See Ya Soon, Chris & John & Girls XXXX

The sample postcard illustrates a number of the aspects we have discussed above and shows some additional features of the corpus as a whole which I wish to discuss at this point.

The language of the postcards reflects a particular discourse community. In this case the community is composed of young students, who know each other well and interact with each other on a regular basis. There is a high degree of shared knowledge between them and they share common interests, tastes and lifestyles. The postcards show linguistic evidence of considerable interactivity between writer and reader.

Content tends to be expressed in general rather than specific terms. The sample text above shows an example of this general language in this case to express location: 'here in Florida'. Within the corpus as a whole, *here* is used frequently (47 times) to express location. In very few cases, (5) there is a following qualifier (see Figure 10.1) where the location is mentioned but still at a general rather than specific level (e.g. 'in Florida'; 'in Malta'; 'on Lake Michigan'). Detail in this genre is not required by readers and the use of *here* is exophoric. It is assumed that the reader knows where the writer is and the picture on the postcard gives a further indication of location.

e Saffron Dear Carrodine,Been **here** 2 days. Its cold here on Lake Mich
tby Abbey. It's really beautiful   **here**, surrounded by the Bay. Mary's cou
o see San francisco while I was **here**! Travelled down the West Coast fro
ea. We are enjoying it very much **here** and having fun dodging the sheep o
Anyway must go as they say over **here**, See you soon, Graham & Jill Dear
family. Yours John Hello I'm **here**, safe and sound. The camp is set i
e. We are having a great holiday **here** - the weather has been super. Its
ppens it is, 'cos its great down **here**. The only draw back being no wind.
talks and workshops. The people **here** are really friendly and kind. I've
Bill Hello Carrodine, Well I'm **here** feeling very spiritual in this com
There are lots of things to do up **here** with our friends Jenny and Mark. H
X   Dear Jane, Well, **here** I am sitting in glorious sunshine
Love Phill Dearest Carrodene, **Here** I am in the City of extremes. It's
hilling to think it all happened **here**. Girl, I've walked & walked & walk
camels for company. It's great **here**, ballroom dancing everynight at th
ined. Oh well I'd rather get wet **here** than stay dry in London Best Wish
ad a good holiday. Wish you were **here**. Susan Dear Diane. We are having
Dear Chris, Having a great time **here** in Florida. The weather's sunny &
ou? Well I'm having a brill time **here** in Malta. I've got a suntan alread
hrough that you made. Anyway I'm **here** in the City of Angels and having a
Love, Lynne X Monday. Arrived **here** in Rome today after travelling thr
dine, Been here 2 days. Its cold **here** on Lake Michigan. Been to top of S
ear Carrodine, Hi there. Made it **here**, after driving for 13 hrs.   It's v
X   Hello Mark, I'm down **here** for a long weekend while Paula "su
d of September, so I'm a tourist **here** for the next 2 weeks. My Dads com
he car we set off at 5.00 & were **here** for quater to 7 & its sun shining.
it's so brill that I could stay **here** for at least a year! See you soon
& Phil & Girls XXXX Dear Chris, **Here** is the promised postcard. I'm havi
retentious rat race!. Everything **here** is simple and basic. Except the pe
Janet, Have a nice rest, weather **here** is very mixed we certainly having
ve M XX Dear Jane, The weather **here** is very nice and we have been in t
ay. Pizzas are something special **here**. Nikkis appartment is nice, she ha
y Dear Christine, Finally "Wer'e **here**" Lots of sun good food and not fo
trivial pursuit.   You'd love it **here** - lots of brown bods etc !! We may
. Have been doing some gardening **here**, lots to do in & around the house,
& Cameron. Having lovely weather **here**, boys are in the sea. The caravan
way, I'm so glad none of yoo are **here** - that makes a good time in itself
pite returning before this card, **here** it is! Having a wonderful time etc
Well? where to start?   We've been **here** just over a week now - what a plac
ou see this.   I've enjoyed myself **here** but its been hard work. My job fi
me and Cameron. It is really hot **here** about 32 (dc) The house is lovely
h to last me. Its not that cheap **here**. You have to pay tax on top of eve
boiling hot, 40's (dc) have come **here** today Antrodine. It's a really bea
ugh there's plenty of fit fellas **here**. Anyway see you when I get home

ved home at 11.45 ppm It's nice **here** - mostly farm land. I'll be back i
d.   I'm having a great time over **here**. My legs are agony at the moment a
ese).   They have black squirrels **here** - very gothic. Vancouver city grea

Figure 10.1 Concordance showing instances of *here*

Any specificity in terms of location is confined to a narrative consisting of listings of iconic sights or places visited en route. Thus we find:

we drove to Roskilde ... and took a train into Copenhagen

and, another example,

So far, done Cairo, the Pyramids, the Egyptian Museum and now in Luxur

In the example above, the individual sights are listed as touristic objects to be consumed or 'done' (on tourism and commodification, see Corkery & Bailey, 1994; Markwick, 2001). This example also illustrates another striking element in the data, namely the concentration on 'things' and events, with little reference to human participants apart from the writer (expressed through often ellipted *I/we*) and the reader (*you*). Not counting ellipted forms which are difficult to retrieve, the number of occurrences of *I/we* is 199 (the most frequent item in the corpus). *You* is the fifth most frequent lexical item (127 instances) after 'I/we', 'the', 'a' and 'to'. The communication is, therefore, highly personalised with two main protagonists, the writer and the reader. The sample postcard text above illustrates this well with six out of the seven grammatical subjects being stated or ellipted *we*.

In contrast, other human actors in the holiday events are referred to rarely and non-specifically as 'people' (only five occurrences referring to local inhabitants; three occurrences to other holiday makers, see below). 'Locals' are referred to once in the context of 'haggling' referring to tourist traders, and there is a generalised use of 'they'. This has the effect of foregrounding the writers and readers as participants and distancing other participants, including the inhabitants of the country or region, from the activities and interest of the tourists. Local people are surprisingly invisible in the text. One exception is the mention (three examples) of 'men', where the reference is sexual and part of the tourist experience of self-gratification. These examples are presented in Figure 10.2.

As we have seen above, because of the restricted purpose and the contextual limitations, information content is low, and tends to be kept at a general non-specific level. Writer comment on the context outside the positive evaluation of places and events is rare, with just one mention of the writer's inability to speak the language and one comment on social divisions within the country. Topics include more mundane aspects such as physical appearance (including sunbathing and tanning); hotels; beaches, sun; sea; sand; weather; and sex. Archetypal activities include eating and drinking (often to excess), seeing the sights, and general enjoyment.

---

of the time so far haggling with **locals** every time we go anywhere or bu
lesbians, shame about the young **men**, to be redundant at such a tender
ave to try this place....   plenty **men**!! See you soon, Phil, Deb, Laura &
alked but its well worth it. The **men** are really, really letcherous, its
g time - so far Great country & **people** eating too much as usual - all t
cheap (hic!) John says he hates **people** with bronzed bodies so Deb and I
y Sunday! Hotel is great and the **people** are very friendly - a bit too fr
escapes.   I expected to see more **people** begging and crazy folk - Maybe I
tual in this community. I've met **people** from all walks of life. Everyone
 is simple and basic.   Except the **people** (simple I mean) Have an enjoyabl
promises!!! Don't know who these **people** are, must be famous particularly
resting talks and workshops. The **people** here are really friendly and kin
ting used to. Anyway must go as **they** say over here, See you soon, Graha
naire! Having lots of cocktails.   **They** do a wonderful rum punch. See you
three weeks of cottage cheese).   **They** have black squirrels here - very g

---

Figure 10.2 Concordance showing instances of *people/locals/men*

Evaluation

Purposes of evaluation

Whenever we communicate whether in speech or writing we present what has been variously referred to as propositions, referential content or facts (Georgakopoulou & Goutsos, 1997). However, merely presenting facts with no speaker/writer comment on those facts is in fact extremely difficult for a writer. My use, in the last sentence, of 'merely/extremely/difficult' are all ways of commenting on the propositional content of the sentence. This involvement of the writer in propositional content and the expression of the writer's views, opinions and feelings I shall refer to as evaluation. The use of the term 'evaluation' is admittedly potentially confusing since it operates at a number of levels. It can refer to the use of individual lexical items (as in the example above), but it can also refer to stretches or 'chunks' of discourse (Hoey, 2001), and later I shall refer to the overall purpose of the holiday postcard text as evaluative. In this chapter I shall be using the term evaluation generally to refer to word and phrase level, but I shall also refer to evaluative purpose below in the section on textual semantic prosody.

Evaluation (according to Hunston & Thompson, 2000) is used for four purposes: (1) to express the writer's opinion; (2) to reflect the value system of the writer (and we might add the identity of the writer); (3) to maintain relations between writer and reader, and; (4) to organise the discourse. We find all four aspects of evaluation operating in the language of holiday postcards. Since we are not dealing here with transactional texts, evaluation in order to express opinions is not as relevant to the corpus as evaluation to express feelings and attitudes. The postcard texts are based more around affect than cognition and evaluation is used to a large extent to express the writers' views of what they have seen and done. There is little opinion expressed within the genre, it is rather a heavily evaluated narrative of events and activities. The genre is characterised as we shall see by widespread use of positive evaluation.

The content and topics of the discourse (part of the ideational component in Halliday's language model referred to above) and the way they are evaluated by the writer reveal a value system deriving from the culture or sub-culture of the readers and writers. To take a simple and obvious example, the frequent mention of drinking, often to excess, clearly belongs to the sub-culture of the student writers represented in the corpus. Such content and positive evaluation of it might not appear so frequently, if at all, with representatives from a different culture or sub-culture. The value system is linked to the identity the writer wishes to represent to the reader. The identity may be created for the purpose of the genre and may be exaggerated by using evaluative language. There is a sense in which writers of this genre, at least as presented by the sub-group represented in the corpus, aim to impress their readers, presenting an identity which may conform to perceptions of a student tourist stereotype but may not be the reality. It is as if the writers are living up to an expected student tourist role.

We have already mentioned that holiday postcard texts are relational rather than transactional, and evaluation is part of this relationship preserving and building the interpersonal between writer and reader. Evaluation is used to organise the discourse, though this feature is not as widespread as the other three. An evaluation device is used for example to signal the conclusion of the discourse 'clear skies and warm. Just perfect! Love Mary'.

The discussion that follows exemplifies the first three purposes of evaluation – the writers' views and attitudes, writer/reader value systems and identities, and writer/reader interaction. I have not attempted to deal with each feature in isolation. Such a programmatic approach rarely works in practice since all three features tend to operate at the same time, and isolating one feature at the expense of another does not do justice to the complexity of the discourse.

Positive evaluation

There appears to be a social rule operating that the sender should project a positive image of the activities presented in the postcard – the overall impact on the reader is one of positive evaluation. It is expected and accepted that negative elements should generally be suppressed or at least minimised. Holidays should be presented as enjoyable experiences and it is not acceptable to admit to any problem, unless it is to turn it into a joke or exaggerate it so that it becomes unreal. A form of positive and negative politeness operates (Brown & Levinson, 1987). Senders wish to save their own face by not admitting to problems out of their control, and not admitting the failure of their holiday investment. At the same time, they take care to minimise the imposition on recipients by avoiding bad news so that recipients are not socially obliged to react sympathetically. As we shall see, where negative statements do occur, hedging is used as a politeness device to attenuate the potentially negative impact on the reader.

Tourists and holidaymakers (senders in this context) have access to a form of social capital that recipients (since they are not tourists themselves) do not possess at the time the postcard is sent. As a consequence, senders possess a degree of symbolic power over recipients (cf. Bourdieu, 1991). Such power needs to handled carefully if the friendships between senders and recipients are to be preserved. Senders need to respond to expectations that the power confers on them, hence the high degree of positive evaluation in holiday postcards, and should not admit the failure of that power through negative evaluation. At the same time, admitting the power too openly could damage relations between sender and recipient so we find exaggeration and humour used in the narrative, not only, as we mentioned above, to minimise the negative, but to make the power more covert and unreal.

Textual semantic prosody

'Semantic prosody' has been used by writers before to refer to the positive or negative interpretation we put on words and phrases in a text. Certain words seem to carry negative or positive meanings with them independent of their dictionary meanings and seem to attract other words around them to create a texture of negative or positive meaning. Sinclair (2003) gives the example of *regime*, which he shows from a corpus analysis is a lexical item generally associated with negative meanings. Thus when we look at the words with which *regime* is associated in texts we find for example *fascist/authoritarian/repressive/collapse/control/killed*. I want to suggest here that in the context of the holiday postcard we can extend this useful notion so that it applies not only to single words and phrases but to the production and interpretation of whole texts. I have called this extension from word to text 'textual semantic prosody'.

As we have seen, one of the major social purposes driving the production of the text is to present to the reader a positive writer-view of the holiday experience. The reader of the text is as aware of this social fact as the writer. It is part of the writer's and reader's knowledge of the genre, acquired by being a member of the particular discourse and cultural group producing and receiving holiday postcards. So readers know that the frame around the holiday postcard genre is overwhelmingly positive and are therefore 'primed' to interpret any term or phrase used within the text as positive. This is what I have called textual semantic prosody where semantic prosody operates at a whole-text level leading the reader in the case of the texts discussed here to take the default position of interpreting lexical items as positive. (Other texts from different genres may of course have negative default positions). This explains, for example, why the lexical item *lazy* in the context of the postcard corpus is clearly meant to be interpreted by the reader not as a negative but as a positive comment, and further examples are given below.

We can help to explain textual semantic prosody in the case of holiday postcards with reference to Labov's comment that evaluation is achieved by comparing two things – the thing being compared contrasted with a norm (Labov, 1972). If 'A is better (bigger/smaller) than B', then in Labov's terms, the norm is B and A is contrasted with it. In some cases the comparison may be less explicit. If we say 'A is terrible', A is being compared with an implied norm B. This is, as we shall see, a linguistic strategy used with isolated events described in the postcard message. 'Weather perfect' compares an unstated norm ('imperfect' weather) with the (*perfect*) weather being experienced by the tourist. However, I suggest that comparison (and hence evaluation) is the motivation underlying the creation of the postcard genre as a whole. The purpose of the postcard writer is to contrast domestic reality 'outside' the holiday (the norm) with the ideal unreality of tourist life, so evaluation in this sense underpins the creation of the text. The writer creates a text where the positive ideal (the holiday) is contrasted extremely favourably with the negative reality of everyday life (the norm) and we can see this in the wide use of positive evaluation used throughout the text. Although we find clear examples of positive evaluation in the text which need little reader interpretation, the effect of the underlying evaluative motivation behind the creation of the text is to create textual semantic prosody where the reader comes to the text expecting to interpret the text and its content in terms of positive evaluation, including those lexical items which are not inherently positive. Examples are given below.

Readers of holiday postcards as I have explained are primed to regard the whole text as an instance of positive evaluation. However, at the level of individual lexical items and phrases, there is a cline of interpretation which requires more or less interpretative 'work' on the part of readers.

At one end of the cline, little interpretation is required by the reader since the items are clearly to be read as positive and the interpretative work required by the reader is slight. The following two short extracts indicate this end of the cline:

I'm having a brill time – I've got a suntan already
the weather is brill

At other times the positive evaluation is built into the text and can only be interpreted positively if both reader and writer share the same cultural values, e.g.:

lying in a hammock under trees contemplating a large glass of the local vino.

To evaluate the extract positively the reader has to appreciate the positive cultural associations of a hammock in the shade and the enjoyment of wine. More interpretation work is required with facts and figures which are presented in order to impress. 'A waterfall with a 3/400 foot drop' and 'a mountain a mile high' are meant to be interpreted as larger than the norm and hence in this context positively evaluated. At the far end of the textual prosody cline requiring a great deal of interpretative work we have such phrases as:

chased by a snake, hustled, and sun burnt

and

so hot it bleaches hair and reddens all else

Whereas in a different genre the activities described in the two examples might well be interpreted negatively, in the holiday postcard genre, because the overall context is one of positive evaluation, even potential negativity tends to be construed by the reader as positive. The negatives are embedded in a positive context. They describe dramatic by-products of positive experiences pushing the reader towards positive evaluation as a default response. We shall now look at further linguistic exemplification of positive evaluation and reader interpretation.

Examples of the language of evaluation

Attitudinal epithets
Much evaluation is expressed directly through adjectives used as modifiers and attributively. The adjectives are of a generalised kind and

belong to a specific sub-set that seems to be associated with this genre in that they represent an excessive subjective appreciation. Thus we find in order of frequency:

great (36 occurrences)
good (21)
lovely (12)
nice (13)
beautiful (8)
brill/brilliant (8)
friendly (6)
perfect (6)
wonderful (6)
sunny (4)
fantastic (3)
glorious (2)
unbelievable (2)
(the following occur once only)
ecstatic
excellent
exciting
exhilarating
fantastic
first class
gorgeous
grand
hair-raising
huge
idyllic
impressive
refreshing
relaxing
remote
stunning
sunny
terrific
total

The instances of _lovely_ are presented as an illustration in Figure 10.3.

Several adjectives are further sub-modified with the use of intensifiers (classified as high intensifiers by Downing and Locke, 2002):

here about 32 (dc)   The house is **lovely** and we're both having a good tim
, Having a great time, weather's **lovely** and so is the hotel.   Went to di
yone else who knows me. Having a **lovely** time, weather is awful but food
in the 80's (DC) - I'm turning a **lovely** Pink Colour! Having fun. Love C
Having a real nice time weathers **lovely** & warm. were are going to Prince
nly 2 Tavernas & NO discos. Sea **lovely** n' clean & the weather! has been
r Mart, Linsay & Cameron. Having **lovely** weather here, boys are in the se
t, went to the lake for a swim - **lovely**. It's idyllic. I hope you are we
s. We've got our own pool its a **lovely** apartment. See you soon. Love Li
wn hills to the beach. Resort is **lovely** but the apartment is crap & the
n just aching feet! Have spent a **lovely** day on top of Whistler not list
is looking after me, weather is **lovely** & windy, the sea is a bit stormy

Figure 10.3 Concordance showing instances of *lovely*

very (23 occurrences)
really (20)
truly (2)
(the following occur once only)
thoroughly
just (as in 'just perfect')
absolutely
beautifully
boiling (hot)
highly
incredibly
lovely (pink)
pretty ('pretty exciting')
so (plus adjective)
totally

Such intensifiers reinforce the sense of excess and generally collocate
with the topics we mentioned previously: food, drink, weather, sea, sand,
sun, beach, sights.

These notions of excess and positive evaluation emphasise what
writers/senders explicitly mention in the postcards – escape from a
reality to which they must shortly return. The epithets and their intensifiers are clearly setting up the contrasts between the holiday and 'normal'
life which are part of the evaluative stance of the writers.

Boosters

We have already seen the use of intensifiers to create positive evaluation. Intensifiers may be of two types, boosters or downtoners (see, for

example, Hyland, 2000). As the name implies, boosters raise the positive evaluative impact of the concept being evaluated, downtoners reduce it. As we might expect, writers in this corpus do not use downtoners, but there is frequent use of different types of boosters, two kinds of which I illustrate below.

Quantifiers I have already commented on the fact that evaluation is expressed in terms of excess quantity and that the quantity remains undefined. Activities such as swimming are performed 'every day' and participants eat and drink 'too much'. A further sub-set of lexical items indicating both vagueness (Channell, 1994) and excess (McCarthy & Carter, 2004) are terms normally found in informal spoken English, such as a *lot of, lots of, loads of, plenty of*. These quantifiers collocate in the corpus with things to do and see, food and drink, and sun. The collocates are not specific so that, for example, the food and drink is not specified. The only example of human collocates is in the expressions *plenty of* where the reference is to the availability of men. Figure 10.4 below shows these examples.

's great, & we've been spending **a lot of** time, eating cakes – what a l
Christine, Finally "Wer'e here" **Lots of** sun good food and not forgetti
me meet the millionaire! Having **lots of** cocktails. They do a wonderful
pissed. Had a bon vouyage, ate **lots of** bon bons. Bought a berret & pac
been the attendant's elevenses! **Lots of** lesbians, shame about the young
l pursuit. You'd love it here – **lots of** brown bods etc !! We may spend
Dear Chris, We are getting **lots of** exercise walking up and down h
remote" is the word) and there's **lots of** nature going on. Hope you manag
f coming back is a it daunting – **lots of** tidying to do. Can't say I feel
k Dear Mark, Clear blue skies. **Lots of** walking lots of pub lunches, lo
lear blue skies. Lots of walking **lots of** pub lunches, lots of relaxing.
of walking lots of pub lunches, **lots of** relaxing. Great so far Bon & Da
ing a thoroughly wonderful time, **lots of** sunshine. Somehow managing to d
's great, the food... olive oil (**Loads of** it!) Hope yer jobs still goin
rling Tart, Having a great time, **loads of** shaggin, not so much skiing,
few mountains lately, covered in **loads of** snow - makes it much more fun,
ellent food & congenial company. **Loads of** places to see, numerous pubs s
aved either. Even though there's **plenty of** fit fellas here. Anyway see
ottage in Ocho Rios for 3 weeks. **Plenty of** activities to engage in. Bee

Figure 10.4 Concordance showing instances of *a lot of/lots of/loads of/ plenty of*

All as deictic   *All* is used as a booster in the corpus, reinforcing the element of excess (viewed in this context positively) that we have noted before. Thus, in the first example below, the writer has not only seen 'the sights', but has seen 'all' of them. Notice, too, the reference to food and the body – common topics in the data:

> *done all the sights – eaten most of them too* (ref. food)
> *all with marshmallow frosting* (ref. food)
> *food living up to all expectations* (ref. food)
> *people from all walks of life*
> *we spent all day Sunday at Watermarine*
> *bleaches hair and reddens all else* (ref. body)
> *all this oil* (ref. body)

All is also used as a positive evaluation to summarise the preceding discourse:

> *all in all, it's so brill that I could stay here for at least a year*
> *been in a helicopter for a hair-raising trip..all this in one afternoon*
> *John is very enthusiastic about it all,*

and to initiate a positive discourse:

> *it's all I imagined…*

There is only one occurrence (out of 14 instances) of *all* used negatively: 'today it has rained all day', although this is contrasted with the more positive: 'yesterday it was sunny' in the same sentence. The phrase: 'we all got sunburnt' is an example of the text prosody mentioned above. Although in another context the concept of sunburn might be taken to be negative, it is clear from the text that this 'misfortune' is to be read as part of the almost sybaritic experience of the writer, the reader is accordingly triggered to evaluate positively, and the phrase is interpreted as positive.

Evaluative stance and negative items

One of the most interesting aspects of the stance (Biber *et al.*, 2000) of the writers is their use of negative elements, for example, *no/not/none/ nothing*. There are few (all positive) instances of *none* (1) and *nothing* (2), so I shall concentrate on *no* and *not/n't*. Negative items, although indicating an absence, have different meanings depending whether the lack is interpreted positively or negatively in the context. *No snow* means different things for a skier (negative meaning) and a gardener (positive), for example. In this corpus the use of such negative items conforms to the overall pattern of positive evaluation that we have seen.

No

Used as a determiner before a noun, there were only eight examples and three of those instances were found in one postcard as part of a list of three positive elements, the repetition reinforcing the evaluation

no cars, no neon signs, no noise

This repetition is then immediately contrasted with the following:

only the gentle sound of water

Of the remaining five examples, one was a similar celebration of the absence of the disadvantages of modern life:

A really nice quiet bar... NO discos,

emphasising the idea of escape represented by the postcards. The (negative) norm is represented by features of urban life (cars, signs, noise, discos) and is contrasted with features of nature. The 'sound of water' is interpreted as positive because of the contrast (if you omit 'gentle', the interpretation is still positive). The 'quiet bay', which in another context could be negative, is clearly positive and reinforced by the modifier 'nice' and intensifying pre-modifier 'really'. Of the remaining four examples of *no*, one was a positive generalisation ('no problem'), and one referred to lack of space on the postcard ('no more room') and was, therefore, external to the content.

The remaining two instances were apparently negative. In the first case, 'no booze killing me, seven days without a fag, living death', the humorous exaggeration acts as a form of hedging so that the reader does not take the negative aspect seriously. The writer continues to mitigate the negative by saying that he promised before the holiday to give up drinking and smoking (i.e. it was his decision and therefore the lack of such pleasures is not an intrinsic feature of the holiday itself). He then ends the postcard by commenting 'enjoying the complete lack of work', underlining the positive aspect of the text once again. In the second case the text reads:

It's great down here. The only draw back being no wind. There you go!

The potentially negative element ('no wind') is minimised. The lack of wind is referred to as 'the only drawback' (i.e. all the other elements of the holiday are positive); the negative phrase is preceded by a positive phrase ('it's great down here') and the text ends with the idiom 'there you go', a form of hedging used to attenuate the negative aspect. Thus, of the two instances of *no* that might be interpreted as having negative meaning, we have seen that the writer minimises the negative aspect.

Not/n't

Out of 24 examples in the corpus using *not/n't*, there is only one example which is an explicit unhedged negative evaluation referring to the holiday – 'We have not got time to look around' – though even in this case the negative occurs within the context of a generally positive text. In all other cases, as we shall see, the negative particle signals either a positive evaluation or is hedged to minimise negative reader perception. Let us look first at those negatives which are hedged in some way:

> *weather not so bad*
> *weather's not been too good*
> *not so sunny Scotland*
> *it's not that cheap here*
> *it wasn't too impressive*
> *I don't think $320 will be enough*

In the first two examples, the weather has been bad, but the writer chooses a hedged form of denial, and the remaining examples use similar hedging devices. The last example is a rare example of relatively low modality in the corpus, i.e. the author expressing some degree of uncertainty of the state of reported affairs. Other cases exist where the meaning of a phrase is reversed by the negative particle:

> *It doesn't shock me*
> *I wasn't afraid*
> *We haven't argued yet*
> *I haven't misbehaved*

In each case the feelings and behaviours of the writer are expressed as positive meanings. In other instances the negative evaluation is minimised by the surrounding co-text. Thus, a walk up the Eiffel Tower is presented as a positive experience and a solution to a problem ('We don't have enough money to pay for a lift'). 'Kath and I are not popular' refers to an attitude by another member of the group who does not like tanned bodies, which are however clearly positive for the writer and her companion. A negative comment ('ballroom dancing every night!') is denied by the exclamation 'Not really!' and finally 'I can't speak the language' is countered later by 'It's been a pretty exciting trip'. In all four instances the negatives are attenuated.

Negative meaning

Where a negative aspect is mentioned it is counterbalanced immediately by positive follow-up with mitigation markers.

1 In the examples below, part A of the phrase (negative) is counterbalanced by part B (mitigation):

(A) *overcast* (B) *since sunny and hot*
(A) *first ever powercut – typical –* (B) *never mind we're off to Disneyworld tomorrow*
(A) *when it rained –* (B) *still I'd rather be wet here than dry in London*
(A) *my tan is rapidly fading in the storms we're having –* (B) *oh well I suppose it fades the sunburn too*
(A) *pissing down with rain –* (B) *stopped now*

2 *but* is often used to signal the switch from the negative to the positive as in the following examples:

weather has been a bit dodgy but we are being very brave
weather is awful but food makes up for it
hot outside of the shade but I'm sure we can cope
so hot but not humid
courtesy of Disney- but I still enjoyed it!
tidying around the house but it's coming on
it was a shame but I still reached the top
walked and walked but it's well worth it
which is a shame but I'm looking forward to it
what a trial but when in Rome
painful but not serious
may not be paradise on earth but it beats Bradford any day

3 A negative is deliberately set up to be countered:

very hot so have to sleep in afternoon – what a trial!

Irony is employed to create a similar effect:

its such a hard life sitting by the pool
Life's so boring!

Unmitigated negatives are difficult to find. There is one reference to poverty but other negatives refer to what occurs before the holiday destination is reached ('dreadful journey', 'flight out was dreadful', 'recovering from long drive') which then contrast with the positive experience on arrival, downplaying the negative.

Conclusion: The World According to the Postcard Message

I hope to have shown in this article that the holiday postcard is an important genre in tourist culture and that the language used in postcard texts reveals significant information about the attitude of senders and recipients towards each other and towards the activities they engage in and the events they experience. I have suggested that positive evaluation is the motivation underlying the creation of the text for reasons of power and politeness and that evaluation is centred around a contrast between the holiday as an ideal and the reality of everyday life. The overriding presence of positive evaluation is revealed through a wide range of lexical items including attitudinal epithets, intensifiers and boosters. Negative particles are used with positive meaning and there are few examples of any negative evaluation, which is not contrasted with the positive and hence mitigated. Language that expresses specificity is avoided and content is expressed in vague general terms, which emphasise excess, viewed positively. Writers/senders narrate their contact with the tourist environment in terms of general activities but there appears to be little contact with or awareness of local populations at least as expressed in the postcards.

Linguistic approaches to the genre of holiday postcards have been relatively rare till now and there is much opportunity for further research. It would be interesting to compare the results obtained from this specific discourse community (British male and female undergraduate students) with data from other communities to see whether differences relating to, for example, gender, occupation or age cause differences in the language and content of holiday postcards. In fact, one such study of postcard messages sent to workplace colleagues (Ylänne-McEwen & Lawson, forthcoming) suggests that similar patterns of positive evaluation dominate, although senders may foreground different aspects of their (work-related) identity. A longitudinal approach would also be of benefit so that the language used in postcards written in different time periods could be used to measure diachronic or historical linguistic change. Research should be broadened to include international comparisons of the postcard genre (though see Laakso & Östman, 1999, 2001). It is clear, since tourism is now a global enterprise, that the holiday postcard is used by many national communities, but it is less clear whether the language and discourse produced differs according to the language and culture of senders and recipients. The research reported here was constrained by lack of access to the writers and readers of the postcards. An ethnographic approach would no doubt produce additional valuable contextual and attitudinal information. Senders and recipients could be observed and interviewed, and give accounts of their social and linguistic behaviour during the writing, sending and receiving of postcards, describe their attitudes towards the holiday postcard event, and indicate whether alternative channels of communication such as email are beginning to supplant the traditional holiday postcard.

References

Bhatia, V.K. (1993) *Analysing Genre*. Harlow: Longman.
Biber, D., Johansson, S., Leech, G., Conrad, S. and Finnegan, E. (2000) *Grammar of Spoken and Written English*. Harlow: Longman.
Bourdieu, P. (1991) *Language and Symbolic Power*. London: Polity Press.
Brown P. and Levinson, S.C. (1987) *Politeness: Some Universals in Language Usage*. Cambridge: Cambridge University Press.
Channell, J. (1994) *Vague Language*. Oxford: Oxford University Press.
Corkery, C. and Bailey, A. (1994) Lobster is big in Boston: Postcards, place commodification and tourism. *Geojournal* 34, 491–8.
Coupland, J. (ed.) (2000) *Small Talk*. Harlow: Longman/Pearson Education.
Downing, A. and Locke, P. (2002) *A University Course in English Grammar*. London: Routledge.
Edwards, E. (1996) Postcards: Greetings from another world. In T. Selwyn (ed.) *The Tourist Image* (pp. 197–21). Chichester: John Wiley.
Geary, C. and Webb, V-L. (eds) (1998) *Delivering Views. Distant Cultures in Early Postcards*. Washington, DC: Smithsonian Institution Press.
Georgakopoulou, A. and Goutsos, D. (1997) *Discourse Analysis*. Edinburgh: Edinburgh University Press.
Halliday, M.A.K. (1978) *Language as Social Semiotic*. London: Arnold.
Hoey, M. (2001) *Textual Interaction*. London: Routledge.
Holmes, J. and Stubbe, M. (2003) *Power and Politeness in the Workplace*. Harlow: Longman/Pearson Education.
Hunston, S. and Thompson, G. (eds) (2000) *Evaluation in Text*. Oxford: Oxford University Press.
Hyland, K. (2000) Hedges, boosters, and lexical invisibility. *Language Awareness* 9, 179–93.
Koester, A. (2002) The performance of speech acts in workplace conversation. *System* 30, 167–84.
Kress, G. and van Leeuwen, T. (2001) *Reading Images*. London: Routledge.
Labov, W. (1972) *Language in the Inner City*. Philadelphia: University of Pennsylvania Press.
Laakso, V. and Östman, J-O. (eds) (1999) *Postikortti diskurssina* [The postcard as dicourse.] Hämeenlinna: Korttien Talo.
Laakso, V. and Östman, J-O. (eds) (2001) *Postikortti sosiaalisessa kontekstissa*. [The postcard in its social context.] Hämeenlinna: Korttien Talo.
Lodge, D. (1991) *Paradise News*. London: Secker & Warburg.
Lofgren, O. (1986) Wish you were here! Holiday images and picture postcards. In N. Brigeus (ed.) *Man and Picture* (pp. 90–107). Stockholm: Almqvist & Wiksell.
McCarthy, M. and Carter, R. (2004) There's millions of them: Hyberbole in everyday conversation. *Journal of Pragmatics* 36, 149–184.
Markwick, M. (2001) Postcards from Malta. Image, consumption, context. *Annals of Tourism Research* 28, 417–38.
Phillips, T. (2000) *The Postcard Century: 2000 Cards and their Messages*. London: Thames & Hudson.

Pritchard, A. and Morgan, N. (2003) Mythic geographies of representation and identity: Contemporary postcards of Wales. *Journal of Tourism and Cultural Change* 1 (2), 111–30.

Sinclair, J. (2003) *Reading Concordances*. Harlow: Longman/Pearson Education.

Street, B. (1995) *Social Literacies*. Harlow: Longman.

Swales, J.M. (1990) *Genre Analysis: English in Academic and Research Settings*. Cambridge: Cambridge University Press.

Whittaker, E. (2000) A century of indigenous images: The world according to the tourist postcard. In M. Robinson, P. Long, N. Evans, R. Sharply and J. Swarbrooke (eds) *Expressions of Culture, Identity and Meaning in Tourism* (pp. 425–37). Newcastle and Sheffield: Universities of Northumbria and Sheffield Hallam.

Ylänne-McEwen, V. and Lawson, S. (forthcoming). Colleagues as tourists: Analysis of postcards sent to the workplace. In N. Morgan and M. Robinson (eds) *Cultures Through the Post: Essays on Tourism and Postcards*. Clevedon: Channel View Publications.

Index